DYNAMICS
of
GROUPS AT WORK

By HERBERT A. THELEN

DYNAMICS

of

GROUPS AT WORK

THE UNIVERSITY OF CHICAGO PRESS

THE UNIVERSITY OF CHICAGO PRESS, CHICAGO 37
Cambridge University Press, London, N.W. 1, England
The University of Toronto Press, Toronto 5, Canada

Preface

The face-to-face group working on a problem is the meeting ground of individual personality and society. It is in the group that personality is modified and socialized; and it is through the workings of groups that society is changed and adapted to its times. These two processes are not separate; they are merely two aspects of the same phenomenon. Moreover, they are necessary to each other: without social purposes shared with others there would be no basis for the give-and-take through which the individual develops his capabilities, and without the differences among individual personalities there would be no basis for the creation of new and better solutions to the problems of living.

Both the relationships between these two processes and the slanting of group experience toward personal growth or social purposes differ from group to group and are determined by leadership. Effective leadership depends on understanding these two processes, and it facilitates both. It recognizes that every group has purposes to be achieved, that it has problems of organizing itself and utilizing the resources of its members to achieve these purposes, and that its members have problems of assimilating their experiences in the group within their own private worlds. The goal of effective leadership is to encourage behaviors that contribute simultaneously to the solution of these fundamental problems.

These, then, are the matters with which this book is concerned, and two kinds of approach are used. The first is "practical." It assumes that basic principles and understandings can be found from the analysis of successful practice in such areas as citizen participation, classroom teaching, in-service professional training, administration and management, human relations training, and public meetings. Part I devotes one chapter to each of these technologies. Each chapter pays particular attention to the things that "stand out" most. Thus, the distinctive feature of citizen programs is that participation is voluntary; of classroom teaching, that it demands so many roles of the teacher and is concerned with so wide an array of student needs; of in-service training, that it changes the character of an institution through individual growth; of administration and management, that it involves the exercise of power; of human relations training, that it is based on the continual diagnosis of emotion; of public meetings, that they represent a patterning of activities in a sequence to achieve carefully defined and limited goals.

Behind these differences, however, are fundamental similarities. Part II is concerned with concepts useful in thinking about group activity regardless of its social purposes or particular clientele. The six chapters of Part II present a development of ideas beginning with the meaning for individuals of group membership and then considering in turn the processes of experiencing by individuals, the kinds of facts with which a group operates, the nature of group control, the problems of leadership, and, finally, the community as the context for group activity. It is in this part that we attempt to weave together many ideas from the social sciences.

To aid the reader in seeing how the material in the various chapters fits together, we have included in each chapter references to other parts of the book that are particularly revealing by way of illustration, amplification, or explanation. An annotated list of selected readings is given at the end of this book.

The background of this book can perhaps be seen in the acknowledgments made below. I owe a great deal to a great many people: to Professor Lawrence F. Foster (Supervisor of Practice Teaching, Education Department, University of California), for showing me that teaching is a continuous adventure, challenging one's faculties of creativity and objectivity; to the late Professor E. D. Eastman (Chemistry Department, University of California) for understanding of the scientific method of inquiry as guided by human imagination; to Dean R. W. Tyler (Social Sciences Division, University of Chicago) for his insistence on operationality as the sine qua non of meaning in ideas; to Professor Carl Rogers (Department of Psychology, University of Chicago) and Dr. Helmut Baum (Chicago Institute for Psychoanalysis) for insights into the central importance and dynamics of man's subjective life; to the writings of Kurt Lewin and John Dewey for understanding of the basic approach to human behavior—as interactions participated in by the whole person; to the writings of Dr. W. R. Bion for a psychiatric approach to the group as a whole; to the late Tom Wright (Chicago Commission on Human Relations) for his brilliant insights into the social meaning of urban group activity.

I am indebted to many people and groups for making possible the wide range of research and practical experience on which this work is based: to the Chairman of the Department of Education, Maurice Seay (University of Chicago); to Howard Page and Joan Criswell of the Human Relations and Morale Division, Office of Naval Research, for support of theoretical and methodological investigations; to the Education Directorate, Human Resources Research Institute at Air University, for opportunity for applied research with learning groups; to the Wieboldt Foundation for support of community action research; to the National Training Laboratory for Group Development for induction into, and experience with, human relations training; to the Chicago Commission on Human Relations for partnership in our citizen action workshops; and, finally, to a large number of classes, citizens' organizations, professional conferences, and research project seminars for the opportunity to work with them in exploring better methods of group operation.

Lastly, I wish to acknowledge with deepest gratitude the emotional support, stimulation, and inspiration of my research students and associates; my professional colleagues Hugh Coffey, John R. P. French, Don Nylen, Freed Bales, Alvin Zander, Ron Lippitt, Floyd Reeves, Bruno Bettelheim, Leland Bradford, Helen Jennings, Fritz Redl, Kenneth Benne, Ted Newcomb; my journalistic mentors, Stuart and Marian Chase; my indefatigable secretary, Mrs. Pearl Bunton; and, above all, my wife, Leonora Elizabeth Thelen.

HERBERT A. THELEN

HUMAN DYNAMICS LABORATORY
DEPARTMENT OF EDUCATION
UNIVERSITY OF CHICAGO
January 1954

Contents

PART I

SIX TECHNOLOGIES

A PRELIMINARY NOTE

A technology is a set of principles useful to bring about change toward desired ends. One distinguishing feature of a particular technology, then, is its target for change—the individuals, groups, or objective conditions which it is designed to alter.

The right to influence others is founded upon some kind of authority, and this is best symbolized in the leadership of the group trying to promote change. A second difference among technologies, then, is the source of the authority of leadership.

A third difference is the role of the member in the group trying to produce and maintain changes. This is defined by the expectations he and the other members hold for his performance and action.

A fourth difference is in the method of group control employed. In each situation there will be a distribution of emphases on problem-solving, on maintenance of the change-group, or on problems of individuals within the group.

A fifth difference is in the relationships between the group promoting change and the other groups with which it communicates; and the ways of communication also vary.

We shall begin each of the next six chapters with a brief comment on the nature of the technology and shall then characterize it with respect to each of the five features noted above. It is hoped that these introductory statements will facilitate comparisons among the technologies as here presented. We shall close each of the next six chapters with further identification of some of the theoretical problems behind the practices described, and we shall indicate sections in Part II which are particularly relevant to these problems.

CHAPTER 1

When citizens get together and share ideas and feelings, they tend to shake off their apathy and become ready for work. When they deal with problems they feel strongly about—in their own neighborhoods—they improve the community and learn what it means to be citizens. The whole political and friendship climate changes. But for success there must be proper leadership and training and the support of a parent organization.

DISTINCTIVE FEATURES

Participation in the program of citizen action is voluntary, and this means that the authority of leadership is the shared and mobilized optimism, determination—or possibly resentment—of the citizens. The primary target of change is a set of community standards. These are standards which sanction inactivity, exploitation, and the every-man-for-himself attitude. The change required is an awakened and maintained social consciousness and conscience. The role of members in the organization is defined by the expectations that they will take care of their own social and financial investments, come to meetings, recruit others, work in committees and projects agreed upon by their group, and, possibly, undergo training for leadership. The method of control of meetings is through the development of group commitment to particular projects, and then satisfaction of the demands of these projects; behavior is relevant and useful when it contributes to getting the job done, and it is hindering or nonuseful to the extent that it is a response to ideological, class, or racial factors. The neighborhood group communicates with city officials directly, receives services from a central parent organization, and joins with other neighborhood groups on large-area projects. Unofficial communication to other organizations to which neighbors also belong is through the initiative of individuals.

Rebuilding the Community through Citizen Action

There is only one phenomenon quite as spectacular in its own weird way as the rapid growth of a city, and that is its decline. It is a quiet, spotty, unnoticed decay, neighborhood by neighborhood. Hoopla and excitement attend the opening of the new chrome and glass-incased high school in the currently "nice" part of town; but the overcrowded, beat-up old pride of the eighties on the "wrong" side of the tracks does not even get a decent burial.

A large part of many big cities is middle-aged—neither very "nice" nor very "wrong." These parts, serene and stable to the eye, represent a state of balance between forces of growth and of decay. A school fight every decade, a trickle of ritualistic gossip about the neighbors, an occasional new wing for the hospital, a sudden meteoric business success or failure, the hearings when the transit company replaces streetcars with busses, the annual three-day merchants' shopping event—this is the life of the neighborhood. Dull and comfortable.

It does not take much to put such a neighborhood on the skids. A new superhighway, prosperity, plant shutdowns, influx of population to the city, opening of suburbs, depression, shortage of construction materials, political administration of city services—any or all of these factors can tip the scales in favor of deterioration and blight. World War II, with its massive dislocations, brought to many cities unprecedented prosperity and widespread ruin. The prosperous moved on and out, but the ruined neighborhoods remained.

Accompanying and supporting and causing physical change is social change. Deterioration of a community is not only a matter of crumbling bricks and insecure fences; it is a matter of crumbling morale and insecure people. Maintenance of a community

3

is maintenance of civic consciousness; both must be fed by continual positive communication, planning, and action. These things require the participation of citizens. When citizens lose interest, the balance between growth and decay loses its dynamics, its resilience and restoring force. It no longer can re-establish itself in the face of inevitable changes in the neighborhood.

This chapter presents an exciting story of citizen participation in a community that had one foot on the skids. Through this story we shall investigate the dynamics of action and social problem-solving, and we shall see, on a community-wide scale, the application of the same principles that govern operation in face-to-face groups.

We begin in Chicago in the year 1950.

THE COURSE OF URBAN DETERIORATION[1]

World War II created a vast number of jobs in Chicago's industry. Labor was attracted from all over the country, but especially from the South. During the decade beginning in 1940, there was an increase of 42 per cent among the nonwhite population in Chicago. The construction of houses and other dwelling units did not keep pace with the increase of population, and the resulting shortage of housing became Chicago's number one problem. Two-thirds of the new dwelling units created between 1940 and 1950 failed to meet minimum legal standards of quality. Overcrowding developed and, with it, the decline of morale and communication among neighbors.

The population increases strained the available city services to the utmost. The conditions accompanying overcrowding aggravated still further the problems of maintaining police, fire, and health protection. The average cost of maintenance per citizen increased far beyond what the city budget provided. Many areas were slighted altogether by one or another of the city's services.

1. The next several pages come from a speech more or less as delivered to the Chicago Chapter of the International Society for General Semantics, March 27, 1953. See "Shall We Sit Idly By?" *Etc.*, Vol. XI, No. 1 (fall, 1953). H. A. Thelen and B. B. Sarchet, *Neighbors in Action*, Human Dynamics Laboratory, University of Chicago, 1954, is a considerably expanded discussion of these ideas and practices.

After the United States Supreme Court ruled that bailiffs of federal courts could not be used to enforce restrictive covenants, people began to react not only to the grim facts but also to all sorts of racial fears and fantasies. In some neighborhoods there was panic or rioting when the first Negroes moved in. As residents fled, their places were taken by Negroes, whose need for housing was most desperate—and who were willing to make desperate bargains for property. In some areas, the Negro in-migration took over one block after another, thus in effect simply extending the "black belt."

SOCIAL DISORGANIZATION

The skyrocketing prices of property, the limitation by rent control of income from property, the pressure for housing of any kind—these caused individuals in all parts of the city to decide to sublet or to create new, smaller units in their buildings. In many cases this decision ushered into neighborhoods a hitherto unfamiliar kind of person: the rooming-house tenant. With increased mixing of apartments, rooming-houses, kitchenette flats, and single-family residents came greater mixing of people who differed in their class levels, social backgrounds, values, and ways of life. And these changes were most visible when the incomers were Negroes.

The mixing of class and of caste resulted not only in the breakdown of communication on the block but also in the feeling that communication would now be impossible. Neighbors were no longer seen as people one could identify with; the sense of common cause was lost. People felt more and more reluctant to talk with the neighbors, and their concerns accordingly turned inward on themselves rather than being directed outward as in the past. The deterioration of the physical community seemed to create only personal problems for individual residents, rather than problems for the block or the community as a whole to deal with.[2]

2. It is true, however, that some neighborhoods contained many groups with regular meetings. But these were nonaction groups which provided, perhaps, some feeling of escape from the frustrations of the role of citizen. They contributed very little to the rectification of conditions or to the adjustment of individuals to the conditions.

The feeling of apathy and frustration of neighbors was assimilated into "official" attitudes toward neighborhoods where changes were occurring. There was increasing reluctance of city servants to meet the needs of these areas—and this added fuel to the flames of resentment and frustration. The result was, in effect, that all the usual channels by which citizens normally can get at least some action were gradually blocked off.

Finally, as if to complete this sorry picture of disorganization, there was flight; people moved out, sometimes in blind panic and sometimes to find the better living their war prosperity made possible. In either case, the flight was by people who had enough money to flee; and these people tended to belong to the group which had provided leadership and vigilance in the past. Thus flight was not only the symbol of panic and of defeat in the face of anxiety, but it was also the creator of a vacuum in the power structure of the city. And there was no lack of people ready and able to turn civic disorder into personal wealth. Most notable was the alliance between crime and politics: during the decade it changed from a hothouse plant, delicately and blushingly nurtured by a few, into a rank prairie weed, openly and knowingly nurtured by the many.

PERSONAL DISORGANIZATION

Most citizens were part, parcel, and carrier of the social disorganization. They felt lonely, isolated, cut off from the group. Some felt that they had been singled out for special persecution. Feelings of helplessness became widespread, and, with these feelings, came a stifling blanket of fears. It was, for example, not uncommon for people to be afraid at night to put their autos in the garages on the alley. Along with fear came anxiety and anger at feeling fearful. Out of this arose interpretations that were mostly projections of hostility onto convenient target groups (scapegoats): the Negroes, the cops, the landlords, yes, and even the Democrats.

The fears were expressed in rumors of all sorts; nothing was too silly to be handed on: "the Urban League has a million dollars to break white blocks for Negro occupancy"; "the syndicate wants to convert all the big homes in the Fourth Ward into rooming-houses." Fears and anxieties snowballed because there were no channels for constructive action to relieve frustration. Apathy and defeatism set in, and, with these, hypocrisy and guilt feelings. When one is lonely he thinks it is his own fault; he blames himself and at the same time tries to put up a front both to himself and to the "group," which, he does not realize, exists no longer. These conditions were clearly revealed, for instance, in an interview with a lovely lady who said that she had lived in the neighborhood all her life and intended to finish her days there. In the midst of this painted picture of security and comfort a man in overalls interrupted by ringing the doorbell. He said, "I'm from Ace Moving Company. Is this the house where I am to pick up the furniture?" People would protest they were going to stay in the neighborhood and they loved it—right up to the point where they melted away into the night.

The over-all interpretation of all these things is that individual behavior became more and more determined by self-concern. It expressed reaction to anxiety insufficiently controlled by contact with the world of objective social facts.

FACING FACTS

By November, 1949, the flight of people along Drexel Avenue where the Negroes had moved in threatened serious depletion of the congregations of certain churches. At their request, Tom Wright, director of the Chicago Commission on Human Relations, began preliminary discussions with the Social Order Committee of the 57th Street Meeting of Friends. These led to a meeting of forty concerned citizens from various organizations in the Hyde Park–Kenwood area.[3] The meeting was stormy, and it faced some very sobering facts: (1) that sociologists and planners predicted that the area would be a slum in ten years; (2) that nobody knew of any examples of a community which, when once started on the path of deterioration, had worked its

3. On the South Side: Forty-seventh to Fifty-ninth Streets, Cottage Grove Avenue to Lake Michigan. This was the nucleus of the Hyde Park–Kenwood Community Conference; and the examples used in this chapter all come from the experiences of the Conference. I have been concerned from the beginning in the development of the block program. Another account is by Stuart Chase, in *Reader's Digest*, May, 1953.

way back out; (3) that a whole dynamic pattern of forces toward deterioration was practically unopposed, and that the reversal of these forces would require all-out action on a staggering array of fronts.

The group also saw that there were logically just three alternatives: (1) that citizens could flee from the area, leaving it to exploiters and opportunists to profit from social deterioration; (2) that the group could sit tight and do nothing on the grounds that the problems were too big or that they did not have the required resources; (3) that the group could start to work.

I think that this group recognized that going to work did not necessarily mean success, but that successful or not they must try. Following this feeling of commitment, the group planned a program and talked about what it could do, rather than what it could not do, to get started. Half of the resulting program would be concerned with the pinpointing of specific objectives: enforcing the law, bettering the schools, getting recreation facilities, establishing relations with the building commissioner's office, planning for future development, running a survey of the area to find the extent of deterioration, and so on. As each of these objectives became clarified, working committees would have to be recruited and set up, and they would have to become influential in mobilizing pressures strategically to get decisions changed or improved for the benefit of the community.

It was seen that the second half of the program would need to be concerned with what sometimes has been called the grass roots aspects. Basically, the origin of this part of the program was the realization, in general terms, that no one group of forty dedicated individuals could possibly provide the man-hours, skill, and energy required to reverse the whole pattern of social action in the community. A veritable army, co-ordinated and energetic, would be required.

It was recognized that the area was unstable in the sense that its ultimate fate was in doubt. In such communities, the positive forces of growth appear to have been halted, but deterioration has not yet progressed to the point of slum conditions. For slum conditions, incidentally, there is a pat answer: bring in the bulldozer and knock everything down, relocate the citizens, build new buildings, then move some of the people back in. This area had not run down that far. It was seen that progress or deterioration in the area would depend upon the cumulative wisdom of the thousands of decisions made by citizens every day.

Some of the individual activities which would forecast the community's future were:

1. Decisions about how extensively and how adequately to keep up property.

2. Decisions about the use to which property will be put, particularly with respect to the type of dwelling units and number of people living in each.

3. Initiation of actions and follow-up requests for city services.

4. Participation in neighborhood conversation to share ideas of the standards to be maintained.

5. Expression of attitudes of friendliness or indifference or hostility which foster concern for the welfare of all or which indicate only concern for one's self.

6. Maintenance of an attitude of objectivity toward rumors: the tendency to make objective inquiry and the feeling of trusting other people's common sense, so that one does not rush off always believing the worst.

Since these and many other everyday behaviors of citizens were seen to determine the fate of the community, it was necessary to try to reach everybody under conditions which would result in the most intelligent behavior possible.

Following this analysis of what would be required to stop deterioration and rebuild the community, the initial group of forty citizens talked with officers of existing improvement and planning councils and associations. None were ready to spearhead the immense effort that would be required.

A new organization, the Hyde Park–Kenwood Community Conference, was formed. It set up working committees to study problems of law enforcement, schools, recreation, planning, zoning, and the like. The Conference also created the program of "block organization," through which it hoped to enlist every citizen into a massive, co-ordinated, and self-disciplined movement to halt deterioration and to rebuild the community.

Before finally adopting the program of block organization, the

Conference decided to try the idea of neighborly meetings in one block first. A certain block on Drexel Avenue held the first meeting in January, 1950; it illustrates many of the principles and characteristics of subsequent block meetings.[4]

As it turned out, this block meeting was planned at a strategic time—when rumors were sweeping the block that a house was about to be sold to exploiters who would pack a Negro family into each room. People were concerned, and they knew that each of the others was concerned; there was something to discuss, no question about that! As soon as the rumors swept the block, four people put their houses up for sale.

Everybody in a row of fifteen owner-occupied houses was invited to the meeting by a small planning group of four. These four personally visited the families with whom they were already acquainted—it was easier that way. As the people came into the house, it was clear that they had different expectations, ranging from the notion that we were met to consider strategies to keep the Negroes out to the feeling that we ought to invite Negroes in and turn the neighborhood into an interracial paradise. These attitudes were expressed fairly readily by people in small discussion groups which had formed before the meeting started.

After about twenty minutes, the feeling arose that we should get started, and there were many glances toward the chairman and host. An old man about eighty climbed up on the stair landing and opened the meeting with this gem: "What do you want me to tell you about those damn niggers?" There was a decidedly awkward pause. The leader replied that while listening to the informal conversations before the meeting opened he had discovered that we had a wide range of feelings about Negroes among us, and he suggested that we might as well accept this as a fact about ourselves about which we could do nothing. He pointed out, however, that Negroes had bought the apartment building across the street and he felt that the block faced certain objective possibilities:

1. It could form a pitchfork mob to try to drive the Negroes out.
2. It could attempt to ignore them.

4. The following account is from H. A. Thelen, "Social Process versus Community Deterioration," *Group Psychotherapy,* IV (December, 1951), 209–10.

3. It could attempt to establish communication with them with the idea of explaining the block's determination to prevent physical deterioration and to make the block a pleasant place in which to live.

Posed in this way, looking toward alternative possibilities for action growing out of a real situation, the group quickly decided to begin talking to people. A committee, combining the features of investigating team and friendship group, was appointed to go calling on the new neighbors. The Negroes, fortunately, could see the committee's embarrassment and were mature enough to help them establish communication. The fact that members of the committee did not have strong feelings either way about Negroes undoubtedly made matters easier.

Three other actions were taken at the first meeting; and the second meeting started with a report of these actions, the introduction of new people, and the setting-up of an agenda consisting of the things people on the block thought were problems to be looked into.

As the neighbors left the first meeting they felt considerable relief from anxiety. The meeting had not yet done anything very important by way of taking action but the neighbors had found out something that they knew intellectually but could never have really felt if they had not been called together to enter into action. They had found out that there were a lot of people just as concerned and just as frustrated as they were. Instead of feeling that "everybody else is perfectly able to cope with the situation, but I am not," the individual found that everybody was equally unable to cope with the situation, so that the feeling of inadequacy dissolved and was replaced by the much more objective perception that the group as a whole had problems. Thus the feeling of being out of the group, of being a helpless spectator on the sidelines—feelings which had led individuals to turn inwardly on themselves and feel lonely—these were replaced by a complete reversal of the relationship to the group. The group of neighbors was felt now to be supportive; one was no longer alone. Under these conditions of establishment of communication and support the individual could feel free to act intelligently rather than out of anxiety.

The restoration of communication thus grew around the need

for reducing anxiety, but it continued as a new pattern on the block. The neighbors had become acquainted at the block meeting, and each day, as they passed up and down the block, they would greet each other. The network of communication on the block was reinforced and grew because it became a part of the way of life on the block.

The reduction of anxiety freed the group for active problem-solving efforts. To feel better was nice—and the neighbors openly acknowledged it. But they also saw that improvement of the neighborhood requires people to take action; feeling good makes action possible, but does not, by itself, rebuild the block.

Thus there arose spontaneously from the meeting a demand for subcommittees to get busy. The group identified a wide range of practical problems: the moving of abandoned cars, the installing of porch lights to dispel darkness, the prompt reporting of movements of materials into houses so that the plans for conversions could be checked, the development of tot-lot and recreational space, the collective buying and sharing of garden implements. Working committees arose from volunteers who felt strongly about one or another of these problems. And committee action, supported, encouraged, and supervised by the block group, resulted in positive acts of neighborhood improvement.

The actions resulting from working together had their effect on the physical community. In addition, during the processes of co-operation, neighbors began to make some highly significant personal discoveries about themselves and each other. They learned that the things they used to worry about don't need to matter. A Negro worker or a low-income renter can have just as useful ideas, make as many phone calls, dig out just as valuable facts, and be just as helpful as anyone else. Through these discoveries, the neighborhood as a community of people became stabilized. The block began to feel like home; life on the block acquired new richness of meaning and satisfaction. The neighbors learned that the physical and social communities are inextricably linked: actions are taken to maintain and improve the physical community, but it is the way in which neighbors participate to take action that maintains and improves the social community.

With the first successful actions, the neighbors began to think of themselves as a group. They gave their group a name, an identity. They developed loyalty to the group, and standards of upkeep which strengthened their individual desires to keep their own houses in order. The group found the language in which to state its goals, and it began to take a long look outside itself at the city government. As time went on and other neighborhood groups developed under the leadership of the Conference, loyalty spread from the block to the community, and, through the central Conference organization, community feelings and pressures began to be felt in many offices of the city hall. The local organizations, which had not been ready for action in the beginning, began, one by one, to respond to the new attitudes of the citizens, and to add their efforts to the program. At the end of four years, it is literally true that practically every major institution of the community is actively participating in the total program.

Events in the Hyde Park–Kenwood community have amply demonstrated the importance for community betterment of massive, creative participation by the citizenry.

We will, in the remainder of this chapter, try to transfer to more general terms and for use in other areas, some of the experience gained in the Hyde Park–Kenwood Community Conference program in Chicago.

PRINCIPLES OF THE BLOCK PROGRAMS

PROBLEMS FOR BLOCKS TO WORK ON

It is clear that there are certain kinds of problems that every block needs to work on. There are, in addition, many types of projects which seem to be congenial to certain blocks but not necessarily to others.

Thus, the problems all blocks must be concerned with include:

1. Setting up block standards, for example, of quality for dwelling units, or of behavior that the block expects from its residents. In the development of such standards through discussion and in participation in them, a coercive group force arises which prevents many selfish impulses from finding expression.

2. The range of city services available to citizens for maintaining and servicing the neighborhood. Continual alertness in

checking these and, if necessary, complaining about their in-adequacy might be thought of as vigilance functions. The most important of these from a community standpoint are probably those centering around the reporting of suspected illegal con-versions and the reporting of crime.

3. The typical type of improvement project—putting in tot-lots, installing lights, planting flowers, and so on—has been dis-cussed above.

In addition to these three basic kinds of effort some of the following types of projects have been undertaken:

4. Joining with other blocks on an area job, such as cleaning up the length of a business street or digging out all the fireplugs in the area when they become covered with snow.

5. Collective private enterprises, such as equipping a shop or running of hobby nights and sharing of tools.

6. Recreational or social activities, such as parties, square dancing, and poker festivals to raise money for tot-lots and the like.

7. Educational programs, featuring speakers who can tell the neighbors what they can do to make their homes less attractive to burglars, what to do about auto larcenies, or how to have a beautiful lawn.

PRINCIPLES OF BLOCK LEADERSHIP

In conducting meetings to attain these objectives, a number of important principles have been identified. These have become, in effect, the bases for the training of leadership. Let us take a look at some of these principles, not necessarily arranged in order of importance.

1. *Participation depends on reward.*—For the neighbors to remain involved and interested over a long period of time, they must re-ceive rewards at a sufficient rate. The two kinds of rewards possible are *gratification* of individual need for such things as dominance, friendship, intimacy with certain people, opportu-nity to test ideas, and so forth; and *satisfaction* with group ac-complishment of tasks. Particularly at the beginning it is evident that the reward for task accomplishment will not be sufficiently great and frequent to avoid discouragement and to maintain in-

volvement. Therefore, the meetings by design should be given a quasi-social character so that through parties, the sharing of hobbies and games, and informal conversation of all sorts people can obtain rewards over and above the rewards of work.

2. *The block works on "felt" problems.*—The only matters on which people will expend energy are these which they feel are problems, things about which people have feelings which they must deal with. Therefore, the survey of problems suggested by members is the starting event of the meetings, so that the group will not inadvertently commit itself to action along lines nobody will be motivated to carry through.

3. *Leadership is by team.*—The kind of leadership required encourages free expression of feelings and opinions, sifts these to help diagnose problems realistically, and guides the group into action. This requires a range of skill greater than most men can provide. A leadership team is therefore far more effective than a single leader: it will make a more objective analysis of how the last meeting went and it will have more information and understanding to use in planning and conducting the next meeting. The team concept also includes getting the help one needs from anyone who can supply it.

4. *Movement spreads through friends.*—A component of the initial attitudes of people in disorganized areas is the feeling of lack of trust; they are suspicious of each other. Meetings can be organized most successfully when friends call on friends so that the initial hurdle of distrust does not have to be overcome.

5. *Membership is based on willingness to work, not on ideology.*— The basis of participation in block meetings is merely that one lives on the block. There is no test of ideology because it is not what people say they believe that is important so much as their willingness to work on problems. As long as there is willingness to work on problems, ideological differences can be settled or avoided. Moreover, the people who are out of sympathy with the movement are very likely to be the ones whose actions are most damaging to the block; therefore, special effort is put forth to have them participate in the meetings.

6. *Discussion focuses on concrete problems.*—Arguing about "ideologies," making grand generalizations which take in all the

territory from here to Alaska—these behaviors are gratifying to some individuals, but they are irrelevant to the action part of the block meeting. When the group is trying to select problems, define them, and work on them, it gathers steam and enthusiasm through being able to see more and more clearly what the problem is and what acts will be appropriate. In short, the discussion marches along and leads to action when arguments are settled and generalizations are tested by getting concrete—talking about particular times, places, peoples, and behaviors. The first requirement for carrying the discussion beyond its initial questions is the production of the necessary facts, either from informed people at the meeting or through the efforts of a committee between meetings.

In general, it is assumed that people will hold different opinions about Negroes, city offices, liberals, real estate agents, etc. These differences of opinion can be accepted as differences of opinion rather than as the start of a battle. Decisions for action are sound when they are based on relevant facts, not on opinions, and the number of facts needed is the number required to make a confident choice among the suggested actions. Whatever one's opinions, attitudes, or ideology, he is pretty likely to join with his neighbors to get a wrecked jalopy off the street, a rat colony discouraged, or a new landlord indoctrinated.

7. *All decisions are subject to revision as a result of taking action.*— A "good" decision results in action which remedies the situation. A "bad" decision results in action which makes people even more uncomfortable, apathetic, or frustrated. It is possible for a group to make the wisest decision of which it is capable and then find that when it acts on the decision matters get worse. The value of a decision cannot be known at the time the decision is made; it can be known only through study of what happens during action.

Thus it is possible—although it has not yet happened in our community—that a block might, after sober discussion, decide to sell property only to white people. If this is a "bad" decision for that block to make, then acting on the decision should produce evidence that the situation on the block has been made worse. We should expect people to discover such things as feelings of guilt, of fear of being called into court, of loss of self-respect, and of weakness. The decision would hang like a heavy cloud over the block; spontaneity of discussion would be reduced, and every time a Negro walked down the street people would have uncomfortable feelings. Needless to say, there would be a greater wish to flee the neighborhood, and a developing mistrust of the suddenly increased protestations that people are going to stay. This is, of course, an extreme example, but it is an instructive one because it reminds us that the evidence to be taken into account must include information about how people feel. In any case, decisions should always be kept open for review as evidence accumulates, understanding that behavior depends more on how people feel than on what people say. The example is instructive also because it indicates rather clearly why some property owners' associations have typically contributed to the deterioration of the community.

8. *Each block group determines its own autonomy.*—The fact is that the existence, success, and prospects of most block groups are in no small measure owing to the efforts of the Conference organization. Block groups, however, react in different ways to this fact. Some will deny it; others will accept it gladly and look to the parent organization for much help; still others will feel little concern one way or the other. Some block groups develop jealous loyalty to themselves; others, to the community. In any case, the way a block group feels toward the parent organization changes from time to time. Generally, as the group matures, it tends to be able to be loyal not only to itself but to the parent organization and to any other group perceived to be working for the community.

Members of the block group are likely to differ in their knowledge about and attitude toward the parent organization. If the block leaders received help from the Conference to get started, they are likely to belong to the Conference, and to feel they ought to try to get all the neighbors to belong also. Further, the block group receives services from the parent group, which also helps make the local efforts "add up" through the development of other groups which can reinforce each other's demands. But for most leaders there is considerable embarrassment in asking their neighbors to contribute to some other organization. Block groups are likely to be involved in projects which need money from the neighbors, and to advocate diverting potential contributions to an outside group has some of the feeling of embezzlement. Moreover, leaders hesitate (and rightly) to do anything that will give the impression that membership in the parent organization is a necessary condition for participating in block activities. It seems clear from experience that block groups cannot alone finance the parent organization, and that the people most able and ready to contribute to the parent organization are likely *not* to be the ones most active in block groups. Block leaders can help the general fund-raising activities such as theater parties, community fairs, and rummage sales.

IMPLEMENTING THE PROGRAM OF PARTICIPATION BY CITIZENS

The difference between an occasional meeting on one block and a vigorous widespread program of citizen activity is a matter of services helpfully rendered. Potential leaders must be found and recruited, advice and training must be given to those needing it, the community must be informed as to what is going on, action channels to the city hall must be opened and maintained, new methods for dealing with the wide vista of community problems must be continually developed and pooled, encouragement must be maintained for all workers, a place must be found for everyone to help, and competent professional help must be enlisted and made available to all.

The list of facilitating services is long and demanding. And no less demanding is the spirit of co-operation which must be consistently maintained in the offering of all services, and, indeed, throughout all communications with everyone in the community. It is not always easy to put problem-solving ahead of prestige; to refer decisions to the good of all rather than to the need for organizational power; to welcome all who will help regardless of personality, beliefs, or vested interests; to accept help of people on their own terms rather than on your terms; to regard attacks by organizations and individuals as a sign that efforts to co-operate must be redoubled, rather than as the signal for counterattack; to confine publicity stories to the records of accomplishments for the community, even in the face of requests from the papers for "news"; to develop and make room for new leadership at the top, and to allow those who want retirement to pass on to their new opportunities; always to stand ready to interpret any part of the program to anyone who asks—for whatever reason; to resist the temptation to overload a willing volunteer or one's friends with chores; constantly and forever to concentrate on improving the ongoing processes of problem-solving rather than to go around taking a stand on every attractive issue or campaigning for one's own solutions to problems.

The principles and attitudes which govern the friendly meeting of neighbors on the block must also govern the entire community enterprise. The social and neighborly situation of the block meeting is the model for the organization as a whole. Executive secretaries who love to give orders, nonworking boards of directors, jealous and ego-inflated working committees, chronic advice givers, dogmatic idealists—these have no place in the setup. The pitfalls are greatest at the level of over-all organization because the status rewards are greatest and because the contact with the community problems is most remote. The organizational leaders do not directly experience the conditions they are trying to alleviate; they know of slums through the testimony of others, but they do not know slums. It is always someone else whose experience tests the wisdom of actions by the board.

Finally, the central organization has a complicated problem of working methods to clarify for itself: one co-operates with others in his group or in his community, but one makes a show of power to groups outside the community. Within the council chambers of the city, one more neighborhood organization is always just a group that wants something for itself, and its chances for success are proportional to the pressure the organization is perceived as controlling. But the same pressure ideology—epitomized by the business deal—that works when groups are in competition with each other is fatal to the development of a program of voluntary participation.

The importance of co-operative attitudes is so great that one almost hesitates to discuss specific techniques of operation. A co-operative group with poor techniques will develop the tools it needs; a nonco-operative spirit, manifesting itself through the most up-to-the-minute techniques that can be devised, still adds up to exactly nothing of long-range significance. On the other hand, a preaching of attitudes is not likely to change attitudes either. Understanding and practice and objective study of results are the ways to the learning we all need for effective community work. The following discussion of the facilitating services required for development and maintenance of the action program can suggest techniques that have been found useful under at least some conditions. And we can try, in discussing these, to spell out some of the meanings of the co-operative method of community problem-solving.

DEVELOPING LEADERSHIP

RECRUITMENT

There seems to be no systematic and certain way to locate and recruit leaders, possibly because there are so many different possible motivations for becoming a leader. Recruitment is an everlasting job for everyone concerned with the program. Finding leaders can have much the same zest as hunting big game, although in some respects the rules are different.

Several neighbors on a block can usually put their heads together and suggest possible leaders. Many a leader has been nominated at a bridge party, baseball game, local supermarket, and husbands' night at the PTA. Anyone who shows leadership talent in the Rotary Club, Scouts, rummage sale, or anywhere else can be marked down as a candidate for a cozy interview. A person who calls up to ask questions or make complaints is displaying that rare jewel, initiative, and should be followed up. A properly planned community meeting, with a sober discussion of community problems, can end with everyone being asked to fill in a card indicating the ways he can help. Certain categories of people, such as housewives whose youngest child has just entered school, and who have had jobs working with people, may be appropriate material for leadership in some communities. Librarians, ministers, doctors, and others can be more useful informants if they are given a general description of the sort of person sought.

Whatever the method of identifying likely people to contact, the next step is to present them with information in such a way that they can make a wise decision about their own participation. The most common mistakes are probably presentation of the wrong sorts of information, and presentation of too little information. A leader can hardly make a realistic decision until he has decided that the problems to be solved are important to him, the amount of time and skill required are within his reach, and the rewards he hopes to get for serving as leader are attainable. In general, the potential leader should be able to visualize the sort of meetings he will help lead, should talk with other leaders, and should attend at least one training session or neighborhood meeting so that he will know what to do and whether he can do it.

Whatever information the potential leader has is never adequate to guarantee to him that he will get what he wants from the experience of leading. Volunteering for anything always involves taking a calculated risk. Most people make up for their lack of information by putting their trust in another person. It follows from this that it is decidedly worth while to pay attention to the selection of the director or block leader who should talk with or sponsor the candidate.

TRAINING

Most people know by now that running meetings successfully is a somewhat more complicated art than falling off a log. Adequate information, creative knowledge of techniques, and appropriate attitudes are all required. The maintenance and spread of the action program is directly proportional to the quality and effectiveness of the training program.

In general, the training program must satisfy two requirements: first, it must get specific help to leaders at the times they need it and in such a way that they can learn from it; and second, it must establish the role of leader as a valued, continuously supported part of the organization. The training program does much to create a leader group which, in some ways, has the characteristics of a profession. The leaders know each other, feel loyal to the group of leaders, recognize certain minimum skill requirements, stand for a set of attitudes—ethics—and have concern for the over-all improvement of leadership in the organization.

Training can be provided in a variety of ways, both formal and informal.

1. *The community clinic.*—This can be developed as the only regularly scheduled, carefully planned public meeting of the parent organization with special effort exerted to get potential and new block leaders to attend. The various features of the agenda reflect some important principles or conditions of training.

The meeting is started with a welcome and a statement of objectives of the program designed to communicate confidence in significant goals. A report from the executive secretary of the parent organization, summarizing actions and events significant to the community, is intended to give people some idea of the range of resources available to block groups and to increase their identification with and understanding of the over-all program.

The third event is informal reporting by block leaders of meetings they have had since the last clinic, telling of problems considered, actions taken, the feelings and hopes of citizens. These reports help people see that the meetings are practical and accomplish results and let them feel the enthusiasm and delight of other leaders, showing leadership as a route to social approval and reward.

Following these reports, the group divides into smaller interest groups to study the various skill problems of calling and conducting meetings, gathering information, and so on. The clinic meeting closes with a report from each skill group as to what problems they have worked on and what bright ideas they wish to pass on to the others.

2. *The training seminar.*—A beginning leadership group has to learn how to organize itself to put on mass meetings and use other recruitment devices, to discover and maintain needed communication with other parts of the organization. It has to understand its own attitudes toward other groups in the community, and it needs to learn the experimental approach to problem-solving, with its emphasis upon firsthand experience and doing things for one's self. The attitudes learned by this executive group pretty

much determine the attitudes of the action people throughout the community.

A training seminar, run with competent professional consultation, is a rapid and effective means to meet these needs for this group. Meeting every week or two for at least eight sessions, and relying heavily on experience-sharing as the people start trying to get blocks going, it develops a strong sense of groupness and dedication, and results in many policy suggestions to the organization's board of directors. The members of the seminar work on their own blocks, and, as the movement grows, take over the administrative problems of the block action program. Representatives of other committees of the parent organization are invited to the seminar so that its developing body of policy can remain coherent.

3. *Congress of block leaders.*—If all block leaders meet together about once a month to share problems and program ideas and responsibilities, they tend to remain active and to contribute to the storehouse of useful suggestions. A congress of leaders may itself have working committees, with specific functions to work on and continuously keep in the awareness of the larger group. They may, for example, concern themselves with the dissemination of program ideas, solicitation of memberships, organization of community clinics, etc. Through these working committees, training for leadership at the organizational level is provided, sharply differentiating the training function of the congress from that of the clinic.

4. *Individual consultation.*—Group training methods can never fully deal with the private doubts and tentative insights of the trainee; it takes an understanding individual to do this. Moreover, in the group methods, the trainee can never get enough information and advice based on specific facts about his own block. Through discussion with someone who can help him sift his perceptions and see which ones make the most difference, the embryo leader can be helped to make realistic and confidence-giving plans. Experienced group leaders very commonly fail to realize the extent of the help they must stand ready to give to the new leader. One result of experience is that we can formulate for ourselves concise formulas and instructions, but

we fail to realize that the meaning of these paradigms and prov-
erbs is in the context of our extensive experience. A variety of
individuals—the officers of the parent organization, the experienced block leaders, interested professionals from schools and
universities and public agencies, and so on—should, as leaders,
stand ready to work with novices.

5. *Local summer workshop.*—The developing principles and
techniques of community participation represent the application
of a rapidly developing body of knowledge in the social sciences to a major social problem. It is clear that both scientists
and community practitioners have much to learn from each
other, and that the problems of community action provide an
ideal focus for bringing these groups together. It is also clear that
promising social inventions like the block participation program
should be adaptable to other blocks, and that the general
methodology of the Conference should provide stimulation and
inspiration to churches, youth houses, industries, agencies, and
other groups whose functioning depends on their dynamic relationships to the community.

In the specific case on which this chapter is based, the Human
Dynamics Laboratory of the University of Chicago and the Chicago Commission on Human Relations, with some assistance from
the National Training Laboratory in Group Development, in-
augurated in 1951 annual three-week workshops in the community. At the present writing, the evidence from the first workshop is encouraging. Two neighborhood organizations in other
parts of the city have taken a new lease on life—along conference
lines. The training in face-to-face group operation and urban
sociology has markedly influenced programs of several agencies.
The participants from the workshop have been meeting once a
month to keep alive the communication and mutual supportiveness developed during the summer.

While there are many practical difficulties involved in getting
agencies and organizations to assign their leaders to a three-
week training period, the notion is gradually developing that
community leadership in agencies and organizations is a growing profession. Groups are learning that training is a good investment. In the first nine months following the workshop we

can estimate conservatively that fifty citizens groups got started, all directly traceable to training given during the summer.

FACILITATING SERVICES

The potential effectiveness of a citizen group is determined by the number and quality of the action channels available to it. As co-operative relationships are established with each city office in turn, the possibilities for successful block action increase by just that much. As the legal panel, working with the zoning and housing committees, establishes relations with judges as "friends of the court," the blocks on which housing cases arise can provide more and more effective testimony about the prevailing housing standards to be maintained on the block. As the Conference board joins with other organizations in the city to demand a shake-up in the police department, the block group is encouraged to document and report local instances of misfeasance or faulty enforcement. Similarly, with the real estate, recreation, public schools, and lighting committees.

The pattern is clear and the moral inescapable. Working groups in the community in or out of the Conference can add endlessly to the potential power of the grass roots movement IF there is two-way communication. Moreover, two-way communication keeps the working committees spurred on to greater activity and accomplishment. Probably the most common source of the frustration felt by all too many working groups and social agencies is the feeling that nobody has any expectations for them. And the occupational disease of executive secretaries is the feeling of isolation; they talk to themselves for a while, then fall silent.

Two-way communication is possible under just one set of conditions: both parties have purposes in common and recognize the need for each other. This is the essence of the co-operative relationship. The job of a community conference is clear. It is to facilitate and develop co-operation among all the elements in the community, to align the various forces going our way into one vast drive for betterment. The novel thing about the conference is that it defines and demonstrates an important new social role: that of teacher of methods in community co-operation.

SIGNIFICANCE AND ACCOMPLISHMENTS OF THE PROGRAM OF CITIZEN PARTICIPATION

1. The Community Conference program of the South Side of Chicago has, in a three-year period, been adapted to six other communities in the city. In each case, there has been the initial hue and cry that city dwellers cannot get together on neighborly lines. In each case, as the program started rolling, leadership has been found and blocks have started on the long road from incipient deterioration toward stabilization and recovery. Over two hundred citizen groups are now meeting in Chicago on an average of once a month. In the Conference area, about 2 per cent of the population has attended one or more block meetings.

The spread has been almost entirely the results of voluntary, lay leadership, and it has been most rapid in the areas which had greatest anxiety, usually about (*a*) the in-migration of Negroes; (*b*) the economic problems of keeping up neighborhoods composed of beautiful "white elephant" houses; or (*c*) the neighborhoods where there is greatest concern over crime.

It is interesting to compare this urban movement with the Rochdale (England) co-operative movement, which subsequently spread to Nova Scotia, Denmark, Jamaica, Michigan, and Ohio. The co-operative movement started with economically depressed industrial workers, and its original purpose was to provide food more cheaply. The personal economic base remains, and the movement has caught on most effectively in rural areas, with co-operative self-help as the theme. The conference movement had for its driving force the unrest and anxieties of urban dwellers caught in a period of uncontrolled industrial expansion. The average citizen became submerged; he lost his voice, and with it, to all intents and purposes, he lost his prerogatives as a citizen.

In both movements, however, the individual has found himself by recognizing his interdependence with others in a narrow geographic area. In both cases, the focus of communication is objectively defined problems which are important to the participants. In both cases, the program has been conceived as partly educational. And in both cases, consultative and organizing help has been available through church, government, or university.

The first accomplishment, then, is the fact that needs of citizens are being met, and the evidence is the growth and spread of the movement through voluntary action.

2. The experience of each new conference is that it takes a substantial amount of time and a large number of followed-up demands on the city hall to get for the neighborhoods the city services they should have. In each case, however, the attitude of downtown has gradually changed, and demands for maintenance of services are now met almost routinely. The demonstration of the effectiveness of continually applied, nonhostile demands as a way of getting civic services is a second major accomplishment.

3. There are, in most neighborhoods, other organizations already in existence when the conference begins. The first effort is to try to work through these organizations rather than to start a new one. The typical result has been that none of the other organizations is ready to move along the necessary problem-solving lines. As the program gets going, however, it is usual for the other organizations to become much more active. In effect, the new conference group sets the pace for other groups. In some cases, the renewed activity seems to be an expression of competitiveness; in other cases, of guilt. There may be a renewed optimism and encouragement acquired from people who belong to both groups.

In any case, whatever the reason, the development of the conference, with its co-operative attitudes, results in a parallel reactivation of other groups, and thus vastly increases the total effort going into community problem-solving.

4. There is no question that many neighborhoods with active block organizations have improved physically and have stabilized themselves psychologically. Illegal conversions have been stopped, panic flight no longer happens, and people are investing money in their homes. There is a clear determination to stay on the block, and a feeling that the remaining problems can be solved, and that it is rewarding to try to solve them.

Organized blocks are gradually being recognized as a social fact to be taken into account by real estate operators, housing speculators, and mortgage-loan groups. The average civic spoiler is ambivalent, and his exploitative tactics are often at least partly an expression of insecurities that have little to do with the need for money. The organized block has an effect on such people. The standard of maintenance and the optimistic determination of the group reinforces the positive sides of ambivalence. Thus, most real estate firms do not really set out to wreck a neighborhood; they know that the ruination of housing through speculative exploitation is also, in the long run, the ruination of their own business. Similarly, the mortage-loan people, who, mostly on the basis of racial stereotypes, refuse to loan money on houses in areas where Negroes are moving in, know underneath that such tactics contribute to the creeping blight that eventually destroys their own opportunity to invest their money. Both groups can be influenced by home owners *en masse*.

The psychological stabilization of a neighborhood through meeting the needs of residents develops a positive force which can be applied through organization to the target groups contributing most to decay.

5. Speaking personally, as a methodologist in the field of social action, the block action program outlined in this chapter presents to me three highly exciting demonstrations.

The first demonstration is that there is a vast, almost limitless source of power that can be tapped for the improvement of the community. The source of this power is the individual's need for security and for an adequate way of life. The manifestation of this power is through constructive community activity. And the results of this power are an improvement of conditions which release more activity to improve conditions further. The dynamic of the power is in the processes of re-education and training; a conscious utilization of experience to make the next effort more effective; a renewal of the idea of co-operative self-help. The block program seems to me to be the refutation of the notion that the answer to community problems is the bulldozer, the government planners, or the big life insurance project. These last resorts are just that—the final, desperate effort to buy back, at terrific expense, something that could have been maintained and conserved through maintenance of neighborly interaction.

The second demonstration for me has been the gradual definition of the role of the citizen in urban society. It is a much larger
role than merely that of putting a ballot in the box every couple
of years. The citizen role is not only a political act, it is an aspect
of the role of father, husband, consumer, hobbyist, club member,
and resident. And it is not separate from these things. The actions
and expressed attitudes of each one of us have implications for
the community. In the small town we all know that there is
"feedback," that our acts come home to roost. In the city, we do
not get "feedback"; the influence of our acts is hard to trace; it
spreads outward like the ripples on a pond, and dissipates itself in
many tiny unknowable ways. In a neighborhood, particularly
one with well-defined geographic boundaries and with good
communication among the neighbors, we are more likely to get
"feedback," and we learn from experience that interdependence
exists and that we are a part of it. And thus we have consciousness of our citizenship role.

So far as I know there is no place where the citizen role in this
sense is taught. It probably cannot be taught effectively apart
from its proper context of co-operative action. The block program, it seems to me, can be regarded as a vast adult education
program directed to learning of the operational meanings of
democracy.

The third major demonstration, and one which we shall point
to again and again in many situations, is that there is a close
relationship between the concepts of scientific method and
democracy. Avoiding for the moment the arguments about what
democracy is, still one is impressed by a number of parallels.
Thus the scientific requirement of objectivity as the evaluating
and testing of competent witness is also the reason in the block
group for expecting all the members to help in defining the problems to be tackled. The scientific effort to test hypotheses without inquiring into their origin in creative thought is closely akin
to the block group's problem of weighing opinions in the light of
factual evidence rather than personal status. The scientific concept that an idea is "truthful" if it can be used to predict what
will happen is brother to the block group's testing of action plans

by assessing the results of the first step before planning subsequent steps.

It is my belief that these and other parallels are by no means accidental, and I see these notions, along with characteristics shared by many religious creeds, as evidence that man through various avenues of interpretation of experience is gradually beginning to nail down a basic methodology of human interaction and, with this, the possibilities of a better world for us all.

The problem of the neighborhood group versus the central parent organization involves divided loyalty, the dynamics of which are discussed on pages 231–35. Growth of the citizen group over time will probably generally follow the model given on pages 360–65. The way the neighborhood group operates to reduce racial conflict is examined on pages 349–56. Appropriate attitudes of leadership are described on pages 284–89, and, by implication, in the discussion of two points of view on pages 103–8. Chapter 11 is entirely concerned with problems of leadership.

CHAPTER 2

Classroom teaching is whatever the teacher does in the classroom. He must find ways to keep defined school problems in front of the class, to help the children organize their efforts to attack these problems, and to arrange opportunities for them to obtain insight as to what it all means to themselves.

The teacher guides the class by shifting his own role experimentally in response to his diagnosis of the kind of experience the class needs and is ready for.

DISTINCTIVE FEATURES

In the classroom, the authority of leadership is conferred on the teacher by the community. It is further enhanced by the fact that he is an adult and has special, recognized, and valued competence in the group. The primary target of classroom instruction is the capability of the students, which is to be modified in accordance with particular educational objectives. Secondary targets include parental attitudes toward the school and the children. The role of the student is determined by the will of the teacher—with some qualification by the standards of the peer and family groups to which the student belongs. The method of classroom control is dictated by the teacher's understanding of the conditions required for learning and his ideas as to how these conditions are to be achieved. There may be in addition rules of politeness, courtesy, or other school-sanctioned limits to behavior. The classroom group per se has no direct formalized relationships to other groups, although the teacher represents its needs to service functionaries, and the children act unofficially as ambassadors to family, club, and other groups in the community. The parent-teacher relationships may be formal and group-provided or informal and selective. The principal is typically the spokesman for the school, including the classrooms.

Educating Children through Need-meeting Activity

The Argument and the Problem

It is good practice, if you will forgive a bit of "pedagese," to start with the learners where they are. What are their problems, what are they ready for, what are their capacities and needs?

In education generally, it seems to me that where we teacher-learners are is in the middle of an argument; our problem is to restate the argument in such a way that we can settle it; and what we are ready for is to try to understand what we know about learning wherever it occurs and to see what the implications are for classroom situations. We shall then, depending on our needs and capacities, be in a position to modify classroom experiences for the better.

The first thing that ought to be said about the argument is that it is not just an educational argument; it has been going on in one way or another for as long as there has been a society of men. It is in educational circles, however, that the argument perhaps finds its most direct and hottest expression, partly because "educating" youngsters is safely remote from what we adults do, partly because the classroom is played upon by every segment of community opinion, and partly because everyone has spent at least a few years in school and therefore has a backlog of school experience in terms of which the big issues can be explored.

The second thing that ought to be said about educational argument is that it is contributed to by philosophers, psychologists, teachers, politicians, welfare workers, sociologists, manufacturers, educators, journalists, judges; and that somehow, out of the welter of many voices and many points of view, there has emerged a first-class list of "either-ors." In other words, the battle lines seem to have been drawn, and the resulting unreasonableness and heat underscore the point that we have here no mere argument

33

about education but rather a basic conflict cutting across all aspects of society.

We shall, however, attempt to consider the argument simply in its relevance to classroom teaching, even though we shall need to range far beyond the classroom to find the light we need.

The most simple expression of the argument is through a sampling of the conflicts it contains. Stated as either-ors, we have:

Individual	versus	society
Child-centered	versus	subject-centered
Guidance	versus	instruction
Discussion	versus	lecture
Pupil planning	versus	teacher planning
Intrinsic motivation	versus	extrinsic motivation
Insight learning	versus	drill and practice
Growth	versus	achievement
Firsthand experience	versus	vicarious experience
Freedom	versus	dominance
Democratic	versus	authoritarian
Subjective world	versus	objective world
Spontaneity	versus	conformity

The terms on the left-hand side of all these "versuses" fit into a pattern; see if you recognize this theme song:

"I want my child to be treated as an *individual* by teachers who *center* their attention on the *children* and see themselves essentially as *guides*. Children are capable of *planning* and *discussing* their experiences, of being *guided from within*. The important thing is understanding and *insight* that leads to *growth*. I want them through *firsthand experience* to learn the meaning of *freedom,* to understand and be committed to a *democratic* way of life. But, above all, I want them to be adequate people, with a rich and ennobling *subjective inner life;* only thus can they achieve the creative *spontaneity* which is man's most precious attribute."

But the terms on the right-hand side cannot be ignored; here is another theme song:

The teacher is an instrument of *society* and he is hired primarily because of his mastery of the sciences and the arts as arranged in *school subjects*. His job is to give *instruction* and to communicate not single interesting facts but rather ideas organized in meaningful relationship to each other, as in a *lecture*. The *teacher* knows the material to be covered, and it is his responsibility *to plan* in such a way that it will be covered. The teacher knows that getting ahead in this world requires ability to meet the *demands of the community*, and that only through *drill and practice* can school *achievement* become part of one's habit pattern. Many of the important things in life were discovered by others and are learned through *vicarious experience dominated* by these great *authorities*. The child is free to think as he wishes, but in the *objective world* of action he must *conform* to the standards of the community."

It is interesting to note the grammar of these theme songs. The first makes use of the words "I want"—it is a statement of wishes and values. The second song uses the word "is"—it is a statement of facts. (Not all of them are correct, incidentally.)

This observation makes clear why the argument has existed so long and also why it is not a real argument at all. The confusion lies in the assumption that stating values (first song, "I want . . .") immediately implies specific instructional procedures, which it does not; and in the assumption that stating social facts (second song, "The teacher is . . .") immediately implies specific instructional procedures, which it does not. From these two assumptions then follows a lot of discussion and taking sides about what ought to be done in the classroom. Actually, of course, there is no argument between facts and values, between what is and what we want. There is, however, a gap and a question: Taking the facts into account, how do we get what we want; how do we move from where we are to where we want to be?

This is a question of method of instruction. And the method can be created only by considering both the facts and the values. It cannot be deduced from one or the other alone. Let us note that the little phrase "how do we get what we want?" requires two kinds of thinking: first, what is the nature of the means by which we get what we want, and, second, what kinds of changes are to be brought about by these means? In other words, what does a class look like when it is learning, and what changes in behavior occur as a result of learning? The teacher's image of what a class looks like when it is learning determines his behavior while teaching. The teacher's idea of what changes in behavior are required determines his construction of examinations and his assignment of grades to students. The two questions together determine his planning of instructional activities.

THE PICTURE IN OUR MINDS

As one watches different classrooms, he notes that each teacher has a style of his own. He is quite consistent in the way he operates: the amount of challenge to the class, the depth or superficiality of his comments, the feelings about his job. It is as if he had a model in mind and operated consistently to make the classroom conform to this model; it represents the teacher's idea of what the classroom should be like. When the classroom situation deviates from this image, the teacher then tries to rectify matters by taking action: making more of an explanation, reassigning working partners, bringing in a personal experience to increase interest, stopping talking so that the students have a chance, and so on. The teacher's model summarizes for him the principles of learning; his action is taken to maintain the model, using principles of educational method as his guide.

Let us look at a number of models which teachers have used.

MODEL 1: SOCRATIC DISCUSSION

The image is of a wise, somewhat crusty philosopher getting into arguments with more naive people. The issues discussed are known to both Socrates and the other party, and both have adequate factual knowledge for the discussion. Socrates shows the other up by pointing to inconsistencies in his logic. The arguments are primarily to clarify concepts and values.

As applied to classrooms, this type of discussion is an aid to the assimilation of ideas. *After* the children have learned some facts and had some experiences together, the teacher-Socrates can challenge the class and test their conclusions. The teacher has a central role, and the discussion has much of the emotionality of argumentation.

MODEL 2: THE TOWN MEETING

The image is of a group of citizens whose lives are interdependent meeting together to decide on courses of action required to solve problems. These problems are objectively defined in terms of acts of God, services needed, demands to be met. The group draws on the experiences, feelings, and thoughts of each other, and the method is co-operative. The leader is a moderator rather than an expert. The most appropriate action is decided by vote of the majority.

As applied to classrooms, this type of discussion best fits teacher-class planning of activity, in which the task is to decide how to organize to carry out specified learning activities. Some differences between class and town hall, however, are that the neighbors immediately recognize the problem to be solved as important, whereas the students do not; the action to be selected makes a financial or status or other difference to all the citizens, whereas there are fewer "real" consequences for the students; the citizens are competent to testify because they have all experienced the problem, whereas the students do not have such backing of relevant experience; the moderator is simply looking for the most complete consensus he can get, whereas the teacher must also give information and the results of his past experience.

MODEL 3: APPRENTICESHIP

The image is of a young person's life being "taken over" by an older one. The apprentice learns a trade, how to behave in the social-class level of his chosen occupation, how to be a parent in the family, and so on. The master is teacher, father, friend, colleague, and boss. Psychologically, the apprentice identifies himself with and imitates the master: he is there to learn how to be like the master and to live like him.

Some of the dynamics of apprenticeship apply in the classroom. The student does identify himself with the teacher, and he learns many attitudes in imitation of the teacher. And many teachers, basically, attempt to make the student over into their own image (as they perceive it). Much of the master's warmth and concern for the welfare of the apprentice is appropriate for the teacher also. In many universities today, training for the Ph.D. has considerable resemblance to apprenticeship experience.

MODEL 4: BOSS-EMPLOYEE, OR ARMY MODEL

The image here is of a person who has higher status and also the power to reward or punish, telling others what to do and how to do it, then seeing that it gets done, and, finally, evaluating how good a job he thinks it is. It is not necessary that the relationship be harsh or unfriendly, but it is necessary that there be considerable acceptance of many kinds of dependency by the subordinate. The rather small minority of people who thrive best as dependents may be quite creative in this situation.

This is probably the most prevalent model of the classroom, although there is wide variation in the extent to which the model is "softened up" by procedures for taking account of what the students feel about the teacher's demands. In other words, the teacher has to modify the image in the direction of more attention to pupil motivation and interest. This image is realistic for skill learnings like typing in which the requirement is to practice objectively described behaviors until a clearly defined level of performance is reached. It is also realistic with respect to a class working on a project involving physical work laid out according to plan.

MODEL 5: THE BUSINESS DEAL

The image is of one person with money (or some other inducement) making a bargain for the services of someone else. Thus one might pay a cabinetmaker to build him a chair. He would discuss specifications for the object, be available for making some decisions as the work progressed, and would finally decide whether to accept or reject the object.

This is essentially the "contract plan," in which the teacher makes the best deal he can with each individual workman (student) and consults with him as the work proceeds. The advantage of this model is that the child assumes a high degree of responsibility and the contract can be written to fit reasonable expectations of him. The disadvantages are that the teacher has to supervise a wide variety of different jobs, and the social factor and possibilities of learning better through working together are either denied or ignored.

MODEL 6: THE GOOD OLD TEAM

The image is of a group of players listening to the coach between quarters of the football game. This is followed by inspired playing which defeats the opposing team. The coach's objective is to get better playing, and almost any devices of persuasion or threats or promises that will produce high-level performance are accepted as legitimate.

This is an unrealistic model for the classroom, although its use is sometimes encouraged. The coach is working for a quick spurt rather than for long-range effects; there has to be an "enemy" team to compete with; the product to be evaluated is a score run-up by the group, rather than individual achievement; the team players are required to submerge all but very limited aspects of their individuality as completely as possible; and finally, the team is primarily an instrument for expressing the will of the coach. Few of these characteristics can really be found in the teacher-pupil relationship.

MODEL 7: THE GUIDED TOUR

The image here is of a group of interested children following closely behind a mature guide as he leads them through the jungle, brewery, courthouse, or wherever. From time to time he calls their attention to objects he wants to tell them about, and he gives them information, stories, and opinions. He also answers questions. He maintains order and sees to it that the number of children who arrive home equals the number who set out in the morning. He may or may not plan with them certain questions or major categories of information the field trip is supposed to answer.

The acceptance by the teacher of the fact that he has been "over the field" before and has much to tell should be realistic. His personal enthusiasm and ability to "let the class see for itself" help motivate the children and arouse their interest. The experience of learning names for objects is a rather small intellectual task, and usually is inadequate to absorb the class's energies. The guided tour (e.g., survey course) is a quick way to cultural ornamentation but the "knowledge" learned may be unrelated to possibilities of personal use.

The fact that so many models or analogies are possible underscores the complexity of classroom teaching. The fact that there may be particular times when each of these models is most appropriate points to the vast array of roles in which the teacher must act at different times. Even within the space of a very few minutes, the teacher may have to show considerable flexibility. He may speak as a representative of the group or culture he grew up in, act as social analyst to help the class evaluate the opinions he expresses, give expert answers or facts about subject matter or school rules, consult with the class on how to proceed to next steps, act as counselor to some child needing help, act as symbol for parent, sweetheart, or generalized adult authority in the eyes of children "working on" such problems.[1]

Actually, however, nobody has an unlimited repertoire of roles. In general, the attractiveness for a particular teacher of the model he has adopted or worked out lies partly in the fact that it enables him "to play the role" which is most congenial to himself. The teacher's identifications with business, sport, government, wisdom—these are expressed through his playing, in effect, the role of businessman, coach, moderator, Socrates. Each of these occupations also is characteristic of a social class position in the community, and the wish we all have for belonging to some particular class enters into the choice. We could guess that in communities where the teacher's position has little prestige, where control is in the hands of groups who have little communication with the school, the teacher would feel strongly the pull of some class and occupation group other than his own. The place in the teacher's life where he is free to act out his wishes of belonging to another group is the classroom, because there the teacher has sufficient power and control to mold its culture to almost any shape he desires.

Models like the above help the teacher define the working relationship between himself and his class. They serve to clarify the role of the teacher: his power, his concerns, his style of teaching. The roles of the students are not differentiated in these models—

1. Thelen and Tyler, "Implications for Improving Instruction in the High School," chap. 12, *Learning and Instruction*, 49th Yearbook, National Society for the Study of Education, 1950.

all the students are expected to behave alike in ways which enable the teacher to enforce *his* role.

The view of teaching implied by the existence of these models is realistic, but it is also inadequate. It is realistic in recognizing that the only behavior under the direct control of the teacher is his own; and the teacher, by virtue of the authority of his position, age, and professional competence has the power to determine his behavior pretty much apart from consideration of student needs. The models also realistically recognize that the roles possible to the students depend upon the role that the teacher chooses to play. In effect, the freedom of students is with respect to whatever functions the teacher does not pre-empt for himself. These two basic principles provide us with clues for understanding how the teacher consciously and by design alters the activities in the classroom.

The inadequacy of the models becomes apparent with the realization that they only illuminate half the problem of method. The models make clear what is expected of teacher and students once the teacher's role is decided. They do not, however, give any basis for determining the appropriate role of the teacher, and they start from the needs of the teacher rather than from an analysis of the requirements of learning situations. Effective thinking about the design and control of educative activity must begin with the question "What sort of participatory role must students have, to learn what they need to learn and are supposed to learn?" Only after this question has been answered quite apart from any consideration of the teacher's needs can we begin to see the sort of role the teacher must play if student experience is to be educative. The most significant quality of a good teacher is that he is able to meet his own needs through playing the roles required to make activities educative for students.

The question of the sort of role-participation required for learning by the students is complicated by the facts that different kinds of learning require different roles, and that learning experience is complex, involving thoughts, feelings, actions, emotions, and desires. To give students the kinds of experiences they need demands from us first that we understand the nature of classroom experience. What, then, are the facts?

THE FACTS IN THE CASE

What I am about to describe as an accurate picture of the state of affairs in the classroom would, I think, be agreed to by many competent students of education who are concerned with the social-psychological factors which influence learning. Nonetheless, these comments, if they are to fit the "typical" classroom, must be generalizations, and, as such, I shall submit them as hypotheses which are suggestive and probably correct, but which have not been rigorously, i.e., competently, demonstrated.

The first important facts represent a set of rules that the child has to accept. He didn't make them, and in most communities he has no effective way of rebelling against or changing them.

The basic rule is that the child must go to school. Other rules are that he must accept as teachers the people he is assigned to; that he must accept the other pupils as fellow-members of the classroom group; that he must learn whatever he is told to learn up to some minimum level of competence as given by the authorities.

The facts are legislated. They could be changed by the proper authorities, but they operate like laws; in fact, in most states there *are* laws governing many of these requirements. For many students, these rules are so fully accepted that their existence as limits to behavior is very rarely felt; for others, the whole school experience is colored by the existence of the rules. These students are like the man who loves to speed on a Sunday outing. He is so concerned with lawmen that he misses the scenery—and pays an occasional fine.

A second important set of facts represents description of the child's firsthand experience. The most fundamental thing about classroom experience is that it is social; it is a continual set of interactions with other people. I call this the most fundamental thing because there is no escape; the demands are there, and they must be met. You can ignore what a dead author has left behind on a printed page, but you cannot ignore the youngster behind you snapping with a rubber band. You can know that a story about how Horatius held the bridge is just a story; but teacher holding the class after school is no mere journalistic creation.

These interactions are most fundamental for another reason: they make a difference in the learning process. I do not now remember who and what was involved in 1066, but my interactions with Miss Burke still color my feelings and attitudes about Latin. I have forgotten most of the formulas in statistics that I learned in summer school; but I married a girl I met in that class. No matter how deeply immersed in play the nursery school's four-year-olds may be, every time the door opens every head turns toward it to see if Mike, the bully, has arrived. One girl in my present seminar never participates except immediately after another girl has spoken; one boy in the group says very little when I, the teacher, am present; but when I am absent he says many good things to the group. Social interactions set the conditions under which learning occurs.

These interactions are most fundamental for still another reason: they involve direct feedback. If Willy hits Mary in class, he can't just pretend that it did not happen. He has to face a return behavior from Mary, the teacher, or another child. If Willy reads into O. Henry's story "The Ransom of Red Chief" the principle that a boy who is naughty enough can control the adults in his life, nothing happens. There is no direct test of his belief until he starts acting toward people as if he believed it, and by then, his citing of O. Henry as his authority will be pooh-poohed as a "rationalization." I still do not know whether the lesson from college ROTC was (*a*) that with proper equipment and skill we can beat the enemy, or (*b*) that war is futile because the other side can manufacture equipment, strategies, and soldiers too. There was never any occasion in ROTC to test which of these morals made most sense, and I sometimes still wonder what was intended. But there was plenty of opportunity for an immediate test of the idea that, while a cat can sneer at a king, a private had better not sneer at a major. When I taught high-school physics, I had two beginning classes which, as far as I could tell, were composed of children who were equally bright, had equal social standing in the community, and, on individual interview, expressed the same range of interest in physics. Yet teaching one class was like pulling teeth and teaching the other was like singing around the piano. In one class, I had the immediate response of apathy to everything I did; in the other class, the feedback was of challenging questions and meaningful ideas for the group to pursue.

Every one of these illustrations points to the compelling nature of interactions with other people in the classroom. The highest priority needs of students are to find their places in the group, to work through their anxieties about their competences, to adjust to authority, to explore and define their growing social capacities. These needs determine much of the quality of classroom experience, and they color the meanings of the subject matter learned. Good school achievement is usually the socially approved way of getting commendation from other people, or the way of withdrawing from social interaction, or the victory one gets from successful competition, or all of these. It is part of a socially determined pattern, produced through interaction with other people in and out of the classroom. Most school learning is partly a means to some other end.

A third set of important facts helps us to assess the probable meaningfulness of classroom experience over and beyond its social implications. There are two conditions under which ideas are meaningful. First, they have been connected through direct experience to real feelings so that they have color and richness; and, second, they have been assimilated into the student's fund of previously learned ideas so that they serve as doorways to whole structures of thought. But thoughts without organization and without associated feeling are basically nonsense; they have little usefulness of any kind to their host.

Ask any six people what they visualize when you say, "Columbus discovered America in 1492," or what you should do now that you know that the density of lead is 11.35 (11.35 *what*, for Heaven's sake!). What comes into your mind when I say that "frustration leads to aggression," or when I quote that dear old chestnut of the child-development courses: "Ontogeny recapitulates phylogeny" (or is it the other way around?)? I just opened a book I studied in anatomy, and I am trying to figure out why I once underlined in red the following: "The nuclei or centers of several cranial nerves lie in the gray matter of the medulla immediately under the floor of the fourth ventricle." I have, of course, taken these ideas out of context, and that is my point: out of context they are dream stuff. But in what context did they have reality and meaning?

One kind of meaning is "developmental." At one stage of life, Columbus represents high adventure, and studying about him can be gratifying. A few years later, Columbus can be pretty dull.

Another kind of meaning comes with problem-solving. The figure for the density of lead could make sense if I were building a model boat and wanted to know the dimensions of an appropriately weighted lead keel. Of course, if I just imagined I was building a boat, the fact would be only academic and it wouldn't matter whether lead's density is 4.5, 11.35, or 26. In either case, however, the context is that of a practical problem to be solved.

Thus learning is useful or real if it makes a difference or helps solve a problem—in other words, if it has a meaningful context in purposive experience. The "problem" may be one of taking action, organizing ideas within a consistent framework, getting out of emotional conflict, and so on. But for an idea to be useful there must be not only a use for it; in addition, the idea must be usable. Thus we all have uses for ideas about democracy, but many of our notions about democracy are not usable. They are either high-sounding phrases which, on examination, are either meaningless or else mean something other than what they sound as if they ought to mean; or they are misunderstood assertions such as "all men are created equal," which, if taken literally, would refute the known facts of biology and psychology. The test of the usability of an idea is that when one operates in accordance with it, the results have the expected consequences.

The facts about classroom experience are, in brief:

1. Classroom experience occurs in classrooms set up and operated by authorities for children who have to participate.

2. The firsthand tested experience of the child is one of interaction with other people.

3. On top of this experience is grafted a great deal of "school subject content" which may or may not have any reality and meaning for the child, depending on the conditions under which it is taught.

THE THREE BASIC ASPECTS OF THE TEACHING
AND LEARNING EXPERIENCE

"Teaching method" is the set of policies used by the teacher to guide or control activity in the classroom. Control is exercised through the fact that the teacher is the "authority" in the sense that nothing can be planned without his acquiescence or permission. Under proper conditions, the teacher exercises this control through continuous definition of purposes and expectations rather than through threat of punishment. The matters for which the teacher assumes responsibility include the particular school achievements to be striven for, the ways of working together, and some of the kinds of socially authorized meanings of the experiences of children. The way the control is exercised—the feelings responded to and the timing of the response—determines both the fruitfulness of the immediate activity and the motivation for future learning. By influencing the children's participation in immediate activity, the teacher determines what they have a chance to learn; and the quality of reward or punishment in his relationship to the children determines their taste for further activity along the same lines. The acts by which a teacher controls the situation and, through this, the participation of the children have both long- and short-range effects.

As we now examine the three facts about classroom experience in the light of the foregoing facts about teacher control, we shall see that the quality of the total classroom experience is woven from three distinguishable but ever present aspects of all activity.

The first fact of classroom experience, that "classrooms [are] set up and operated by authorities for children who have to participate" tells us that the community expects teachers to teach. And teaching is, in this context, the "transmission of the funded capital of human experience"—an elegant way of saying that the preservation of the community requires everyone to know some things that have been learned by other men. But the first fact alone, that authorities determine subject matter, does not tell *how* to teach. In general terms, at least, the answer is perfectly clear: the "funded capital of human experience" is more successfully transmitted through a goal-seeking type of experience than through a formally organized passing-on of information "from the notes of the instructor to the notes of the student without passing through the mind of either." It is certainly well established that content is better retained and creatively used when it is learned in response to a sense of problem than when it is simply passively absorbed.

We may, therefore, think of control of the conscious goal-seeking or problem-solving aspects of experience as one basic function of teaching. And we can see that the objective sciences and technologies, with their easy-to-obtain data and their possibilities of incontrovertible proof of propositions, offer the opportunity *par excellence* for demonstrating to children the methods, meanings, and satisfactions of problem solving. We conclude that one requirement of teaching method is that it must enable the teacher to accept contributions from children within a framework of problem solving. Chapter 1, dealing with community problem-solving, delineates many of the attitudes the teacher needs in order to facilitate learning of school subjects.

Our second fact presented above, that "the firsthand tested experience of the child is one of interaction with other people," also has implications for teaching method. The social interactions of the classroom appear to be viewed in different ways. To some, they are distracting occurrences to be suppressed in the service of orderliness, discipline, or learning. To others, they are the most important expressions of individual personality, and they should therefore be encouraged and, in some magical way, guided and controlled. Our point of view is that through social interaction, conversation, and expression of feeling the group exerts its influence on the individual and the individual on the group; the problem of control is not to prevent these kinds of influencings but to try to obtain a quality of influencing that improves learning.

A genuine learning situation is one which involves the emotions of the learner; the social conditions in the group determine whether the necessary emotionality will be facilitating, distracting, or inhibiting of learning. Successful methods of teaching do control emotional phenomena or "group process" in such a way that learning is better motivated, challenge is greatest, and accomplishment is the goal of the group.

Control of social interaction—of side-conversations, of expression of opinion, of relaxation into humorous episodes, of work stoppage—is legitimately for one purpose: to increase learning. It is by now quite clear that the appropriate qualities of informality, concentration, rigorousness, and expressiveness differ from activity to activity, depending upon purpose. A freewheeling "bright-idea" session is far different from a careful attempt to deduce courses of action from explicitly stated principles. The amount of frustration and difficulty that can be tolerated and worked through depends very much on the extent to which people can share with each other their feelings about the situation. It follows, then, that there cannot be any one specific model for social interaction; the quality of interaction is good when it is appropriate to the task and to the purposes. Without a clearly defined achievement task, there is no precise way to judge the appropriateness of social interaction.

It is true, of course, that there are some limits. Murder is not admissible regardless of the learning task. Licentious activities which place a burden of guilt on students should not be allowed to occur, regardless of the state of definition of the achievement problems. Aside from the prevention of events that are bad from a mental hygiene standpoint, there are no criteria to be applied to social interaction beyond the requirements of behavior appropriate to the learning task. Thus the notion that a classroom should always give the appearance of "co-operation" and "shipboard intimacy" implies that these conditions are in themselves good, quite apart from what people learn under these conditions. Actually, when dealing with ideas, learning probably occurs under conditions of conflict over ideas, accompanied by sharing of feelings about common purposes, and subconscious agreement that hostility is not meant personally. If a teacher likes an orderly, quiet classroom, there is only one legitimate way to obtain it: make the work so interesting and challenging and need-meeting that the students naturally work in an orderly and absorbed way. It is probable, however, that such periods of orderliness will be interspersed with periods of give-and-take, during which students are preparing for the more studious activity.

Just as students need to learn the discipline of problem solving so they can know how to participate for school achievement, they also need to learn the discipline of group management and organization so they can deal with their problems of security, belongingness, and individuality within the classroom group. The social sciences—sociology, civics, history, psychology, anthropology—should be taught in such a way as to illuminate these matters.

The second aspect of experience to be guided, controlled, and understood by adequate teaching method is social interaction. It is required that the teacher be able to diagnose from the contributions of the children the appropriateness to learning of the particular state of social interaction, and that he then be able to steer the classroom experience as a result of such diagnosis. Chapter 5, dealing with human relations training, shows what is involved in these skills.

The third fact is that " 'school subject content' . . . may or may not have any reality and meaning for the child, depending on the conditions under which it is taught." This statement asks us to recognize the ultimate fact about classroom instruction: that its purpose is to enrich the lives and capacities of all of the students. The aspects of experience important here are the self-discovering and reality-testing parts. The quality of these experiences probably determines whether knowledge is for power or merely for social ornamentation, whether it is an instrument for creativity or simply more material for the dead files.

The development of these experiences is referred to in various ways: the development of an effective personality, the development of personal objectivity, the learning of appropriate personal-social attitudes, the integration of thought and feeling, the gaining of personal security, the getting in touch with reality. However it may be referred to, the kind of experience required is clear: one must have opportunity, with appropriate guidance, to reflect upon and understand his own reactions to immediate experience. And the most useful content of experience from which to start in such a discussion is the feelings the individual is aware of having had. To explain our feelings we must study our participation within a total framework of self-knowledge. Gradually we learn to use this knowledge to help decide in each new situation how to participate, i.e., what behaviors to present to the group.

The method of teaching should enable the student to relate the personal meaning of his experience to his individual behavior and to ascertain the appropriateness of his behavior both for himself and for others. If Jack wants affection but all his behaviors antagonize people, then he needs some personal re-education. If Joe distorts all experience to prove over and over to himself that getting ahead is primarily a matter of "pull" and favoritism, then Joe needs to reinterpret his own experience along more realistic lines.

The fundamental point is that the quality of the inner subjective world, created by each individual and used by him to guide his impulses into behavior, is the heart of the educative process. It is not enough to say that "every individual is free to think as he pleases" any more than it is appropriate to try to mold individual thinking into the teacher's pattern. But if an individual reacts unrealistically, then his inner world needs modification; his concepts and theories, whatever they are, are inadequate.

The third aspect of experiencing to be guided and controlled by the method of teaching is the connecting of problem solving and social participation to the private inner subjective world of the individual. This is the process of finding meaning in experience, of understanding, experimenting with, and modifying one's orientation to the world in the light of new learning. The arts, particularly literary and dramatic, have a contribution to make to the student's understanding of this aspect of experiencing.

We conclude that the method of teaching guides three basic aspects of experiencing: conscious goal seeking or problem solving, group process, and individual meaning. Instead of being "society-centered," or "subject-centered," or "group-centered," or "child-centered," respectively, the teacher needs to be *reality-centered*. He must determine his behavior in such a way that all three aspects of experiencing fit together and enrich the education of the child.

How is this to be done?

THE METHOD IN OPERATION

We have suggested that, within a classroom learning activity, energy goes into three types of processes: (1) working with school subject matter, preferably within the context of problem solving; (2) organizing social relations to maintain greatest support for and participation in learning activities; and (3) discovering, formulating, and testing meanings of experience for one's self.

We shall refer to these three types of processes as three aspects of classroom experiencing. We believe that these three aspects provide the functional framework for learning, and that at any time, as needed, any aspect may become the central object of attention, the central organizing principle for learning experience.

The problems we are confronted with in implementing these ideas in the classroom may be identified as follows:

1. How can the understanding of these three aspects in their relationships to learning become part of the classroom culture?

2. How can the teacher and class diagnose which aspect should be central to activity at any given time?

3. How can shifts in focus on the three aspects be accomplished without producing ambiguity and confusion?

4. How can needed activities of the three types be created?

5. How can the class be organized to carry out the needed types of activity?

PROBLEM 1. HOW CAN THE UNDERSTANDING OF THESE THREE
ASPECTS IN THEIR RELATIONSHIPS TO LEARNING
BECOME PART OF THE CLASSROOM CULTURE?

The assumption behind this question is that the class and teacher, in so far as they operate together, do so on the basis of shared expectancies about what is important, necessary, desirable, and possible. Among the shared expectancies and agreements, which constitute the culture of the group, are: (*a*) that the course is concerned with problems of school achievement; (*b*) that in working on these problems it will be necessary to pay attention to the part played by the teacher and by the students, and that these role-definitions may change from activity to activity;

and (c) that the conclusions individuals are drawing about themselves, the others, and the work need to be understood, tested, and used as data in planning activities.

Ultimately, of course, such understandings should be part of the total school culture, and at such a time they will be acted upon as a matter of course. Assuming, however, that these expectancies are not yet institutionalized in the school, the teacher has the problem of getting them incorporated into the group culture. The simplest way to accomplish this is for the teacher to act as if he believed them and to make clear to the group why he proposes each activity he does. Thus it is easy for the teacher to say, for example, "It seems to me that we have talked about a lot of factors that influence public opinion at election time and I believe we ought now to think about which ones would influence each of us, and why. I propose, therefore, that we break up into twosomes, and each of you can try to persuade the other to vote for, let us say, Mr. Smith for mayor. Use all the appeals we have been talking about. Then you can discuss which appeals seemed to work and why you thought so. After we have done this, we can compare notes in the class as a whole." Thus the teacher could move from the level of general group discussion of objective facts about elections to the level of individual feelings, resistances, and needs.

Such simple explanations not only instruct the group well enough so that it can carry out the activity; they also, if consistently offered and discussed as necessary, rather rapidly lead to the development of expectancies for the three types of basic experience.

Questions that the class needs to understand as part of the various basic experiences are:

For problem solving:
  What is the nature of the problem?
  What factors are involved in a specific instance of the problem?
  What will have to happen if the problem is to be solved?
  What are the ways of getting these things to happen?
  How can we judge which suggested way is the best in our situation?
  How can we test whether the way we select really is effective?
  How can we explain why it worked the way it did?
  Etc.

For group membership and management:

What kinds of ideas or facts do we need now?

How shall we organize ourselves to get these needed ideas?

How can we put these ideas together to guide the group?

What provision do we need for special roles: chairman, secretary, blackboard-writer, messenger, boss, etc.

What factors stood in our way of working efficiently?

How does our job today (e.g., reporting facts dug out of books) differ from our job yesterday (e.g., defining the task).

Etc.

For individual meaning:

What disagreements do you have with these conclusions?

What would you do differently as a result of knowing about . . . ?

What other interpretations do you think other people might make of (this information)?

What parts of our (discussion, project, experiment, etc.) seemed most interesting to you? Why?

What things made it (easy) (hard) to participate in the (discussion, etc.)?

Who do you think would find this (information, principle, attitude, etc.) important, and why?

Etc.

The teacher, by asking such questions and helping the group answer and discuss them, gradually establishes the expectancies of the group for the range of qualities of experience required. The best sign of group growth and development of the group culture is that the students themselves begin to pose these questions at the appropriate times. Approval should be given for such efforts and suggestions, so that paying attention to the process of learning becomes in itself a source of reward for the students. The greatest reward, however, probably is not the teacher's expressed approval, except when the class is still new. The greatest reward comes when the class adequately discusses the suggestions and plans its activities as a result of the answers it gets to its own questions.

PROBLEM 2. HOW CAN THE TEACHER AND CLASS DIAGNOSE
WHICH ASPECT SHOULD BE CENTRAL TO ACTIVITY
AT ANY GIVEN TIME?

The basic method of guiding a classroom group is through diagnosis of the problems and needs which the group is expressing as it works. Advance thinking can be helpful, too. A good lesson plan, made the night before, may imply shrewd guesses about developing needs. Thus, if the class is shown a movie which is predicted by the teacher to be highly stimulating, then the teacher is likely to plan a discussion period organized in such a way that the children can express their feelings of enthusiasm, their bright ideas, their identifications with people or problems shown in the picture. Such planning represents the process of "prediction of need"; it is a kind of "diagnosis-in-advance." And, if the children actually are stimulated as anticipated, then the teacher can stay with his plan; but of course he should also have planned what to do in case they were not.

The implications of diagnosis-as-you-go are two: first, running diagnosis is required to assure the teacher that the plan should in fact be followed or to show him that it should be modified; and second, since the plan can never indicate all the details about what is to be done and how, decisions will have to be made on the spot as a result of diagnosis with the class of "where they are." This latter type of planning is essential because it provides for the conscious collection of data and the clarification of next steps.

The purpose of diagnosis is to enable psychologically sound or realistic choices to be made. The responsibility for securing wise choices—that is, choices which result in educative activity—is the teacher's. Many decisions should be made by the teacher alone. In other cases, the teacher may present alternatives for the class to discuss and choose from. Or the teacher may give information from which the class can formulate alternatives and make its choices. Finally, the teacher may suggest that the class is at a "choice-point," and then leave both the decision and the processes of reaching the decision to the class.

The process of diagnosis is both evaluative and explanatory. The teacher is concerned with how well the class is doing, and this is made known to him by the feelings which arise in his automatic and often subconscious application of criteria for good operation. Thus the teacher generally can "feel" whether or not the class is interested in its task. He then checks his feelings by noting signs of attentiveness, ease of distraction, pace of work, the trivial or helpful nature of comments, and the like.

When the class falls short of the teacher's criteria, it is a sign to him that there is some problem to be diagnosed and dealt with. Thus, if the conversation does not seem to be "adding up" and no one is able to summarize the discussion, the teacher may realize that the problem the group is working on is not clearly enough defined; or that the role of the group member is ambiguous, so that the children do not really know what sort of contribution is appropriate; or that some other, more compelling problem is distracting them, so that they cannot concentrate on the task. The kinds of questions listed above under Problem 1 may now be asked in an effort to clarify the difficulty. It may be found necessary to change the focus from attempted problem solving to discovery by each individual of how he feels about the task, so that the group can "get its bearings" and redefine the task in more significant terms.

It is not unusual, for example, for a discussion of a selected problem gradually to lose force because the group needs to change its focus. An initially interesting discussion in civics about how laws are made may have been interesting chiefly as a way of testing whether other people in the class had the feeling that laws are frequently unfair. If the teacher sees that this feeling is shared by the group, and that the discussion is becoming slow and uneasy, he may be justified in surmising that the class really is concerned about the teacher's own rules in the classroom. He may test this notion by interjecting some remark to the effect that as a teacher he has to make rules from time to time, and that it isn't always easy to make fair rules. A response of dead silence, too enthusiastic picking up of the discussion, hasty reassurance that his rules are fine, or too rapid effort to change the subject might seem to the teacher to bear out his diagnosis. In that case, he could propose a shift in the activity, presumably to discussion by smaller groups, since the reactions indicated a reluctance to discuss the problem in the large group of which the teacher is a member. On the other hand, if the class readily falls in with the teacher's suggestion, he could propose a role-played scene in which someone (a boss, for example) hands down rules to his workers, and then the workers discuss the rules among themselves. Class discussion of the way the workers reacted to the boss's edicts would be pretty likely to indicate more clearly where the trouble with the teacher's rules lay.

Thus diagnosis of shifting needs of the group may require modification of activity. The occasional need for emotional catharsis by a classroom group can be accepted by the teacher who, if he has rapport with the group, may even share the feeling. But it does not follow that it is educative or even helpful to the group simply to translate their needs into action without any thought about it. Thus an uncontrolled, emotionalized period of semi-riot, for example, may express a need for catharsis, and it may be better for the group than inhibition of emotional expression; but for educational need-meeting experience there must also be thoughtful discussion of what the feelings are, where they come from, and what sorts of problems this implies. The part the teacher contributes, that the class cannot, is the understanding of *how* needs can be channeled through educative experience rather than just allowed to "blow off."

Teachers learn to diagnose the educational effectiveness of activity and to shift its focus as needed. Thus, when a discussion becomes too academic, interest can often be regained by inviting personal reactions to the material being discussed. When the class seems apathetic and inhibited, the teacher may try to put into words some fear or worry that may be troubling the group, and thus free the group to consider its concerns more objectively. When students are confused or frustrated, it may help to redefine the achievement problem. Personal opinions, tumbling out irresponsibly, may call for some thinking together about the kinds of contributions needed. Too much dependency on the teacher for suggestions may often be overcome by dividing the class into working committees.

PROBLEM 3. HOW CAN SHIFTS OF FOCUS ON THE THREE ASPECTS
BE ACCOMPLISHED WITHOUT PRODUCING AMBIGUITY
AND CONFUSION?

The machinery through which the teacher harnesses the classroom energy into educative work is a set of understandings about how to shift the basic focus of activity in response to diagnosed needs for control.

To comprehend its activities as it shifts from one kind of focus to another, the class needs to have consciousness of itself as a group of individuals trying to work and learn together. The reason for shifting focus is that the group *needs* to do so; and it needs to do so because it has run into a problem which it cannot solve under its present mode of operation.

The first requirement for avoiding confusion, then, is to know why the change is made. This explanation does not need to be a deep, clinical one; it merely involves explicit recognition that the way things are organized now does not give us the chance to really do what we most need to do—or are, in fact, actually trying inefficiently to do. If people are exchanging personal experiences, which are only loosely relevant to the discussion task, the teacher may find it better to figure out how this can be done more efficiently than to worry about how to prevent or stop it. Presumably there is a reason why the discussion has turned to experience swapping. If the teacher knew the reason, he might then approach the real problem more forthrightly.

The simplest type of explanation is, in effect, description of what the group is doing. "We started out to talk about how Hopi children are brought up, but we seem more interested now in talking about what part our own relatives have in *our* bringing up. Why don't we make this our question for the next little while and give everyone a chance to contribute his experience along these lines?" The assumption is that when the group leaves the task and gets involved in another task, it may be appropriate to clarify the new task and accept it as legitimate. Such switches in topic may appear at first to be digressions, but can often be used for contrast or illustration or as the basis of broader generalization. And the fact that they are entered into spontaneously may mean that somehow they are needed to maintain the group as an interactive organism.

A more diagnostic type of explanation is interpretative rather than descriptive. In the case above, for example, one might notice that the spontaneous digression carried with it the quality of complaint: "We don't have it as good as the Hopi children, whose relatives are indulgent and give them more attention than ours give to us." The interpretation might be something like this:

"The last several comments suggest that we are aware of differences between Hopi and American communities with regard to the relationships between children and their relatives." This interpretation then could lead to several follow-up questions for focusing discussion more explicitly: "What do we see the major differences to be?" or "What conditions in Hopi communities might account for these differences?" or "What seem to us to be advantages and disadvantages of the Hopi way as compared to ours?" Thus the purpose of this type of interpretation is to recognize the need for working through the feelings indicated by complaining, and to channel such feelings into relevant school achievement.

If the quality of complaint (to continue with our illustration) were intense, as though the class were really envious of the Hopi children, one might decide that this feeling should be made explicit for what it is rather than simply worked through by recasting the learning problem. In this case, after pointing out the awareness of difference between Hopi and American child-relative relationships, the teacher might decide not to raise questions but rather to set up an activity to make the feeling more explicit. He could propose that the class set up two sets of skits which would reveal their perceptions of differences between Hopi and American ways of dealing with the same situation: scene one might show a child in some naughtiness, such as taking a toy away from a younger brother; scene two might show what the parents would do in this situation; scene three might show what the relatives would do. Following the two sets of scenes, discussion would center about how the child felt in the two cultures, and why all the participants reacted as they did.

A more evaluative type of explanation is to point out the discrepancy between what the group is doing and what it said it was going to do. The purpose here is to get a redefinition of the problem or to get back on the track if the digression represents avoidance rather than reformulation of the problem in more meaningful terms. Such comments as, "We started out to see how many different ways we could find to account for the relationship between mother's brother and child in Hopi communities, and we seem to have lost sight of this task for the present. Have we gone

as far as we can on that task? Or shall we get back to it?" Whichever is done is, at least, explicit, so that the students know what
type of contribution is appropriate.

The answer to the question of how to avoid ambiguity and confusion when activity is shifted from one focus to another is simply
that the teacher makes sure that the students have a satisfactory
explanation. A satisfactory explanation represents the state of
affairs honestly, points the way to activity seen as more appropriate or gratifying than what the group is doing now, and is understandable to the children: neither too deep, complex, nor vague.

Explanations for changes in activity are not fully understood at
the time they are given because they represent untested anticipa-
tions of experience. To some extent, then, students have to trust
the teacher. The meaning of the explanation becomes clearer,
however, as the activity proceeds, and during this process it may
be necessary to provide clarification of the relationship between
the activity and the plan. Such necessities make themselves
known through difficulties of participation or frustrations about
what to do next.

Finally, the need for explanation and the satisfactoriness of an
explanation are both determined by diagnosis. The behavior to
be diagnosed is the expressed feelings of reluctance, frustration,
conflict, tentativeness, anxiety, and the like. Every time an activity is changed it is important to provide a kind of reasonable
objectivity which makes the expression of such feelings possible.
The simplest way to provide such conditions is to explain can-
didly (leaving out unnecessary threat—or guilt-producing comments) what the activity is about and why it seems necessary.
The simplest way to know how to make such statements in such a
way that the class can understand them is to get some discussion
by the students first, so that one can see how they view what they
are doing and how they feel about it.

PROBLEM 4. HOW DOES THE TEACHER GUIDE THE CREATION
OF NEEDED ACTIVITIES?

The teacher controls the learning situation by controlling his
own role, and his role is different in different types of activity.

With regard to school achievement problems, the teacher is

essentially the leader whose primary loyalty is to the community. He is the boss, and his power is actually less open to question than is the power of the business or factory boss. Because his power is unquestioned, he can afford to be co-operative and friendly. He knows he can get his way with regard to what is to be studied, so he has nothing to lose by talking it over with the children and explaining and developing the logic of the choices of topics.

With regard to the group requirement for organization of effort, differentiation of roles, enforcement of its expectations for itself, development of its natural leadership and the like, the teacher's role is basically consultative. He cannot decide who the natural leaders are to be, but he can help those who are capable of leadership at each time to discover such roles for themselves. He cannot legislate the degree of commitment the group will find toward the achievement tasks, but he can give them a chance to explore the question and develop a group standard about it. He cannot force the group to express creative, personally significant ideas, but he can help them see that such ideas are useful to the group and that they are rewarded when they are expressed.

With regard to the individuals' requirements of personal gratification of their own unique needs, the teacher again provides conditions and opportunities, but he does not demand any particular learning or behavior. As a matter of fact, he seldom has enough relevant information about the children's internal problems to make much of a guess about what will be upsetting, significant, threatening, stimulating, or bothersome to individuals, although he can usually anticipate such reactions from the class as a whole with considerable accuracy. The kind of opportunity required here is for personal interaction between teacher and individual student, or among small groups of friends (under more limited conditions). The teacher's role is that of counselor, and it is not a "put-on" role. It is a side of the teacher which is less evident and available to the students at some times than at others. But it truly represents the teacher's real personality in his relations to individual students.

The appropriate activity, then, is whatever results from the teacher playing the proper role at the proper time; its creation is

a natural process of interaction, of living together. The only behavior the teacher can control directly is his own, and he does
this through diagnosing the class need and then shifting himself
into the type of role needed from him to enable the class to meet
its need. The members of the class must then shift their roles to
accommodate to the teacher; but if his diagnosis and operation is
correct, the class will have high motivation and involvement in
making the shifts in their own roles. If they are unable to accommodate to the teacher's change, then he would be advised to
reconsider his diagnosis, timing, or skills.

In actual practice, the teacher tests whether to shift his role by
tentative probing, by beginning to act in the new role and assessing the class's reaction. If they accept the new role, immediately shift their own participation to maintain interaction, and
start moving effectively, then the teacher knows that his diagnosis was correct. As soon as the class has operated on the new
basis long enough that it can be clearly seen that the shift has
occurred, then the teacher may raise the question of proceeding
along the same lines, but more efficiently.

Thus, "readiness" is not something to discuss, but rather to act.
The evidence that the group is ready for a change of activity is
that, given the chance, it changes its activity. On the other hand,
the efficiency of activity depends upon the explicitness with which
the member role, during the activity, is visualized by the children.
Such explicitness is achieved by talking about the activity: by
planning together. But effective planning is possible only when
the group is committed, and knows that it is committed, to stated
goals. Changes in the way of working demonstrate to the class
that they have a new commitment to "something"; and their
diagnosis of the new things they are doing tells them what the
"something" is. At this point, planning activity more directly to
achieve the goal becomes not only reasonable but inevitable.
Planning is complete when each individual has a clear picture of
what sort of participation is required from him and also when he
is motivated to accept the challenge to produce the needed types
of behaviors—in other words, when he is ready to experiment
with his own role, his own ideas and feelings.

PROBLEM 5. HOW CAN THE CLASS BE ORGANIZED TO
CARRY OUT THE NEEDED ACTIVITIES?

This is the problem of what things need to be taken into account during planning, and how this is to be done.

The class and teacher take direct and explicit account of the objective requirements—of what must be done to solve the problem. The students, as individuals, are affected by their perception of opportunity to meet certain personal needs; this is their vested interest.

Instrumental to these considerations is the central concern over who should work with whom, and under what conditions. One way to think of the question of how to organize effort is in these terms: How can the people who will stimulate the best in each other, who possess among themselves the needed resources to avoid frustration and to keep their groups going, who have with each other the kind of relationship which best promotes exploration of personal meanings and, therefore, the internalization of experience—how can these people be put together, and under what circumstances should they be put together?

There are some general principles that are relevant to this problem:

1. Subgroups composed of friends are likely to have more energy to spend in participating.

2. Groups composed of friends are more likely to deal with whatever problem they need to, whether it is centered around school achievement or not.

3. Individuals, when among friends, can express their real feelings easier, and are threatened less and supported more by the others.

The use of friends is advocated when the going is tough, as in diagnosing what is wrong, or in creating a wide range of ideas, or in working under pressure.

On the other hand, there is another side of the question, indicated by the following generalizations:

1. When members of the group get into conflict everyone tends to get involved rapidly (as in a debate situation, for example).

2. People need challenge and stimulation to cause them to think through their ideas.

3. When a person is undecided about some issue, it helps to let him see people who are committed to the two sides of the problem "fight it out."

The use of groups with some possibilities of clash is advocated in situations which require aggression and where taking things for granted might jeopardize success. Thus, after a tentative plan has been formulated, its possible bugs are more likely to be found by its opponents than by its friends.

The amount of clash that can be tolerated depends upon the possibilities of channeling aggression into work. If the job is clearly defined so that everyone can tell what is relevant, then aggression can be channeled by the group.

The size of the subgroup and its relation to the total group both affect participation by individuals:

1. The smaller the learning committee, the more time is available for each person to test his ideas directly through overt participation.

2. The smaller the learning committee, the less clearly defined the problem has to be for them to be able to work on it.

3. The smaller the learning committee, the greater pressure each individual feels to participate, and the more visible is his nonparticipation.

4. The smaller the working committee, the easier it is to express intimate thoughts and feelings.

5. The smaller the working committee, the less are its potential resources, but the greater is its motivation.

6. The smaller the working committee, the greater the influence of each individual, including the "blockers" and "wreckers."

7. The clearer the expectations of the total group for a given product, the harder the working committee will work to produce it.

8. The status of the working committee within the total group is of no direct significance, but the desires of the subgroup for mobility and improvement of status are significant motivating or blocking factors.

In general, the simplest way to express what is required to organize subgroups for *most* achievement related tasks is: that the members be well enough acquainted that they can communicate fairly readily; that there be enough range of temperament that they challenge each other; that they have among them enough skills of group process (socialization skills) that they can work together; that they have enough resources and enthusiasm for the achievement problem that they keep going on that; and that they have a secure enough role in the total group that they do not waste much energy comparing themselves to or belittling the other subgroups. And finally, that the difficult children are in groups that can handle them, either by containment, giving of security, or meeting them on their own terms.[2]

The different subgroups may or may not be given the same assignment:

1. The problem of steering the group is aided best by having several subgroups working on the same assignment, followed by total group debate about differences in the subgroup findings.

2. The problem of extending the range of experience to increase its significance is probably best dealt with by having the subgroups working on different but complementary assignments.

3. The greatest account of individual differences can be taken by having students choose their subgroups on the basis of interest in the topic assigned to that subgroup. But such choosing should not be permitted until there has been adequate discussion in the total group of what is expected with respect to each interest-task.

The strategy of breaking down the achievement of purposes into specific problems to be assigned to subgroups is decided by: the extent to which the subgroup experience is to be the basis for deciding on next purposes of the total group, the extent to which the subgroup is primarily to help the individuals find more of a place for themselves, and the extent to which the product of the subgroups, when put together, "closes out" the unit.

The total group can delegate particular functions to working committees:

1. Working committees, set up after short preliminary discussion, are used to give each person a better opportunity to find out what he thinks and feels through informal discussion in a con-

2. H. A. Thelen, "Group Dynamics in Instruction: The Principle of Least Group Size," *School Review* (March, 1949), pp. 139–48.

genial group. Reporting, in this case, is of whatever any individual wishes to report.

2. Working committees, set up to produce plans, hypotheses, or analyses, have the job also of preparing a formal set of conclusions. These may be reported back in a panel discussion composed of representatives of each working committee.

3. Working committees, set up to extend the range of experience of the class, have the task of "walking" the total group through a brief recapitulation of their own experiences. They can do this best by some variant of a developmental discussion, planned by the committee and directed by it.

4. Whatever the assignment of the working committee, it must also identify and lay before the total group any reservations, or problems, or needs of the group in order to clarify the purposes, directions, or means used in the total group working together.

5. Working committees can be set up completely informally to make whatever use of a period of free time they wish. This is primarily for individuals to express their ideas and feelings, following a significant amount of study and experience with a unit. Their only responsibility in this case is to indicate what use they made of the time so that their new readiness for learning can be assessed as a basis for further planning. A steering committee, made up of leaders of the working committees, can make a preliminary diagnosis of possible new directions and present them to the class as a series of alternative proposals.

6. Working committees, delegations from working committees, or individuals may bring to the teacher any question they wish for clarification. The teacher can use such questions to decide what the problem is, who is involved in it, and what further checking he ought to do, either to ameliorate conditions or to capitalize on the issue for the good of the class.

The generalizations simply spell out the fact that no matter what the assigned focus of the working committee is, attention must always be paid to the objective achievement problem, the problems of social co-operation, and the typical needs or problems of individuals.

The teacher's job is to be helpful at all times. The following suggestions may be useful to him:

1. The teacher prevents the waste of effort on planning activities outside the competence of the group by telling them, as needed, the limits within which they may work. Thus a teacher should not allow a working committee to operate on the fantasy that it can make decisions for the total group.

2. The teacher attempts to understand the problems as they are seen by the children, and he helps them deal with these problems primarily by helping them take into account the factors of which they are unaware, and by redefining the task in such a way that they can deal with it.

3. The teacher joins working committees as a consultant only when asked, and he clarifies his own role with the committee before proceeding to offer advice or suggestions.

4. In follow-up discussions with the total group, the teacher acknowledges the contributions of the working committees, and helps them report such parts of their experience as the teacher feels will be helpful to the total group.

5. The teacher, particularly on long assignments, keeps track of the progress of the working committees, preferably through short questionnaires filled out by each person at the end of each working period.

6. The teacher encourages working committees to make use of each other as resources during working periods, by arranging joint meetings or visitation among committees.

7. At all times, the teacher is concerned with maintaining work as a learning experience. He can do this to the extent that the children themselves want to learn, and he does it by challenging them to create new solutions and to deal maturely with all suggestions.

8. After making recommendations to a group, the teacher then withdraws from the group so they can make their own decision. The teacher, however, does not abdicate responsibility for seeing to it that the decisions of working committees are properly tested against reality by the committees before they have committed themselves to a good deal of effort which can only end in failure.

9. Such disciplining as a working committee needs is adminis-

tered by the teacher through redefinition of the requirements of the task and of the expectancies of the total group for a useful subgroup product. He may need to shift students from one group to another in order to get each student into a group in which he accepts the challenge to work constructively.

10. The teacher is always ready to represent the group to the outside world if their work takes them out of the classroom into the school or community. But his representation is mostly in affirming to others the need of the children to communicate with them. It is up to the children to represent their own needs or wishes, in their own way.

11. In so far as possible, the teacher helps the children find resources other than himself for work on objectively defined problems. On the other hand, he is also concerned that the children gain help from these resources commensurate with the effort expended. He avoids sending them on wild-goose chases, and he answers simple, direct questions if they can be answered without consideration of a broad context of facts or experiences. He helps them clarify their questions in such a way that the available resources can be helpful.

RECAPITULATION

The foregoing discussion endeavors to spell out the following basic assumptions about classroom learning:

1. The purpose of the classroom is to change people as a result of their own experiences.

2. Experiencing is an active process of working with others for common goals. In the classroom these goals are related to school achievement.

3. Experience is educative to the extent that it involves thinking about what one is doing, why he is doing it, and the general significance, usefulness, and applicability of the methods he is using in doing it.

4. The control of learning is through the use of consciousness. While all experience may produce changes in a student, the part that is educative is the part that is understood through conscious thought processes.

5. Utilization of consciousness to guide experience, and to im-

prove the constructiveness of subsequent experience, requires that experience be seen as inquiry; and this includes such functions as explanation, experimentation, and test of the consequences of behavior.

6. The guidance of education requires that teachers strive at all times for the needed and, therefore, appropriate distribution of energy into these objectives: the defined and required school achievement, co-operation within the group, and the formulation of individualized meanings of experiences. Inquiry is directed to all three of these objectives.

For elaboration of the kinds of facts with which teachers deal, see chapter 9. Some obstacles to learning are considered from the social standpoint in chapter 7, and from the psychological standpoint in chapter 8. Chapter 1 indicates by analogy the nature of motivated participation in projects, and chapter 5 exposes in detail how a group is steered in response to its relatively deep needs. Administrative Propositions I and II, on pages 114–26, are highly relevant to setting up and controlling subgroup activity within the classroom.

CHAPTER 3

The improvement of performance by professionals is self-stimulated. Teachers, nurses, engineers, lawyers, have to train themselves on the job. This requires opportunity, under group-supportive conditions, for studying their own professional skills.

But the efforts toward self-improvement of small groups within an institution succeed only if there is an over-all program which involves working with other groups in the community.

DISTINCTIVE FEATURES

In the plan here discussed, the motivation of the teachers for self-training is a combination of professional drives, desires for gratification in small groups, loyalty to the faculty and desire for advancement, and expectations of citizens with whom the teacher co-operates. The authority of leadership is the combination of these commitments, and is delegated to teachers chosen by their peers. The primary targets of change are teaching methods, to be improved, and school programs and curricula to be advanced. Secondary targets are youth-serving agencies in the community, businessmen, and others co-operating in the training of students. The role expectations of faculty members are: initiative in working on teaching problems in their small groups, co-operation with certain citizens in giving training, and participation in professional discussion within the total faculty group. The method of control is through organized faculty leadership, which plans and executes agenda in accordance with the canvassed interests of the faculty. The relationships with other groups include co-operation of individual teachers with citizens, two-way conversation with the school administration, and individual and small-group participation in out-of-school training classes, workshops, and the like.

Developing the School through Faculty Self-training

View X: "The supervisor used to come snooping around my class, but I cured him. How? It's easy! I just turned the class over to him. Boy, did he fall for it!"

View XI: "If I get put on one more faculty committee I'll scream."

View XII: "Well, you know where *that* idea came from, don't you? It's that English Department trying to build up its position."

View XIII: "You know, he was caught writing a letter while his class was working in the laboratory. . . . The new crop of teachers just doesn't have the old professional discipline."

View XIV: "I so admire the way you teach. . . . I hope after I get the house fixed up a little better we can get together and really *talk*."

View XV: Add a few of your own.

It seems fair to say that a school can be a pretty complicated institution. The problem of being a professional person without the status of a professional; the fear of being misunderstood by the parents if anything is said that they don't agree with; the nuisance of being saddled with blue forms, pink forms, reports, societies, PTA meetings, room meetings; the diplomacy required to thread one's way through the maze of cliques; the confusion between one's desires to try new things and yet not be seen by the others as a threat to them—these are no mean problems.

On top of all these matters, as a sort of last straw in many schools, is a half-hearted effort to "improve the instructional program."

It is easy to be critical, particularly if you have to sit through department meetings when you know you should be preparing the next day's work. It is easy to be bored if you are an old-timer getting acquainted with one more freshly scrubbed new principal. It is easy to be discouraged if everyone else leaves promptly with the closing bell so they can work in their gardens. It is convenient to be dependent if the principal throws his weight around.

Given the complicated, busy confusion of the school, and the typical overloading of work onto the staff, and the difficulty of finding energy for long-range concerns when forced to meet the deadline of a new class lesson every fifty minutes—given all these things, it is clear that the in-service training program cannot be just one more task piled on top of teaching: it must be a part of operation, part of the way of life in the school; and it must be continuously rewarding and adaptable to individual teachers; yet—it must add up to a better school program.

The purpose of this chapter is to analyze what is involved in in-service training, to make explicit some of the major principles guiding in-service training, and to suggest a concrete plan. We shall discuss the problem in terms of schools, but the same general principles and many characteristics of the plan would fit hospitals, engineering firms, large libraries, and other professional institutions. The plan has been tried in part, in various ways, but never in its entirety. It cannot be offered as a blueprint, but it may be a model against which present practice can be examined and improved. The plan will be developed step by step and will be organized around a series of assumptions.

DEFINITION OF AIM

Instruction occurs in classrooms and its effectiveness depends upon the teacher. The teacher guides instruction by what he says and does; by the ideas, wishes, attitudes, feelings, and values he communicates to the class. Those which he communicates outside the classroom to other teachers or to parents or in written articles affect the class's learning indirectly—if at all. The quality of learning by the class is determined to a very large extent by the classroom performance of the teacher. The creation of effective performance is a continuous production job which is affected by fatigue, skill, imagination, insight, anxiety, possibilities of reward, personal needs, and many other factors. But the central fact that must never be forgotten is that all efforts to improve instruction succeed or fail by the criterion of better performance by teachers in their classrooms.

THE OBJECTIVES OF IN-SERVICE TRAINING

Teaching is what the teacher does. To change teaching means that the teacher himself must, in some respects at least, change. And only the teacher can change the teacher.

Not all changes are equally possible or equally desirable. The most appropriate changes for any teacher are toward improved ability to cope with the problems of educating children—that is, of giving instruction more creatively and more realistically.

Coping with a situation is actually coping with one's self in a situation. And, more precisely, it is coping with one's feelings as he interacts in a situation. This may be done in a number of ways. The teacher can pretend, against all evidence, that certain feelings do not exist. He can deny feelings of inadequacy with respect to his rapport with children. Or, he can recognize the feelings, try to understand them, and then consciously set about to acquire the information, emotional orientation, or skill required to do better next time, i.e., to feel more satisfied with his improved operation. Feelings can also be fought, projected on others, run away from, and so on.

The changes that a teacher can be motivated to produce through training experience are the ones he wants and which are not surrounded by feelings of threat, coercion, fear, or other blocking emotions. These appropriate, desirable changes will differ from one teacher to another. The training objectives for each teacher should be formulated from interpretations of feelings he is aware of in the classroom. Since interpretation of one's feelings is a personal matter, it is clear that, for training to succeed, the teacher must be deeply involved in it; training for the total creative act of educating children is not a matter of gimmicks or superficial knowledge—it is a matter of integrated changes within one's total self.

RESISTANCE TO CHANGE

To understand the conditions required for training, we might profitably start with the question: Why haven't the needed changes happened? If these changes are really profitable to the teacher to make, and, in fact, even necessary to individual functioning, what stands in the way of their occurring spontaneously?

We assume that the reason needed changes have not occurred is that there are blockages, or obstacles to change. These barriers may operate to prevent awareness of the relevant feelings, or diagnosis of the particular types of problems encountered by the teacher, or the formulation of new alternatives and experimentation in new ways. Thus, for example: in some schools, when the teacher feels that he does not like certain pupils, he also feels threatened because of a group standard that "we are all unprejudiced here"; in others, the school's strong insistence on a "good solid academic program," and the greater prestige of academic teachers, could make him hesitate a long time before diagnosing that the content he is supposed to teach is simply unsuitable to the needs of his pupils; and experimentation with teacher-pupil planning can be suicidal in any school which goes on the basic assumption (whether it admits it or not) that all children are alike and teacher, by definition, always knows best.

In addition to such faculty-maintained group standards, designed, by defining the acceptable orthodoxy, to preserve one from discomfort, there are many more important possible barriers within the self:

1. A person may need to maintain illusions of expertness or infallibility, and to do this, he may rationalize failure as success. "Well, the class sure got into a mess today, just as I predicted it would"; or "We didn't get anywhere on the lesson, but we had a good experience together."

2. A person may also feel that the job is too big, too demanding: he simply cannot muster the energy required to tackle it. Thus: "To move into the project method is really asking me to prepare ten different lessons each day for each class." "To give students more freedom of choice would really require that I change my whole method of teaching." "How can I get permission to experiment with those new workbooks now that the official textbook list has been turned in?"

3. A person knows subconsciously that any significant change in himself as a teacher also means a change in his role or position in the total faculty. Thus a professional person is almost inevitably an advocate of his own methods; he is expected to "represent his professional point of view" to his colleagues. He can fear new learning because it changes his role in the group: others have to accommodate to it through revision of their expectations. Thus a teacher who has been seen as the leader of the academic subject-matter crowd might find it difficult to contemplate giving up the rewards of this role for the frustrations of a neophyte in the child-

centered approach. A teacher who was safely pegged by the faculty as a rather ineffective academician suddenly became a severe threat to her colleagues when she introduced role-playing into her classroom. A science teacher who went away to a workshop and returned as an expert on evaluation suddenly found himself snowed under with a new testing program.

Changes in competence mean changes in what a teacher is perceived as advocating, as being able to do, and as wanting to push others into doing. He can fear upsetting expectations of others, threatening others, or being given new responsibility.

4. Another kind of resistance to change comes from the fear of ambiguity or lack of guideposts. To experiment with new ways always means to strike out into the unknown. The teacher may not have confidence that his past experience and old habits can be relied on: he is "on his own."

It is commonly accepted that people have a vested interest in their professional practices. What we need to see is that this is a *total* vested interest, not only in the ways of doing things but also in one's position in the group, his confidence in himself, his ways of regarding the world, and his image of himself as a special kind of person. And this total vested interest means that resistance to change is inevitable—even with regard to changes that one knows might represent real improvement.

With regard to self-changes, the typical state of affairs, at least initially, is ambivalence. We have impulses to change, to try new things; but at the same time we have impulses to go back to the safe and certain and easy and rewarding. People cover up or deny ambivalence through such means as too much enthusiasm, too much dependence on the literally interpreted word of a new authority, overassertive attempts to persuade others, increased hostility to the people still doing things the old way, and the like. The most significant problem of changing is the problem of dealing with ambivalence with regard to the changes about to be produced.

A person who is ambivalent needs to resolve the ambivalence. A person who is ambivalent with regard to learning needs to resolve the ambivalence in favor of, rather than against, learning.

THE NEED FOR GROUP SUPPORT

Resolution of ambivalence is facilitated by working in the right kind of small group. The "right kind" is one in which a participant can express his feelings of doubt, hostility, excitement. It is one whose other members can give him reasonably accurate perceptions of his work. It is one with the group goal of improvement. It is a group of friendly well-motivated colleagues who feel that they are mutually benefited by working together.

Such a group supports a member in many ways: It enables him to face feelings which he could not otherwise face, through his discovery that others feel the same way. It encourages him to produce, so that he will have something to talk about and be rewarded for. It helps him face the total group by backing up his opinions or at least by helping him get a fair hearing. And its other members articulate openly the sides of the conflict he has not yet been able to formulate in words for himself.[1]

The first organizational principle of in-service training is to get each person into a small, supportive group in which the member's responsibility is to help the others.

Such groups can help some people merely by talking. But for any direct effectiveness, they must actually know at first hand how their members perform. In other words, these small groups need to have the opportunity to watch their members' work from time to time—and possibly to help carry out new kinds of activity. The ideal would be realized when a teacher, about to try out a new activity, could get the help of the others in planning it, could get their observations and reactions to the procedure as actually tried, and could then discuss it with them.

The small group could begin simply by having the members observe each other in a period of regular work. Discussion would be for the purpose of diagnosis and for comparing notes on the shared experience. This is a quick way to get into communication and develop common assumptions about what the members

1. Bruno Bettelheim and M. E. Sylvester, "Therapeutic Influence of the Group upon the Individual," *American Journal of Orthopsychiatry*, XXVII (October, 1947). The kind of group we envision has many characteristics of a psyche-group. See also Helen H. Jennings, *Sociometry of Leadership* (Sociometry Monograph No. 14 [New York: Beacon House, 1947]).

are looking for or working toward. For such operation during the working day, the school administrator will have to co-operate. He may need to provide a substitute teacher from time to time, mobilize parents in the community to help with classes temporarily left by their teachers, or sanction arrangements for handling classes together every so often.

ADDITIONAL RESOURCES FOR SMALL TRAINING GROUPS

Most of us working with people in groups would improve remarkably if we could suddenly understand all that we know. In other words, very few of us, including teachers, are limited by lack of resources as much as by the unavailability of the resources we have.

Nevertheless, the small training groups will need help from time to time. The difficulty may be in their own processes of operation, it may be a lack of knowledge of available techniques or materials, or it may be simply a lack of confidence in their own new planning operations. Effort on the part of the administrator to have resources made specially available is reassuring, too, provided the principal does not insist that his resource people be used.

There are few communities in which the schools have made serious efforts to catalogue the resources and consultant help that would be readily accessible to teachers and students. Schools could have lists of citizens who are willing and, in fact, eager to make their past experience in teaching available. There are, in most communities, people competently trained in human psychology and with experience in consulting with business and other institutions. There are people who have had illuminating adventures, or who are knowledgeable about workshop techniques (useful in classrooms), or who know visiting dignitaries well enough to get them out to help a school. There might be a nearby university which would be willing to exchange its help to the school for opportunity to study the school's program.

The productivity of the small groups will be affected very much by the availability of a wide range of resources. And when the small group is too insecure ever to use outside help, then it needs consultation to improve its own internal functioning.

The generosity of the administrator in seeing to it that many resource people are available is largely canceled out if the administrator cannot also see to it that the use of the resource people is initiated by the small group, and that the resource person is used by the training group in its own way. In other words, to give help you really have to give the help. To accomplish this, a small faculty committee might be put in charge of the resource pool, and it could provide the necessary information to the small training groups to use in whatever way they wished— within faculty-decided policies for communicating with non-school personnel.

The Role of the Total Faculty

It is probably safe to guess that if we were to select all the instances of real growth of teachers on their jobs we would find that in one way or another they had found themselves other persons who could give them the sort of support we have been advocating. In other words, we believe that the small training group must be operating informally wherever one finds the kind of improvement which in-service training ought to be creating. It may operate in a clandestine way and out of school hours in the unfavorable social climate of some schools, or it may be easily visible at a quick glance.

Our planning so far, then, has merely been directed to make explicitly effective a set of necessary processes that go on anyway. The next step is to get larger numbers of people into such relationships, and to produce the kind of incentive and school climate in which, after a time, the small training group becomes an expected and automatic part of the school way of life. This requires certain conditions in the faculty seen in its entirety as a total group.

One of the required conditions is that the prestige system in the total faculty group be based on contribution to the instructional excellence of the school. Past teaching experience, courses taken during the summer, number of years of college work completed, personality, contacts with the right people, and other such factors will probably always have some place in the initial hiring of teachers. But their prestige and pay, once they are hired, should depend only on merit: how well they teach and what they contribute to the teaching of others. The faculty must accept as its major purpose the improvement of its teaching.

A second required condition is that the faculty accept the notion that the end of good teaching can be achieved by a variety of means. There is no one right way to teach, although for any particular teacher in a specified classroom situation there is probably one best thing to do. A faculty concerned with improvement of teaching will encourage development of a variety of methods, rather than demanding conformity to one method. And it will then study these various methods in an effort to see what is common among them, what is different, what method seems to work best under what conditions, and so on. In other words, the other half of the proposition that responsible diversity should be encouraged is that there must also be provision for assimilation.

Diversity is important as the way to encourage development of good ideas and special insights on the part of each teacher. But the school gets maximum profit when it arranges for communication and deliberation on these unique contributions. The simplest communication is through demonstration lessons taught to student volunteers before the total faculty. The most efficient way to make sure that time is well utilized on such occasions is by having a steering committee, perhaps with a consultant to assist it, sift the various available possibilities for demonstration and select the ones offering the most illuminating contrasts, or the most stimulus value, or the greatest modifiability to fit a range of subjects. An effective steering committe will recognize that the other side of the program of small training groups is the total faculty group as audience, encourager, setter of expectancics, challenger, and resource pool. The total group must strive for standards of tolerance of differences in means along with continual reinforcement of the over-all goals.

The dynamics of the total faculty meetings will be a benign type of competition among the small training groups. This is guaranteed to the extent that status depends upon productivity of the small groups, so that the interpersonal motivating factor will be the desire of each to contribute more to the total meeting than the others. The difference between this kind of competition and that between teams is that the aim is to contribute to all rather than to destroy the opponents. The steering committee must be given the responsibility of seeing to it that the rules of competition are fair, opportunities are equal, and rewards are distributed according to contribution. A simple way to achieve this is to have on the steering committee representatives of all the small training groups. These people will help test and check the proposed agendas for faculty meetings.

THE ROLE OF THE PRINCIPAL

The principal is a key figure in in-service training—regardless of what he does about it. By virtue of his position, he has legal responsibility for developing adequate instruction in his school. And he is usually expected by the community to be the spokesman for the school as well as the translator of the community's wishes into school practice.

Within the school, the principal recommends the hiring and firing of teachers, determines their work loads, opens or shuts doors to professional advancement. It is not surprising that the morale of teachers, their creativity, and their dedications to their classrooms are much influenced by their perceptions and interpretations of the attitudes and acts of the principal. For an in-service training program to succeed, the principal must believe in it, express enthusiasm for it, and have a well-defined and accepted role in it.

Defining and fulfilling this role is a difficult business because in many ways the appropriate role in the in-service enterprise is in conflict with the role of administrator and public relations man.

Thus the principal is a facilitator to the in-service program. Essentially he provides services to the teacher group. The teachers are the ones in this situation who must wield the authority and assume the responsibilities. This state of affairs contrasts sharply with the boss-employee relationships typical of action in administrative and public-relations capacities. In these functions, the principal speaks (or should speak) with authority and with full assumption of responsibility. The simple but complicating fact of the matter is that it is not easy to keep distinct two roles which differ so drastically in the way one exercises his authority. The man who hires and fires and is responsible for the teachers' welfare may find it difficult to have faith in their leadership with respect to instructional matters.

The facilitator also works within a different orientation than does the administrator. The facilitator is concerned with the processes of working, and accepts the notion that, so long as the processes are sound, the results will be good. He cannot be sure of what will have been accomplished by next June; he has to believe that whatever does eventuate is sufficient and appropriate. But in his role as administrator, the principal would know that this point of view is suicidal: deadlines must be met, reports prepared, definite promises fulfilled.

The difference is between participation in essentially creative, experimental activity as distinguished from routine or maintenance activity.

At the level of personal relations, too, there are differences. As facilitator, the principal must be equally available and emotionally supportive to all the teachers as they strike out into new realms of experiencing. Trying new ways of doing things is an anxious business. If the principal himself, as administrator, is anxious about the program, he will be of little help to the teachers. Some of the anxieties on both sides are related to the "payoff" value of new efforts; others are related to the problem of adjusting to new prestige and status relationships. The lines of communication on the organization chart of the school are unlikely to be the actual needed lines of communication within the in-service program.

What all this adds up to is the conclusion that determination of the principal's role, like that of each teacher, does not depend simply on the way the individual happens to feel about it. The roles in some respects must be worked out and defined as the enterprise gets under way. Several formal considerations are suggestive. The fact that the principal is spokesman for the school means that the teachers should insist on his being in a role which keeps him informed as to what the teachers are trying to do and what their intentions are. Otherwise, his interpretations to the community may involve illusions about the school which solidify in public expectations and which the teachers feel forced to try to meet—even though they consider them unwarranted.

The fact that the steering committee and the principal are both concerned with the development of the program as a whole suggests that they should have a close relationship. The fact that the principal, in his administrative capacity, can do much to implement the needs which he, as facilitator, can see, suggests that he might well be the executive secretary to the steering committee. Not all principals would be temperamentally able to act in this capacity, however, and in any case it is perfectly proper for the principal and steering committee to experiment to find the best way to define his participation.

THE NEED FOR SCHOOL-WIDE PROGRAMS

We noted that a basic dynamic for training would be benign competition among the small training groups. We saw that the total faculty meetings had, among other purposes, the control of the rules for competing, the bestowal of rewards (e.g., increased status in the group), and, through the steering committee, the provision of services needed by the training groups. All this was seen as necessary to make effective the work of the training groups.

What, however, is to make the total faculty effective as a group? For example, why should *it* develop the set of standards and expectations of creativity, tolerance of new ideas, reflection on and utilization of suggestions? What is to prevent the small group competing in not-so-benign ways for the purpose of taking over the faculty leadership?

If the total faculty group is only a convenience to spur the small training groups, then each training group will expect to use the faculty for testing its ideas and rewarding them. In the absence of any controls, the temptation will be to assume that the best test of quality is influence, and the best test of excellence of ideas is counting the number of teachers who vote for adopting the new gimmick throughout the school. This is, of course, nonsense.

The point is that testing of ideas and acceptance of contribution and insight is not possible except when the total group, as a group, has a purpose of its own over and above the stimulation of members to improve their own skills. What sort of problem—and purpose—can the faculty (as a total professional group) legitimately have? Let us look at some of the possible answers which have been assumed in various schools:

1. The chief problem of the faculty is to educate the children of the community.

Comment: More accurately, the chief job of the teacher is to teach his classes. But one hundred teachers, each teaching his own classes, constitute collective, not group, action. Most schools are actually buildings in which each teacher, with whatever help he needs from the services of the administration and maintenance staffs, does whatever job of teaching he can. It is roughly similar to a hospital clinic except that the "patients" are involuntary groups of children rather than single individuals. Education of children is a job for the school as an institutionalized collection of teachers; it is not a job of the faculty as a group.

2. The purposes for which the faculty acts as a group are to increase wages and get better contracts. Preservation of academic freedom, planning better public relations for a school bond campaign, and the like, are other examples of the same sort.

Comment: These are illustrations of problems tackled by the faculty as a group, and all professional groups engage in such protective activities on behalf of their profession. But the skills required for such activities are not the ones required for teaching, so that contributions of the small training groups are irrelevant to such problems. Ideas created or discovered in the in-service training program cannot therefore be tested against the demands of such problems.

3. The purposes for which the faculty acts as a group are to plan better curricula for the students.

Comment: Meetings for this purpose would probably be along departmental or grade lines, rather than total faculty lines. Such problems *do* provide the *raison d'être* for department meetings because the department bands together to meet demands from the outside. For example, there may be a demand that certain courses be taught, made by the school (principal) presumably acting on behalf of the board, which in turn acts on behalf of the community. Thus planning the various curricula, playground supervision, study halls, after-school programs, etc., are all in response to demands originated from outside the teacher, and the groups for whom meeting these demands is a problem are composed of the people who have to do the work. The faculty as a whole may act in an advisory capacity and as a pool for recruiting manpower, but neither of these functions provides criteria relevant for testing ideas from the in-service program.

4. The purpose of professional faculty meetings is to hear and discuss good ideas about how to teach.

Comment: This is a popular fallacy. It is true, for example, that stimulating ideas from important people from universities or elsewhere can be discussed with pleasure and profit. A few individuals might be induced to try out a new idea, or to feel superior to it, or to reject it flatly; and in so far as this is of value to the individuals, it may be of value to the school. But a more common consequence, however, would be to stir up anxieties on the part of teachers who are not as adequate as the more psychologically sophisticated teachers attending the lecture. Other effects—with respect to a matter like discipline—are likely to include furnishing the "student-centered" teachers ammunition for further battling with the "community-centered," "subject-centered," "reality-centered," or, possibly, "self-centered" factions.

If there are committees working to produce new ideas about school problems, they may present reports to the faculty. These, of course, will be voted acceptance if the principal says the right things about them; otherwise, they will result in nothing because only the people who worked out the ideas have any particular insight or commitment to them. If the report is by one training group, and everyone else is in other training groups, then we can expect the discussion to be primarily the acting-out of the intergroup competition. There could be conflict or withdrawal from the discussion, and ideas might be stimulated. But the ideas will not be realistically tested in their own right because it is the subgroup itself which is on trial, not its ideas. This is the problem which opened this section, and led us into the discussion.

5. The purpose of the faculty meeting as a total group is to consider how better to use the entire community for educative purposes.

Comment: Yes.

To use the community for educational purposes requires collaboration by the faculty with many other groups, businesses, and welfare organizations. Through the processes of collaboration, the faculty can develop meaningful professional relationships with the adult community. And, as these relationships develop, so also do public expectations for the role of faculty member, going beyond the role of caring for children and keeping parents satisfied. The school can move from the occupation of governess within the family of community institutions to the role of active collaborator in solving, through education, community youth problems.

Specifically, the role of a group in the community depends upon the social transactions into which the group enters. The following sorts of collaboration are suggested by way of illustration:

1. Collaboration with merchants and consumers to provide better consumer education
2. Collaboration with civic leaders to devise classroom experience to reduce racial tension
3. Collaboration with parents to evaluate and improve the school's contributions to better living in the family
4. Collaboration with agencies and employers to provide a work-experience program which complements course work in the school
5. Collaboration with a university to aid in the preparation of teachers

The faculty operates in two distinguishable ways within the collaborative relationship. First, it shares in diagnosing problems as they exist in the community, and it trains students in how to behave in their immediate problematic contacts with buying, prejudice, family discipline, etc. These training experiences presumably are set up within the school curriculum, and only a few teachers are actively engaged in direct training with respect to any one type of problem.

Secondly, the faculty has the responsibility of educating children, not just training them, and the entire faculty is involved in this. Thus, with regard to consumer education, for example, the home economics and science teachers may offer to the students training through direct acting-out experiences as young consumers. But the entire faculty is concerned in the development of an understanding of economic interdependence, long- versus short-range values, the nature of wealth, attitudes against waste, appreciation of good design, and the like.

The central curricular problem in most schools is to relate their training functions, which are assigned to different courses and teachers, to their educational functions, which are the province of all. It is no solution to the problem to attempt to squeeze the educational functions into general education, college preparatory, or academic courses; and the training functions into vocational, nonacademic, or professional courses. The most pressing needs of students are to live successfully in a community run by adults, and these needs are satisfied by training through firsthand experiences provided by school and community together. But in the training process, needs arise in the student for understandings and knowledge, for assimilating his experience into his personal scheme of things. These are needs for finding meaning in the relationships between himself and the world, and, by extension, in the world outside his immediate experience. The meeting of these needs is what we mean by "education."

From this analysis, we see that various teachers need to get cooperation from groups and individuals in the community to set up needed training activities, and that the faculty as a whole needs to be concerned with discovering and sharing methods for making these activities educational. We can also see that the results of the faculty's experiences should be communicated or fed back to the various community groups so that they can make such changes as will lead to a more healthy life for youngsters. Thus, we arrive at three possible and complementary roles for the schools as institutions within the community: (1) as collaborators with others in setting up and supervising training experiences; (2) as professional educators working among themselves to improve methods for the simultaneous training and education of children; and (3) as consultants to the collaborating agencies, on aspects of their functioning related to the welfare of students.

The role of collaborator gives individual teachers their place in the community. The professional educator role gives the faculty group as a whole its place among other groups in the community. And the consultative role, usually, but not necessarily, exercised through school officials as representatives of the school, gives the school as an institution its place in the community.

Professional in-service training represents the development of the faculty into the professional educator group. But motivation for this development comes from interactions between the faculty and the outside; motivation depends upon the experiences of teachers in the community and upon the possibilities of reward available to teachers for co-operating in training and for contributing to the consultant role. Aside from its importance to students, the notion of school-wide programming around the problem of how to use the entire community for educational purposes results in demands and expectations from the community. These outside demands require policies and agreements within the total faculty, but it is the small training groups which create the necessary insights and do the necessary preliminary testing and the ultimate implementation of policy. And the need for school-wide policy becomes translated into discipline and encouragement of contributions from the small training groups.

WHERE THE PROGRAM MIGHT LEAD

The small training groups will be in a position to discover a number of helpful administrative revisions. Thus, it may be found that longer periods are needed to enable the class to plan an activity and carry it through on the same day. Or needs for a broader range of resource materials to replace the single textbook may be seen as desirable. Or the new role of volunteer assistant teacher may be discovered and spelled out, with the consequent recruitment and training of citizens interested in such experience.

The faculty may wish to revise sizes of classes, too. If teachers learn to make much use of discussion, they will wish smaller classes. On the other hand, if they make more use of subgroupings, they may wish larger classes so that there is better opportunity to control the composition of the subgroups.

An additional type of outcome is the diagnosis of further types of experience needed by the faculty. Thus teachers may, after a period of deliberation and thinking together, realize common needs for better training in particular areas, such as discussion leadership and group management. This could lead to a series of faculty workshops, with the help of outside consultant-trainers. The faculty might discover that its greatest concern at some point is to talk over its programs with citizens, and this could lead to the setting up of joint faculty-parent-citizen workshops, meeting on several evenings during the week or on week ends.

If new instructional methods are formulated and consistently used in some classes, the faculty may wish for a careful study of new methods, and it may see a university as helping in this. Similarly, the small training groups will have functioning problems of their own, which could lead to the use of a consultant to talk with some of these groups.

The faculty is likely to feel itself pulled together by its newly found common enterprise, and it may wish to plan a few social events to capitalize on the need-satisfying possibilities of the new closeness and interest in each other as people.

All of these recommendations require collaboration with the school administration.

Some Questions and Answers

1. Does the plan call for forcing every member of the faculty to work in small groups with other members? What if a teacher doesn't want to?

Comment: People cannot be forced to work in the kind of creative relationship required for training, and there are some teachers (and others) who do not work well in this type of small group relationship. They need time to see how it works out with others, and they may need special help or training, as in a summer workshop. In general, the safest principle is to start with the groups that are interested, let them report to the total faculty, and back them up. Motivation is strengthened by the expression of enthusiasm and sympathy for those in the groups, and by understanding of the doubts of those who hold back.

As the program moves along, a group standard and expectation of effective small-group participation will develop, and it will tend to bring in others. If this standard is uncongenial to certain teachers, they may leave. But they obviously must not be fired or driven out: that may be threatening to the ones left behind.

2. Won't the program produce extra difficulties in scheduling classes so that certain teachers have the same period free to work together?

Comment: Yes. This will require administrative ingenuity. If the principal cannot see how to manage it, he should ask the small groups themselves to make suggestions. Finding time for the small groups to meet, and making decisions about how often they should meet, is actually the responsibility of the small group itself. It is up to the administrator to make such arrangements as are possible to help. In those cases where nothing can be done, except perhaps to meet on the teachers' own time, such a decision should be reached jointly by the principal and the teachers concerned.

3. Doesn't this plan assume many more resources than most schools now have?

Comment: No. The plan attempts to make much more effective use of what have always been and always will be the school's most important resource: the teachers. It attempts to develop these resources further, and to make them available to each other. Additional resources are by no means necessary, though there is no doubt that it would be nice to have them from time to time.

4. Do you think that all principals could set up this kind of program and run it successfully?

Comment: Probably not.

5. It seems to me that in a city with several schools, if one school tried this, and it worked, all the teachers would want to come to that school. Wouldn't this disrupt the system?

Comment: Possibly. If the scheme is found to work in one school, then it should be adopted and adapted by other schools throughout the system. Schools which have, through the years, developed firm defenses against new ideas and ways of working might have to be considerably shaken up through transfer of personnel. In this case, the amount of disruption would depend upon the extent to which the community is behind the plan, the extent to which displaced people can be relocated in jobs suitable to their talents, and the rapidity with which early experiences with the new plan are rewarding to participants.

6. Won't such a plan upset the relationships among teachers in the school?

Comment: Indeed yes. Every major change in group activity calls for a reshuffling of status positions. But in so far as prestige has been dependent on worth-while contributions to professional growth, it will not be upset. This would merely provide another route to recognition. In so far as the bases of prestige are reversed or toppled, then the status pattern will change markedly.

7. How can such a plan be set up in a school which has no faculty meetings and no established pattern of working together?

Comment: In most schools where these conditions exist, it is probable that the principal would have to initiate the plan. But the principal does not have to offer the plan "cold." It could be preceded by several faculty meetings devoted to the making of a census of problems the teachers see, or the obstacles to better teaching. The dimensions of these problems or obstacles could be discussed for clarification. Decisive action by the principal to clear away one or more obstacles identified by the faculty will do more to promote the program than any amount of his talking. After the development of initial rapport and trust, the principal and a temporary faculty steering committee can decide on the best means for launching the plan.

Summary of the Plan of In-service Training

We should hardly expect the details of the plan as implemented in different schools to be alike. But we would expect that in one way or another every successful program would meet at least the following specifications:

Specification 1: Improvement of teaching calls for improved performance of teachers in the classroom.

Specification 2: Only the teacher can change the performance of the teacher.

Specification 3: To do this, he requires the emotional support and technical help of a small, friendly group of colleagues (the small training group).

Specification 4: Resources will be needed and should be available to the small training groups.

Specification 5: The total faculty group, with the help of a steering committee, provides the members for the groups, creates expectancy for performance, and assimilates the results of the training groups' experience.

Specification 6: To do this, the total faculty must itself be a group with shared purposes and outside demands or expectancies to be met.

Specification 7: The "outside" must be composed, for this purpose, of responsible citizens representing the community as a whole, or defined groups such as parents, merchants, civic leaders, etc.

Specification 8: Teachers must maintain interactive contact with the outside, so as to get necessary feedback for the faculty as a whole.

Specification 9: As the program rolls along, the faculty must be able to identify its shared needs for further training and make use of faculty-wide workshops and other devices to meet these needs.

All the above specifications and the suggested plan itself (with slight changes in wording) can be seen to apply to in-service training in hospitals, engineering firms, libraries, and other institutions.

The kinds of policies and conclusions about teaching methods with which teachers will be concerned during in-service training are suggested in chapter two and in the pages indicated in the note at the end of that chapter. The problem of building the school as a small community is illuminated on pages 337–41, and the nature of the diversity of faculty attitudes and needs is analogous to the picture presented on pages 341–45. For the planning of effective faculty meetings, the techniques presented on pages 180–217 are suggestive.

CHAPTER 4

For maximum productivity, the individual must have sufficient autonomy that he can be self-directing in his job. This autonomy is based on a thorough understanding of the job and its relation to the work of others. By organizing jobs within co-operative teams responsible for blocks of interlocking functions, individual autonomy, self-direction, and satisfaction can be greatly extended.

The authority of power is used to secure the required communication among the co-operative groups—to insure co-ordination of their activities within the over-all design for production.

DISTINCTIVE FEATURES

Leadership authority exerted on groups is dependent upon the power of superior position in the vertical hierarchy. Leadership authority exerted upon individuals originates in the need of working groups to be governed; and the agent of leadership is usually the boss or other designated official. The primary target of change is defined by institutional purposes, from the processing of raw material in factories to the promotion of research by foundations. Secondary targets of change include the competence and productivity of workers, and the efficiency of communication within the organization. Members of the organization are expected to conform to demands for co-operation in achieving organizational purposes, in return for which they are expected to initiate demands for improvement of their own welfare. The method of control is through feedback of information on productivity, information about changes in the environment that affect operation, and supervision of performance. The relationship between groups arranged "vertically" in the organizational chart is through pressures, both up and down; between groups arranged "horizontally," it is co-operative. Communication with other groups in the community is through spokesmen or officially appointed representatives.

Administration and Management: Group Responsibility and Individual Autonomy

Administrators, managers, and supervisors—like other leaders —are concerned with simultaneous work on three kinds of problems: the task or job functions, the problems of organizing for work, and the problems of individual need-meeting to maintain motivation.

The unique features to be considered in this chapter are *vertical organization* as a way of defining performance expectancies, and *power* as a basis for leadership authority. By virtue of his power alone a boss can overcome resistance to participation by his subordinates. This is not true of community work, in which citizens participate voluntarily, nor of school classrooms in which the student has to attend but does not have to learn.

After considering the nature and types of authority and getting acquainted with a couple of administrators, we shall examine a number of typical conflicts in administration. Then we shall offer two propositions which we think may point the way to considerable improvement of many administration and management situations.

THE CONCEPT OF AUTHORITY

The work of the world is done through the co-ordinated efforts of many people. With respect to some kinds of work, co-ordination is through common adherence to an ideal, a point of view, and a goal. Thus at the beginning of World War II, physical scientists all over the world were building on each other's discoveries to erect the formidable theories of atomic science. The efforts of each man were co-ordinated with those of others through his own processes of reflection and assimilation of ideas. Each man worked at his job because he was interested in it, and the recognition he could get from himself and from his colleagues was his reward. Such leadership functions as "speaking" for a school of thought, convening occasional meetings, and publishing learned journals arose naturally and spontaneously. Efforts to speed up production or to meet deadlines were not part of the picture; it was assumed that findings would become useful in their own good time, and that efforts to hurry the process would be disastrous or wasteful.

Co-ordination of effort through shared ideas and ideals is characteristic of many of the noncommercialized aspects of life. Hobbyists have their shared delights in solving problems and their shared goals of perfection when it comes to model railroading, petunia raising, and wood carving. The ideals of perfection and competition are sufficiently generally understood and shared that people know how to participate in amateur athletics. During the first stages of any club or movement or revolution, activity is co-ordinated through shared social purposes; it is only as the central organizing clique begins to take in members that bylaws are introduced. (The principle that development of hierarchical organization *follows* definition of tasks is discussed in chapter 12.)

In general, co-ordination through shared ideas is possible for those endeavors in which each man fully comprehends the scope of the problems and is competent to weigh, assess, and assimilate the contributions of all other participants.

American technical and productive genius expresses itself in our ability to specialize and to break down complicated operations into simple, easily learned tasks. A factory employing thousands of workers may contain but a handful of men who fully understand the product being manufactured and the details of the manufacturing process. Moreover, men work mostly at one aspect or another of each manufactured item, and no one worker could possibly decide for himself how hard he must work to keep the whole sequence of operations running smoothly. Co-ordination of effort in this kind of situation obviously cannot be left to the voluntary independent decision of each individual.

In such cases, *organization* is introduced. One basic feature of organization is its provision of well-defined *expectancies* as to the behavior of each person. These expectancies can be astonishingly detailed and precise, as in a military post in which both social and professional communications are decided as much by the rank-structure as by the nature of the problems to be solved. But there are certain kinds of expectation that must be maintained and defined in all organizations: who can hire and fire whom; what are reasons for dismissal and for promotion; who are one's superiors, peers, and inferiors; what are the required communications from and to each person.

A second basic feature of organization is *power*. Designated individuals have power over other individuals. This power may be wielded flagrantly or unobtrusively; it may be great or little; it may be with respect to many parts of the job or to only a few. But whatever the exercise or perception people have of power, the fact remains that it is our superiors, not our inferiors or peers, who determine our prospects on the job. In any organization, then, we have two goals: to satisfy the requirements of our job as defined to us, and to please our superiors. In "good" organizations the same behaviors satisfy both conditions.

In general, co-ordination through organization is required for those endeavors in which each man deals with only a part of the product, an aspect of manufacture, a phase of development. Only the men at the top comprehend the total design of the enterprise, and the others *must* rely on the insights and comprehensions of these men for guidance in making many of their own decisions.

Co-ordination of effort solely through shared ideas, on the one hand, and solely through organization, on the other, seldom exists in actual practice. In every job, the worker's actions arise out of two sorts of decisions: genuine decisions made by the worker on the basis of his understanding of acceptable and shared ideas; and deduced or enforced decisions representing implementation of instructions or policies given to the worker by others from whom influence is accepted.

From the standpoint of each individual, these methods of co-ordination are different ways of achieving the same goal: confident knowledge of what to do, when to do it, how to do it, and with whom to do it. When the individual has full knowledge of the total enterprise and when he himself builds a complete product or work of art, he has his greatest freedom and greatest autonomy. He can arrange his own hours of work, set his own standards of performance, communicate when and if he wants to—provided he accepts the authority of the ideals he shares with his community. Whenever he is perplexed as to what to do, he turns to further study leading to reaffirmation of these ideals as the means for resolving his doubts and settling his questions. What we mean by "self-direction" is that to a high degree the authority for one's behavior is one's own understanding of ideas and one's commitment to ideals shared with others.

When the individual comprehends only a fragment of the total enterprise, he depends less on the authority of his own knowledge and more on the authority of other individuals. These others tell him what he needs to know as a basis for whatever decisions his job requires him to make. If the decision involves merely a simple choice between two definite alternatives—e.g., whether to push the red button or the black button on the machine—then, he simply needs to know the appropriate cues for choosing one or the other. The greater the number of available alternatives and the less repetitive the operations on the job, the more insight he must have and the greater the autonomy he needs. If his job requires no decisions at all from him, then his required autonomy is zero.

There is seldom a lack of people willing to tell him what he needs to know. A worker has his own ideas, his colleagues have their interpretations—often different ones—and the boss has his ideas. It is reasonable to assume that each would-be authority is competent with respect to some things, and incompetent with respect to others. The ideal would be that each person would supplement his fragmentary knowledge by getting competent advice or help in finding out each of the things he needed to know. But how is an individual to tell who is competent to give advice in the fields wherein he is ignorant? And who is to advise him where to seek advice in each of these fields? And is it not important that the same interpretations and advice be given to everyone concerned with the same problems?

These questions lead us to consider the functioning of power in the organization. The situation can be put in these terms: "My superior is the person of whom I ask advice. He is the person from whom I accept commands. Because he understands not only my fragment of the total enterprise but also all the other fragments co-ordinate with mine, he has more competence than anyone on my level. And because he supervises all of us, we all get substantially the same set of facts when we go to our boss; hence my work is co-ordinated with that of my colleagues. Moreover, when it comes to decisions about how we at the same level are to work together, the boss gets us all together: he delegates his authority to the group." These statements sound reasonable. They ought to be true. Can they be made true?

There are two ways of making the statements true. The first is to select and train men to wield the kinds of authority their work requires them to exercise, and the second is to invest them with power.

The exercise of power lies in the control of communication. The man with power can enforce his decisions as to who talks to whom about what. The fact that my superior has power over me means that I shall go to him for the things he says I must go to him for. The fact that he has power over me, however, does not automatically insure that he is wiser than I or my colleagues, even though with respect to some matters he ought to be. Under proper conditions, the superior knows the limits of his competence, and his exercise of power is not to set himself up as *the* authority for all matters, but rather to insure that his subordinates make use of the *appropriate* authorities, whoever and wherever they may be.

In other words, power can be authoritarian or it can be facilitative. The former is primarily directed to preservation of power as an end in itself; the latter is directed to getting the job done.

So far we have been contending that action is determined and justified on the basis of some relevant authority. We have talked about the authority of ideas and the authority of position. We have said that the former governs those acts over which an individual has autonomy, and the latter governs those acts which lie outside his autonomy. We have also said that authority of position, based on power, should be used to help subordinates locate the particular authority most appropriate for their problems. But what are the types of authority, and what is the domain over which each is valid?

THE TYPES OF AUTHORITY

Faced with the need to choose among alternative courses of action, to what kinds of authority might one resort?

1. *Dedication.*—When one is dedicated to a goal, the choice among alternative courses of action is a matter of deciding which leads most effectively toward the goal. One's goal dedication is his authority.

2. *Experimentation.*—Choice is made tentatively, and a first action step is taken. Next steps depend upon the results of the first step. The authority is in the empirically appraised nature of the situation as discovered through the first step.

3. *Revelation.*—Choice is based on a dream or "authoritative" advice given by a palmist, numerologist, financial column, friend, etc. Since the advice-giver has a minimum of relevant information to take into account about the particular organizational situation, the basis of his authority is the faith of the advice-seeker in the adviser's hunches or intuition or susceptibility to revelation.

4. *Social standards.*—That alternative is chosen which calls for behavior deemed most acceptable to some group to which one belongs. In any group, an individual does some things but not others, and in the organizational situation, he may try to maintain a code of ethics derived for use by some other group in connection with problems of its own. The authority is a code of ethics which represents the bases of belonging to the group.

5. *Organizational policy.*—Here an ethical position is directly inferable from policies that were made to fit the operating realities of the organization on some previous occasion. The authority is faith in a series of past conclusions about similar situations.

6. *Position.*—Decisions based on concern over one's position are likely to be punitive or aggrandizing. When one feels secure in his position, he is able to distinguish between the functions of his office and the symbols and gestures of its power. The authority, when decisions are based on position, is fear.

7. *Technical expert.*—The man who has had a great deal of experience with the kind of problem under consideration may have valuable notions about what can be done. The authority is prestige based on demonstrated competence.

8. *Personal.*—The personality of a "natural leader" evokes a warm response; he is felt to be talking sense. The authority is in one's wish to identify with, and depend on, someone for help.

9. *Alter ego.*—The assistant-to-the-president and the office "wife" achieve, through identification with a superior, some skill in representing his ways of thinking, and they give substantially the same advice he would. The authority here is that of power transmitted through the power person's alter ego.

ORGANIZATIONAL PROBLEMS

Human relations problems in organizations are likely to be posed by the "top" people. The coldness of a department head, for example, presents the rest of the department with anxieties and inhibitions in their friendship relations. A dogmatic boss sets the stage for undercover revolt and a desire to outmaneuver him by his men. A hesitant or reluctant administrator engenders in workers much anxious conflict over their own roles in the organization. These phenomena are reactions by subordinates to the way their superiors relate to them. The existence of bad feelings within the superior is in itself evidence that he has false expectations about the relationship. False expectations by the top level present subordinates with a prediction of failure, and this strains the relationship further. The existence of false or inappropriate expectations indicates that false prophets have been used—i.e., wrong, inadequate, or inappropriate authority.

The existence of *confused* expectations, in which nobody knows what to expect from himself or anybody else, is an even more serious problem, for it indicates a confusion of the relationships between power and authority. And without clarity in these matters there is no machinery for dealing with any other problem.

The central importance of these propositions is demonstrated by the fact that the "Commandments of Good Organization" are concerned in one way or another with these matters:

1. Define responsibilities.
2. Always give authority with responsibility.
3. Never change job responsibilities without informing all concerned.
4. No man should have more than one boss.
5. Never give orders to another boss's subordinates.
6. Always criticize subordinates in private.

7. Settle promptly every dispute over authority or responsibility.
8. A boss's boss should always approve promotions, raises, and disciplinary actions.
9. Never ask a subordinate to criticize his boss.
10. Give every executive enough help to let him check on the quality of his own work.[1]

When definitions of authority and responsibility are not clear and appropriate to functions, it is necessary for individuals to take matters into their own hands. Each tries in his own way to deal with confusion and demoralization. The situation becomes dominated by a philosophy of "every man for himself," grafted on top of the official but unworkable table of organization. The result is burgeoning of the unofficial and frequently unacknowledged real power structure, as illustrated in the following engaging account of goings-on at Turbid Manufacturing Company.

"Turbid's aggressive managers, however, pay scant attention to jurisdictional distinctions. The industrial relations department's authority, for instance, completely overlaps the personnel department because of (1) the president's enthusiasm for industrial relations, and (2) the emphasis is on public relations in the public utterances of Turbid's dominant board member. Similarly, Turbid's finance chief has so much drag with the president that his department cuts right across all decisions handed down the line of command. The dotted circle (in Turbid's Organizational Chart) symbolizes the post held by the fun-loving brother of Turbid's president, who is incapable of managerial functioning, and dangles—the fruit of nepotism. The president is surrounded by committees, one so dominant it can give orders down the line, as well as advice to him. His young "assistant to" in his confidential status colors much of what the boss hears from the twelve executives who jealously insist on reporting directly to the chief."[2]

If management is to function effectively it must function openly and in an orderly way. If there is to be an informal system of communication outside of the official system, then a vast amount of energy will go into office politics, and decisions will be power

1. Perrin Stryker, "Can Management Be Managed?" *Fortune*, XLVIII, No. 1 (July, 1953), 138. Quoted by permission.
2. *ibid.*, p. 101.

plays rather than problem solutions. But the kind of orderliness and predictability required for honest relationships up and down the hierarchy is based upon the clarity and appropriateness to functioning of authority and responsibility.

One major result of improper or confused selection of authority and the relationship between authority and power is administrative ulcers. The administrator is extremely vulnerable to confusion in authority because he plays a number of different roles. Thus he is (*a*) petitioner on behalf of his men to the group above; (*b*) designated leader of his subordinates; (*c*) a subordinate to the levels above him; (*d*) consultant to his men on interpersonal process problems, and so on. If the complex of leadership expectations is unclear, the administrator may find himself unable to bring all these roles into relationship within his personality.

THE ADMINISTRATIVE PERSONALITY

The manager, functioning to co-ordinate operational efforts; the administrator, functioning to form policy and facilitate long-range welfare; the supervisor, functioning to improve efficiency of the men—all these are wielders of power. The quality of each person's need, use, and wish for power, and his fantasies about destructive and constructive possibilities of power enter very decisively into his predispositions for and objectivity about the different sorts of authority to be favored.

Let us quote soliloquies of two hypothetical administrators in order to get some feeling for the orientation of their ways of life around concepts of power and its uses.

One point of view.—"I worked hard to get into my present position of power. The fact that I succeeded is prima-facie evidence of my superiority. To get where I am meant that I had to see facts straight and realistically. It meant being able to assume responsibility and deliver the goods. When I make a decision it is probably better than the decision that could be made by the people I boss. If they could make better decisions, they would be my bosses. I go around with other people like myself, and we tend to run things, both in the plant and in the community, although we delegate a lot of the community running to our wives. We married women who, by and large, would be assets to us in the community, and we're a pretty decent set of people, if I do say so.

"We think well of the people who work for us, and we know that they must be kept reasonably happy and secure and satisfied. When outsiders come in and stir up trouble we resent it because we are always willing to meet the employees halfway and there's no sense in trying to do things by violence when peaceful means are available. Our competitors, too, we respect. There's plenty of room for competing companies, and their advertising budgets, added to ours, increases the public's demand for our products. And we work together to head off unfavorable legislation. Of course, we are not in business for our health, and any time we can run a competitor to the wall it is our obligation to the stockholders to do so. Everyone in business knows this, and he accepts these rules as part of the game when he goes into business. We neither ask nor give any quarter.

"My personal life? What does that matter to you? Well, sure, I suppose you might say that my group pretty well controls the investment of money in our town. It's a fine town, and our company, through providing jobs all these years, and through taxes and voluntary contributions, has done a lot to make it a *great* town. Look at the way our population has grown! You know, a high percentage of these new people—fine people,too—came to town to work in our company. No, I don't know where they live —over on the South Side, I expect. Yes, I have heard that the housing over there is pretty bad, but I guess it's at least as good as the people are used to, or they wouldn't live there. Every man to his desserts, I say."

Another point of view.—"Sure, I worked hard to get where I am. My wife tells me I'm sort of compulsively ambitious, and maybe I am. All I know about that is I like to get ahead. I enjoy prestige and being listened to. I guess I'm personally sort of competitive. Of course, I'll admit I got some good breaks. When I first came to the plant I was pretty green, and old 'Doc' Saunders sort of took me in hand. I owe a lot to him. And I owe a lot to the other fellows on the bench alongside me, although I didn't realize it at the time. Our first boss was pretty rough, and we used to have to calm each other down every so often. When we found out we all hated him it made things easier, and we learned how to handle him. And he gave us a square deal when it came time for promotions.

"Ever since then I've sort of had the habit of listening to what people say. When I make a decision it is usually a pretty good one, but the reason is that I know my men and how they look at things. They make a good team. Of course, I have to lay down the law every so often, and sometimes they get mad about it, but we generally talk it through. You know, when I finally got up into this high-level bracket, I palled around at the country club with the other execs, and I still do. But I get tired of doing everything with the same people, and I've recently gotten out the old fishing tackle. I found a local group of anglers—the Isaak Walton Association—and the leader of the group is one of our foremen. We've had some pretty fine trips, too, although my wife is suspicious of them.

"Are our workmen happy? Golly, I wouldn't know how to answer that. What I mean is that that's really up to them. Every so often an organizer comes around the plant, and I always try to be sure that he gets a fair hearing if a group of the men are interested in what he has to say. One fellow made a lot of headway telling them they were being exploited; so I suggested they appoint a committee and go over our books with the auditor. No, that wasn't my idea. It was tried in another company in the East somewhere, and the workers decided not to ask for the raise. In our case, we figured out with them what would be fair wages, and we made some adjustments. That committee really impressed our management board, and they have consulted with us about a lot of things since. I don't know whether they will formalize it as the nucleus for a union or not. I have offered to see what can be done to get them good training in union management if they want to try it.

"Sure, we have problems. Our expansion during the war brought in a lot of new people, and it's been hard to find places for them to live. We don't think it's up to the company to provide them housing—we see it as a problem for the entire community, and we have been putting money and staff time into a new civic organization to study what to do. It's discouraging, though. That

South Side housing just isn't good enough for our new laborers. Sure, its as good as they were used to where they came from, but everyone lived that way there. They're not living there now, they're living here, and our community has a higher standard of living. We'll have to see what can be done about it."

These two points of view are admittedly extreme, although I have actually known men who held them. The two men represented in these interviews have different concepts of the sources of their success, different ways of relating themselves to other people, different concepts of the autonomy of their companies, different perspectives on plant operation.

It would be a mistake to dismiss this pattern of differences with some phrase such as "Oh, that's just the way people are!" It is true that there is a relationship between a man's personality and the beliefs he holds. But these beliefs and ways of working come from living in our culture, which offers both the alternatives given above.

In a situation where such divergent ways of life are available —a matter of choice, so to speak, of each individual—we need to find some way to make the choice, not "once and for all" but creatively, in terms of the requirements of each situation. The way of life we need is illuminated by principles and understandings: it is the method of intelligence—relevant facts plus appropriate interpretation and decision. These conditions are not easy to achieve because the culturally induced administrative confusion extends to methods of thinking.

Methods of thinking in administration are based on concepts of authority. Thus, the man who sees himself as the authority, who uses only his own experience as the basis of decision, tends to set up his own private theories of administration, and these are generally not very well articulated simply because they are private. Such explanations as he makes for his policies often strike the outsider as rationalizations, and these policies may be quite inconsistent from one situation to the next. Thus, one can hold the policy that promotion is based on merit in one case, that it is based on need in another case, and that it is for the good of the group to kick the man upstairs in still another case. To the outsider, this adds up to three ways of explaining rather personal prejudices. The person who bases his action primarily on his own experience, interpreted by his own private theories, also tends to limit the range of his experience. He surrounds himself with yes men, which means that he uses other people simply for the reassurance that he is adequate. In effect, such people talk to themselves because they are basically afraid to talk with others. Their approach to management is likely to be in terms of pressure.

The man who believes that the source of authority is the experience of all those concerned in the operations he governs, has to make his methods explicit so that others can give him relevant information. In the process of this communication, his theories get tested and ironed out, and they become part of the rationale of the group rather than his private property. Such a man tends to surround himself with those people who are most competent to help with respect to each major kind of problem. This kind of administrator admits to himself that he is not the most competent person to decide everything, and he learns how to use the competence of others. When he gets differing advice from competent people, he makes the decision tentatively and with some provision for testing and revising in the light of experience.

Such an administrator can add to the skills that got him to the top in the first place additional skills in dealing with groups through the use of an open-minded experimental approach—he grows on the job. There are times when he acts alone on his hunches, but these are either emergencies or familiar situations. He tends to look far enough ahead that things can be checked before they reach a crisis stage, and he tends to develop through experience shared with others new areas of judgment in which his competence is clearly that of the expert. The methods favored by this administrator are those of co-operation.

In comparing our two prototypes, the first man appears to solve problems in whatever way protects or enhances his own position or, by extension, that of his own group. The second man simply tends to solve problems. Such personal vested interest as he has is a partiality for use of the experimental method. This amounts to the conviction that the "right" decision is obtained by "right" methods of decision-making, rather than by having some absolute "rightness" in itself.

Either of these men is probably a better administrator than the one who simply withdraws from the job of administering. Such a person, for example, is likely to act only when he has to, and then in desperation. Desperate decisions are also expedient and unpredictable, so those around such an administrator never know what to expect. We have many examples of this kind of administration given by such city officials as police chiefs, housing commissioners, and mayors who tend to let things slide until a newspaper or some citizen group sets up a clamor and then crack down hard—but only on those most obviously vulnerable. People who "make an example" of occasional incidents, or who plead that every decision is just a matter of opinion, or who listen to everybody without any estimates of their competence, or who judge everything on the basis of personality, or who seem uncommitted to any goals—such people fit this image.

In social terms, the basic conflict of administration, then, is that there is available in our culture a variety of fundamentally conflicting ways of approaching the problems of authority and power, and that to some extent most of us are either unable to act at all or act out of confusion among these conflicting ways.

TYPICAL PROBLEMS OF ADMINISTRATORS

The administrator, in one way or another, has to come to terms with the following conflicts:

1. DIVIDED LOYALTY

When his men express resentment at some new ruling from above, foreman Jackson defends the company. When the division chief complains about occasional lapses in productivity of his men, Jackson defends his men. He now has the uncomfortable feeling that the men think of him as a "company prig" and that the division chief, his boss, thinks of him as being "touchy."

Analysis.—The key word is "defend." The need to defend implies the feeling that an attack is going on, and this implies lack of co-operation between levels, as well as lack of acceptance of the normal gripes that men at one level usually have about men at another level. Jackson's attitude should be that he can help determine the facts, not that he must defend. It may be that he finds it hard to identify or "belong" in the two groups, or that he feels he must select one or the other for his primary loyalty. His indecision is probably uncomfortable to him and angers him. In this case, his defense of the group under attack may serve to reassure him that he feels warmth rather than hostility toward the groups.

Suggestions.—Set up a meeting of Jackson, his men, some other foreman, and Jackson's boss. Let them talk out the problems of what each expects of the other and what criteria of judgment are being used by people at each level in assessing their subordinates. The hope is that this kind of frank and specific talking will increase Jackson's security and belongingness, and will also bring the groups closer together in a reaffirmation of joint purposes.

2. WORK VERSUS AFFECTION

A principal makes it a point to report to meetings of his teachers the latest recommendations and actions of the school board. But he never reports back anything critical of the teachers or the school. He also works long hours on weekends collecting information for reports rather than asking for help from teachers.

Analysis.—This sort of "protectiveness"—which seems more like a fear of imposing on the teachers—is unfortunate, because it makes an additional demand on the principal's time and energy. He not only has the job of running the school, but also of continually reassuring himself that he is giving no cause for dislike.

Suggestions.—His anxiety is probably well communicated, and this is at least one probable cause for his being disliked. He should concentrate on his job of running the school, and pay no attention to whether he is liked or not except in so far as such feelings become forces affecting the school program. He might, for example, get himself a small executive committee from the teachers to talk over the various matters of which teachers should be informed and to decide what recommendations should be made.

3. DELEGATION OF RESPONSIBILITY

In many organizations, the job of the assistant or junior levels is the most difficult, because of the unwillingness of the superiors to delegate definite responsibilities. The juniors have little to do, but they hesitate to ask the chief for work because he gets angry when they do.

Analysis.—Such bosses usually are frightened men, rather than hogs for work. They feel that sharing responsibility also means sharing power, and this is intolerable, either because they feel they do not have enough for themselves or because they fear the use of the shared power against them. By doing all the work, probably better than his subordinates could, the boss reassures himself that he really is entitled to his power—even though he cannot accept or use it intelligently.

Suggestions.—Some superior could point out to the boss that the group standard in the plant is to delegate responsibilities, that this is expected and proper. He could also suggest a self-survey, to discover how present personnel are utilized, and could suggest a discussion between the boss and his assistants to work out an understanding of their several tasks. In these discussions, every effort should be made to reassure the boss that he has earned his power.

4. FINDING OUT "THE TRUTH"

The reaction of the leader to the various categories of information offered by his men will, in the long run, determine the nature of bottom-to-top communication. Most men realize that some things have to be reported upward, and some other things should not be mentioned; they also are aware of an in-between category of relevant information not directly about the jobs but which illuminates what is going on. The problem is to get appropriate communication upward: and this means adequate information undistorted by the personal concerns of the reporter.

Analysis.—Communication upward depends on threat, opportunity, and reward. If information is invited only as a prelude to punishing a culprit or assigning extra work, then distortion of information and reluctance of most men to communicate can be expected. If the only opportunity to communicate is at social functions or during minutes stolen from work, then some men will not initiate communication. If the boss listens gladly to information from some people but brushes off others, then only certain men will have an incentive to volunteer information—and they are likely to be hated by their fellows.

Suggestions.—The routinizing of channels for information-gathering should be discussed with all the people involved in the operation—i.e., with everyone in a position to collect needed information. Agreements are needed on "who communicates what to whom and when." If there are kinds of information the boss cannot accept objectively, then these should be passed to someone else with whom the boss can share responsibility for action. A training session may be set up to help all concerned understand the sorts of information which will be most useful for the improvement of operation.

5. WHEN IS A FRIEND?

The man with enough power to smooth the way for others, but whose power is not enough to take him out of social contact with his subordinates, is likely to find that he has many "friends." And he may feel (properly) that his attractiveness to all these people is not solely due to his personal charm. He will also find that many of his former friends no longer seek him out if he is promoted, and he may assume that they are jealous of him. In any case, the man with power is like a debutante with a two-million-dollar inhertance: neither can ever really be sure of the motivations of their "friends."

Analysis.—The merging or confusing of a man's private world (friendships) with his public world (job) can lead to problems of partisanship and double standards. When the boss cannot separate the two worlds—so that he judges technical skill by the warmth of a smile—there is considerable anxiety aroused in all because the rules for job and pay competition are now obscured by caprice. The informal structure of the organization loses its legitimate adjustive and ameliorative functions and becomes decisive with regard to jobs.

Suggestions.—The formal work structure should be kept separate from the informal interpersonal structure. To keep them separate requires provision within the formal structure for all the work-required types of communication. A further useful policy may be to achieve more remoteness from the social needs of the men by assigning responsibilities to groups rather than to individuals. This would require the primary social interactions of the men to remain among themselves rather than with the boss; but it would leave the door open for necessary discussion of job-related matters with the boss. (This is, in effect, the "project" method of organization.)

6. "NOBLESSE OBLIGE" VERSUS "CHANNELS"

This is a conflict not only with reference to the way people work together, but also to the way they feel about each other, and the extent to which they identify with each other. The "stickler for form" makes everyone fill out all slips in quadruplicate, as a general principle, and he also usually questions the right of others to make requests of him. He simply does not trust others, and he does not trust himself either; which is why he hides behind his tablets and rubber stamps. At the opposite end of the scale is the expansive fellow who will give anybody anything; he seldom has any records to show who now has possession of the calculator or the last annual report or the model of the proposed new product.

Analysis.—These are caricatures of two conditions: first, that channels and procedures exist and are needed for the orderly operation of an organization; and second, that formal communication through channels is basically facilitative of informal agreements reached earlier and noted in private memoranda. Both types of communication are needed, but they operate on very different assumptions. The informal agreement can be used under certain conditions: the participants trust each other, their verbal agreement is as good as a contract; the participants probably identify with each other as members of the same class or social group, and they have enough power to impose their judgments on the "channels," so that clerks are recording-instruments rather than policy-makers. But in the absence of these conditions for informality, the clerks are likely to take over.

Suggestions.—The *sine qua non* for mutual trust is that people have facts rather than fantasies about each other's work in relation to their own. This is accomplished through advisory boards which hear about project plans, successes, and failures. Outside friendships and social functions can help, of course, but they should not be required; they can be carried to the point of unwarranted interference in private lives.

7. LONG-RANGE VERSUS SHORT-RANGE IMPLICATIONS

Administrative behavior has two kinds of consequences. First, as action, it brings about some sort of immediate change; and second, the attitude communicated with the action may reinforce or change relations among people. This latter change carries with it the probability of changes in motivation, readiness, trust, confidence, and the like. The feelings going with administrative action, then, bring about changes the implications of which are long range. Every administrator knows that many of his acts imply relative judgments about the men he judges to be helpful for various purposes, those he sees as co-operative, those whose ideas he most wants, and so on. Similarly, punitive measures are at least as important for their effects on the group as they are for correcting an individual.

Analysis.—There are many times when "doing it one's self," or picking out a pleasant youngster for a task ordinarily done by one of the older people, or making a casual remark in front of a group instead of in the office would be easy and natural to do. But those behaviors, inevitably related to personal problems, are likely to be interpreted differently by every spectator, and even the simplest nonwork gesture of an administrator can be the topic of considerable speculation.

Suggestions.—Action should be governed by two sets of criteria, not one. The first set defines what it is hoped the action will accomplish. The second set defines the characteristics of action: the right of the agent to take action, the amount of consultation with those affected by it, the use during its consideration of existing groups whose jurisdiction can be extended, etc. Finally, each discussion of action also should be partly a training session for setting conditions favorable to the growth and long-range strength of the groups.

Two Central Propositions

One implication of the above discussion is that administrative behavior is perceived and reacted to by many people; and that the behaviors of the administrator are themselves affected by the perceptions and feelings of those about him.

This leads to the suggestion that administration and management may be thought of as *functions* arising within the organization, rather than merely as roles played by a handful of people. Our first proposition, then, is: Proposition I: Not all systems or organizations are equally susceptible to administration or management. The one best administered in the long run is the one in which the power of position is least often exercised, individuals have belongingness in groups to which responsibilities are assigned, and the autonomy of each individual is agreed upon in group discussion in which he participates.

This proposition implies in effect that a vast percentage of the industrial work of the nation is poorly organized. It seems to me that this is indeed the case. The fragmentation of complex manufacturing arts into sequences of simple repetitive operations has gone so far that many workers are mere machines, living in a state of suspended animation during the day and living as persons only after work hours are over. We seem to have sacrificed creativity for productivity; and worth-while living for a high standard of living. But, in the light of Proposition I, this is not unalterable.

Take the case of a punch press operator, assigned to a machine eight hours a day, five days a week. How can our talk of group discussion and individual autonomy affect him?

One suggestion is that possibly a man shold not be assigned to a punch press eight hours a day, five days a week. The reasoning of this chapter would suggest that *a group of men should be assigned to a group of operations*, and they should decide among themselves how to man the machines.

The cluster of operations assigned to each group should be visibly interrelated in the product. Thus, if Jim forms the aluminum, Joe drills holes in it, Jerry inserts the waggobbles into the holes, Jack tightens them in place, and Jacqueline tests them to be sure they operate—then this much of an assembly enables all five workers to see their work in relation to each of the other four. Their work has meaning with respect to other work, and they have a place with respect to other people who share the same purpose. And their team can have relationships to other teams.

Suppose there are 40 of each of the punch presses, drill presses, waggobble bins, tightening wrenches, and inspecting instruments. Suppose one person is assigned to each. This makes 200 workers. Suppose there is a foreman for every 20 workers. Our proposal would be that each foreman plus 20 workers constitute a group. This group would be given the responsibility of organizing itself into 4 teams of 5 persons each to turn out subassemblies.

They could form their teams in any way they wanted to, and divide up the five jobs among the five team members in any way the team desired. Rotation would be possible at will,[3] and so would reconstitution of the teams. The group of four teams could work out its own plan for breaking in new workers.

Under these conditions, the job itself would have far more meaning, more challenge, and more reward. The robot concept of workers would pass from the scene. And each person would have a clearly defined part in certain decisions relevant to his work. Thus his individuality would be enhanced and his autonomy increased.

There are further implications, too: Instead of the personnel department's trying to select each individual for one rigidly described "slot," it would be possible to accommodate a wider range of temperaments in the team groups. Thus the team idea makes it easier to use whatever workers are available at the time they are needed.

It will take ingenuity to redesign plant layouts and job coordination to make use of these principles. Some unit operations

---

3. The following item appeared in the business section of *Newsweek* on March 22, 1954, under the heading "How They Got More Done": "While the boss was away, some factory workers in Endicott, N.Y., switched jobs, just to break up the boredom. Result: it turned out to be just what the doctor ordered. By the time the switch was discovered, the men were all doing so much better that the boss decided to rotate jobs in his department—at an International Business Machines plant—as a matter of policy. That was a year ago. Since then manufacturing costs in the department have dropped about 19 per cent. If nobody gets bored by the routine of rotation, everything will be dandy." Comment: If the boss maintains the kind of relationship that allowes this spontaneous action of the workers to occur, he will keep production up. If he imposes rotation as a gimmick, the effect will be only temporary.

are faster than others. One man might service several teams. The continual challenge is to maintain the basic psychological conditions through whatever adaptations of the simple model arc required.

In general, Proposition I calls for explicit effort to develop worker groups. By and large, workers *are* in groups which strongly affect their productivity already, so that we are advocating making conscious use of a situation that already exists. The evidence for the assertion that worker groups exist anyway is the fact of interdependence: what one man does influences others, and vice versa.

There are different degrees and qualities of such horizontal interdependence:

1. The interdependence may be as *members of a team in competition* with other teams. *Examples:* A team tending a blast furnace; a small in-service training group within a school; subgroups of different academic specialties within a university department. In these cases, each member of the team has somewhat different responsibilities, and each other person is affected by the manner in which he does his job.

2. The interdependence may be in the *setting of standards* governing essentially parallel activity. *Examples:* Pieceworkers all doing the same job will gradually arrive at coercive standards of production; regardless of individual skill and apparent motivation, all the workers turn out finished pieces at approximately the same rate. Salesmen in widely separated territories tend to have common standards of honesty and diligence. In a university, there tend to be group standards for research productivity; in a school, for concern over children; in a factory, over waste, workmanship, quality and kind of supervision, and so on.

These standards usually express the feeling of the group toward its job. A major factor influencing them is the shared feeling about the people who control the job. Interaction with the superior may be private and separate among individual workers, but they find ways to compare notes and to set up standards for their own "protection" in the face of demands seen as coming from the boss—whether he is a foreman, plant manager, or the executive head of a corporation.

3. The interdependence within the group may be through its power to *regulate the pressure of its own work*. *Examples:* Initiating an active faculty committee results in a general increase in responsibility; a bottleneck on the production line reduces the rate of work all down the line; the acceptance of money by the directors of an organization means that more work must be turned out by operating personnel. The interdependence here is essentially sequential: the effects of events at some one place may gradually fan out through the entire institution. These changes can often be anticipated, and can be a source of concern long before they become real. The best example of this situation is probably a change in top leadership, but the place where the accommodations are successively made is within each horizontal level.

Thus, we note that people within a given level may be in face-to-face contact, finding that the way in which they operate is dependent upon each other's actions; or they may simply share the same ideas about themselves and the "proper" rate of production, a common perception of the boss, the general expectancy of fair or capricious treatment, and the like. Finally, they may be affected by fluctuations in operations prior to their own, and these may be fluctuations in the flow of materials, rumors, or rewards.

Our first assumption, then, is that because of these interdependences within each horizontal level, we may think of the workers within each level as constituting a "group." Each group has a designated "leader." Each group meets demands from "above," and the experience of each group contributes to policy which affects the nature of those demands.

Assuming that we now have defined each job in such a way that one can have significant experience through his work, and that we have done this through the creation of worker groups, then our next problem is to co-ordinate these groups of workers within the hierarchical situation. We note that the group has a boss or supervisor, who provides leadership to the group, and who also communicates between the group and the other superior and inferior groups. It is almost inevitable that the administrator finds himself caught in a conflict among his various roles, and that conflict would be greatest when he is wielding administrative power. Thus, consider the situation when the boss brings to his group a new set of demands or regulations from "upstairs":

1. Demands from "upstairs" are *pressures* on the group from a superior or dominant group. These pressures may be seen as reasonable or not, but the group must meet them.

2. The group meets these pressures by mobilizing its resources, as if against a common "enemy." The process of pulling together is one of co-operation.

3. The job of the boss as leader is to help the group co-operate efficiently to deal with the pressures.

4. In dynamic terms, the basic conflict of the administrator is a real one: he is seen as putting pressure on *at the same time* that he must also help the group co-operate to meet the pressure. He is essentially "enemy" and "leader against the enemy" at the same time. The administrator thus finds himself in a very difficult role conflict.

There are several ways to deal with the conflict. One is to deny one or the other of the roles. Thus, the administrator or supervisor can say that his job is to tell his men what to do. He includes, in the definition of the demand, instructions of how to meet the demand. In other words, he squeezes out the place of co-operation among the men, and establishes basically a one-to-one relationship between each man and himself. This, of course, loses the resources of the group, removes a number of important interpersonal types of gratification and involvement, and may set the men competitively against each other.

The administrator can also deny the other role, that of communicating demands to the group. He cannot, of course, fail to transmit demands, but he can fail to communicate them. Thus, he can post a memorandum on the bulletin board rather than talk directly to the men. In this case, he knows what the demands are, but the group actually discovers them to be only barriers to operation: it is as though a new "house rule" were suddenly invoked against them every time they got rolling. The group can never define the extent of its autonomy under such conditions. It would be justified in gradually sinking into a state of dependency and apathy as a way of avoiding the continual disappointments of being constantly interfered with. The point is that demands from "upstairs" actually become part of the facts, the "given's," with which a group must operate. These facts should be told them.

A common way in which administrators react to conflict in their role is to muddle things up—to exert pressure at times and to co-operate at times, without understanding when and how to do which. Possibly a basic cause of such muddling is the administrator's inability to distinguish a demand from "upstairs" from his own demands upon the group. An administrator whose security depends mostly on feeling that he is a part of the "upstairs" group identifies with it, and, therefore, feels that all his pronouncements to his men have the official backing of his superior group. Another administrator may learn that demands from "upstairs" have to be obeyed by his men, whereas things they see only as his personal demands do not; therefore, he may be tempted to imply constantly that what he wants is really a part of the demands from "upstairs." Some administrators act as if the group should arrive by themselves at a formulation of the demands from "upstairs" by some process of spontaneous generation. A final example of muddling is the administrator who swings like a weather vane from pressure tactics to co-operative tactics in an effort to keep everyone happy. This kind of oscillation is easy because the group, too, is subject to the cultural confusion between pressure and co-operation, and from time to time they will make a strong bid for one or the other.

The sequence of thought leading to Proposition II is as follows:

1. Demands from above are made on each group and its leader together. The leader and his group together then face the problem of meeting the demands. This means that the leader, in all his working with his group, never is placed in the position of the demander or "enemy."

2. The demand is made by someone superior to the leader in a meeting with the group. This superior stays around long enough to be sure that the demands are clearly understood. The leader is likely to mediate between the group and the superior: his job is to help the group ask the questions necessary for clarification.

3. Since all demands originate from outside the group, they

can be translated objectively into problems for the group as a whole to solve. The existence of problems to be solved (or changes to be made) provides the necessary focus and discipline for group discussion, and the group has sufficient autonomy to deal with the problem.

4. Since the demand is made by the superior, he is also the person responsible for evaluation of results. It is up to him to decide (preferably with the group's help) just how the evaluation is to be done. He may delegate some of the procedures to the group or to the leader, but he must keep the responsibility.

5. Because the group's leader now has a clearly co-operative role in his group, he is able more accurately to carry the group's thinking "upstairs," and thus is able to help his group exert an influence toward a more realistic formulation of the demands which it receives.

6. Because each man has contact not only with his *immediate* superior but also with higher-ups, he has less feeling of isolation, better understanding of the total operation, and an opportunity to assess the implications of his relation to his leader.

It is clear, in summary, that the intention here is to purify roles so as to avoid ambiguity and confusion. Proposition II may be stated: Each administrator in the heirarchy has three roles, but they operate in defined ways on different occasions. Thus: (*a*) Each man is a *member* of a group, working co-operatively with its leader, to meet work demands from "upstairs" and to formulate policy for the group below. (*b*) Each man is the *leader* of his group of subordinates, and has the responsibility for maintaining conditions of co-operation within the group, for transmitting relevant experience of the group upward, and for transmitting work demands downward. (*c*) Each man is a *transmitter of demands* (superior) to the groups led by his subordinates. His job is to make sure that the demands are understood as problems to be solved by his subordinates' groups; and to check on and evaluate the results of their efforts.

Some Questions and Answers

1. Are you seriously suggesting that the administrator should attend meetings of groups led by his own subordinates?

Comment: Yes, when it is necessary to transmit a demand from "above."

2. Suppose a department manager is responsible for eight subdivisions, and each of these has an average of six sections. Should the manager attend meetings of all forty-eight groups?

Comment: That would be nice, but it may be impractical. If so, the following suggestions might be weighed:

a) He could consider talking to some of the subdivisional sections together. This would succeed to the extent that the same demand, presented in the same way, was equally appropriate to the sections. What he loses by this arrangement is some of the freedom to talk with the men in each section.

b) He could, possibly, send someone in his place. If, for example, he has an assistant who is known to be able to speak for him, this functionary could be sent. What he loses by this arrangement is the opportunity for his men to identify with him as representative to them of "top-level" thinking. The men get less gratification, and may have less motivation to deal with the demand.

c) He could relay the demand through small committees sent by several section groups to talk with him. Thus, one good meeting with sixty representatives might serve to bring the demand to twenty groups. What is lost by this arrangement is the objectivity with which the demand will be presented to the group, and there may be difficulties in clarifying the demand further when the men ask questions.

d) He could write a letter to each of the men, explaining the demand and requesting them to discuss it as a group. In this case, however, he should also be prepared to talk with those who may wish conversation with him; otherwise the communication is just "one-way" and motivation may be low.

e) He might call for some reorganization, on the grounds that eight subdivisions are too many for one man to control.

3. Wouldn't this plan mean that everyone would spend all his time in conferences? When would the work get done?

Comment: There are several relevant considerations here:

a) The "proper" division of time between "working" and

"conferencing" is that division which leads to satisfactory productivity. If another half-hour of talking results in more than half-an-hour's worth of additional production, then the time is well spent. A pointless conference, or one with bad leadership may be a waste of time. All such a failure shows, however, is that someone needs more training.

b) After getting the plan in operation, the need for conferences should decrease quite considerably. Increased co-operation between the boss and his men means more individual initiative, more incentive for men to work things out for themselves rather than to depend on the boss or on a meeting. A co-operative group is one which supports and challenges individual activity and growth; a group which serves as a crutch to lean on or as a pool in which to submerge one's individuality is coercive, not co-operative. As long as the problem to be solved is central, the group spends its time in effective work, whether it be at the conference table or at one's desk. And, by seeing the problem as a whole before beginning work, the men know to whom to go for what further discussion; it is not necessary to call a conference to talk about things that Joe and Mike can take care of in a twenty-minute chat by themselves.

c) At first, time will need to be spent at the conferences defining everyone's role in connection with each new problem. After a while, expectancies will develop, and the roles will be defined much more quickly in connection with new tasks. The groups, under competent leaders, will pick up considerable efficiency in translating demands into problems. They may also earmark certain kinds of demands to be delegated routinely to certain individuals or to "working committees." All delegated activity should, however, be reported to the total group from time to time, and, very probably, the "working committees" should be reconstituted with some frequency.

Two Applications to Administrative Problems

Our proposal is that work in an organizational setting is best produced by small groups which provide scope for significant experience. The internal basis of co-ordination of effort can be found in common ideas and purposes shared among the members. Data gleaned from operating experience are transmitted to superior groups, considered along with other data, and then sent back down in the form of demands or assignments. The demand is made on the group and its leader together. This protects the autonomy of the members and leads to co-operation between group and leaders.

The following represent applications of certain aspects of the model:

1. *Mr. Smith cuts the budget*

Mr. Smith is head of the dormitories at Grip College. Word came down from the business manager that he must operate next year with 10 per cent less funds than he did this year. Smith saw how to cut 4 per cent without hurting the services for which he was responsible. In desperation, he decided to ask his staff to help. He called them together and explained the problem. He was asked to read the letter from the business manager, in which the cut was requested. He read this to the group and they then started making suggestions. No one suggestion represented a major saving, but the staff reapportioned some of its duties so that two men who were leaving would not have to be replaced; they decided to let the students run the snack bar instead of hiring help; and they thought up an altogether new idea: that the students might organize to put on social events on a profit-sharing basis with the dormitory.

Mr. Smith, as spokesman for his staff, came to a meeting between his staff and the dormitory student committee. He presented the suggestion about social events (e.g., he "demanded" that the group consider the suggestion). He then left, and the group considered the plan, finally agreeing on a modified form of it for Mr. Smith to take "higher up" for necessary facilitating policy.

Through these means, Smith saved the college 12 per cent of the usual budget for his operation.[4]

Comment: This illustration fits the model fairly well. The business manager, Mr. Smith's boss, was represented by a letter instead of appearing in person. The business manager lost the op-

4. Related to me by Mr. Smith.

portunity to get suggestions about economizing in other parts of the college, apparently assuming that one can have ideas only about his own little corner.

Mr. Smith's staff, facing the outside demand together, was able to find answers of which Smith alone had not thought, and which he would have thought unacceptable to his staff if he *had* thought of them.

Smith, by presenting the suggestion to the students himself, freed his staff to discuss the matter effectively and without feeling tied to their own vested interests.

2. *General Smith investigates the black market*

General Smith, commanding officer in a corner of the European Theater, heard rumors of black market operations involving the theft of goods from his post and their subsequent possession by "natives." He called in three of his immediate subordinates and told them to bring him the facts "by next week at 2 o'clock." At report time, the subordinates, who had told *their* subordinates to snoop around and interview people, had the names of three malefactors on the base to report. They also had the names of fifty citizens seen with the goods.

The general guessed from the way the reports were made to him that his subordinates were covering up something. He decided to investigate personally.

His subordinates and *their* subordinates received invitations to "come to the game room of the officers club next Wednesday." The invitations were signed by the general. All those invited canceled their other plans and came. The general opened the affair by saying: "Gentlemen, tonight we have the opportunity for a bit of man-to-man talk. I am going to take off all this 'hardware' and pitch it on the table." He peeled off his brass insignia, with a flourish. "I suggest," he continued, "that each of you pitch yours on the table, too." The others followed his suggestion. They had mixed feelings, of apprehension at the unexpected, and of pleasure at the closer identification with the general.

After all were seated again, the general said: "Gentlemen, what are the facts about the black market?"

There was a long silence, during which several men exchanged uneasy glances.

Lt. Jack spoke up: "Do you ever go by the corner of East and Hollyhock?"

The general: "I could."

(*Silence*)

Capt. Tom: "I suppose the stuff gets stored temporarily in warehouses."

The discussion developed in hypothetical language: the men appeared to be planning how to carry out the black market operation instead of talking about actual events. At one point, Lt. Jack said: "If I were the head operator, I'd probably try to get information from someone like the supply officer—even if I had to pay for it." Lt. Jack was the supply officer. The general said: "I suppose the head of the supply depot could refuse to give further useful information, couldn't he?" "Yes," replied Lt. Jack. At no point did anyone have to name names. When it was clear who knew the names, the general gave these people the task of drawing up recommendations for a procedure to learn the names of those people whose initiative kept the business going.

Within five days the black market operation was completely destroyed, and new security provisions, planned in part by men who had connived in the operation, were set up.[5]

Comment: At first glance, one might suppose that this problem was solved by extra-administrative or informal means. But do not be fooled by the stripping off of the insignia. Shedding the "brass" did not mean shedding rank. But it did mean shedding many of the *distractions caused by rank*.

The "problem" as defined by the general was to stop the black market operation and to do what he could to prevent further resumption of the illegal enterprise. He acted on the hunch that these men could stop it, and, with their knowledge and experience, would know how to prevent similar developments in the future. The general may or may not have had any intention of taking punitive action when the meeting began, but he al-

5. I have heard three versions of this story, but am not able to document it. It is a useful story for our purposes, true or not.

lowed each person the opportunity to make such restitution as he could by helping the group more or less anonymously.

By acting informally, without the "hardware," the boss communicated the idea to these men that they were, in effect, his partners—that he accepted them as people, not as cells in the table of organization. He was inviting them to help solve a problem; he was not telling them to answer his questions—or else. His manner put the whole investigation under the rule of *noblesse oblige*, rather than the "big stick." And the group accepted the challenge to act maturely. The general's authority was inherent in his functional relationships to his men—that is not something that he could "put on" every morning with a clean tunic—and this episode probably reinforced his actual authority.

The general made his demands on the two levels just beneath him. These two levels constituted a group, and they quickly set up the group standard of hypothetical discussion. The general was wise enough to let them handle it that way: he wanted to solve a problem, and he knew that they knew that they were not going to leave the room until the general was satisfied. Therefore, the "Old Man," having given them the responsibility and knowing they could not evade it, could afford to relax and let them edge up to the problem in whatever way they could.

RECAPITULATION AND SUMMARY

1. Responsibilities are assigned to small groups whose members co-operate to define the roles of each individual, to train themselves, to induct new members, etc. These small groups have sufficient autonomy to carry out their responsibilities and, also, for their members to meet many personal-social needs in the process. Belongingness in the group gives each person security and emotional support, so that there is minimum need for the self-oriented anxious behaviors so troublesome in administration.

2. The groups meet as they need to, for the accomplishment of various phases of problem-solving: exploration of the problem, planning of individual responsibilities for taking action, and evaluation of results. No man ever acts alone except on behalf of his group.

3. Groups may be recomposed so that the most appropriate

people are working on each problem. Continuous-production groups would presumably make adjustments for turnover and compatibility; problem-solving groups may be *ad hoc* working committees which exist only during the life of the particular problem.

4. Recommendations are formulated during the working of a group and are transmitted by the leader, serving as spokesman, to the group above. Then this receiving group, working co-operatively, translates these (and other recommendations) into policy and into demands to be transmitted downward.

5. Demands are formulated by each group in the vertical hierarchy for transmission by its leader to the group below. This "receiving" group, working co-operatively, translates the demand into problems of changing operation or of finding specific unique solutions. Furthermore, demands may be *initiated* by recommendations coming up from below.

6. The transmission of demands and recommendations up and down the vertical hierarchy constitutes *pressure*, applied through spokesmen, onto the group above or below. The working-out of problems and the taking of action in the horizontal levels constitutes *co-operation*, with the immediate superior serving as leader. The two forms of communication are separated. These two basic modes of operation remain unentangled and unambiguously applicable in their proper situations.

Further discussion of basic principles is offered on pages 181–91. Thirty-four specific empirical generalizations, of considerable help to people concerned with the organization of work for specific purposes, are presented on pages 62–68. Chapter 7 may be useful in understanding the basic nature of loyalty problems, and chapter 12 points to the important relationships, too often ignored by administrators, between organizations and their surrounding community. The principles listed on pages 14–18 apply very well to creative meetings at the staff level, and the principles of group control, pages 284–89, are relevant to understanding the problems of participation by individuals within the organization.

CHAPTER 5

To train people in the skills of group leadership and membership, one must study their behavior in group situations. The trainer's function is to keep the requirements the group needs to meet clearly before it; but he also safeguards the right and opportunity of each individual to experiment with new ways of co-operating to meet the requirements. Thus the "situation" is permissive for the individual, but the "problem" is clearly defined for the group.

DISTINCTIVE FEATURES

The authority by virtue of which the trainer operates is the trainee's trust in and dependence on him. The method of control of the group is through trainer-planned or trainer-approved agreements about activities planned to satisfy the diagnosed needs of the group. The primary target of change is the trainee's competence as a participant in groups; the secondary target is the groups to which the trainees will return after training. The role of the member is defined by the expectation that he will experiment with new behaviors, be loyal to the group, and try, on occasion, to produce behaviors needed by the group. The communication between the training group and other groups is highly individual and unofficial; it ranges from individual resolutions to behave differently in a "back home" group to the utilization of others for "blowing off steam," discussing the training experience, and receiving emotional support from one's own organizations.

Training for Group Participation
The Laboratory Method[1]

During the past decade, an interest in and an extension of the notion that the effectiveness of groups depends to a great extent upon the ways in which they operate has been rapidly gaining force. While personalities, techniques, experience, cultural backgrounds, and education of the participants in groups are important, the fact remains that effectiveness in the use of these resources is largely determined by the individual characteristics of the situation in which they are to be used. And this situation is basically one of interaction among people.

It is possible, for example, for a group whose members are mostly educated, well adjusted, and knowledgeable to get no-

1. The writing of this chapter, and the research mentioned in it, were facilitated by a contract with The Human Relations and Morale Division of the U.S. Office of Naval Research.

The concept of "laboratory method of training" has been developed through the years since 1945 by a number of research men generally identified with the Group Dynamics movement. The core ideas were proposed by the late Kurt Lewin and his followers at the Research Center for Group Dynamics. This group, with the collaboration of the Department of Adult Education, National Education Association, has been the core for operating the National Training Laboratory at Bethel, Maine, which began in the summer of 1947.

Since 1948, the National Training Laboratory has been operated by a Policy and Planning Committee, consisting of men from the original two groups, plus eleven major universities. I joined this group in 1948, and through the years since then have been deeply concerned with the "laboratory method."

During the summer of 1952, at least eight different workshops, run by as many other groups, made use of some modification of the "laboratory method" as a major part of their training programs. The same basic ideas have been modified and applied to three-day conferences, institutes, and even single meetings.

The method of training requires a great deal of insight and skill on the part of the trainer. Each trainer has his own concept of the method, and there has never been (so far as I know) any complete statement of the method. This chapter represents my attempt to formulate such a statement. In doing this, I am speaking out of my own experiences; this is not an official statement from the National Training Laboratory.

where: consider many school faculty meetings. It is possible for administrators marvellously trained to be unable somehow to run successful staff meetings. It is possible for members of a community council, highly successful as leaders in their own organizations, to be unable to work together. It is possible for people trained in research and loaded with information about what happens in groups to be unable to contribute effectively to groups of which they are a part. It is even possible for a group, highly successful in planning policy for its organization's executive secretary, to fail miserably when its co-operation with other groups is required.

The point is that successful group operation is a matter of taking into account not only the characteristics of individuals but also the nature of the problem, the limitations of time and freedom of action imposed by the institution or community, and such "group" factors as morale, expectations, power fantasies, status in the community, and conceptions of the kind of group the members think it is. All these factors come together to determine the quality of experience the group will have, or, to put it in other words, the nature of the "group processes."

The laboratory method of training provides a situation in which group processes can be observed and studied. The objectives are to train members to recognize when these group processes are appropriate to the group task, what the consequences of different sorts of processes are, how members contribute to determine the nature of the processes, how leaders effect these processes, how a group whose processes are inappropriate may be helped to improve. The task of the trainer in such groups is to see to it that the group has significant experiences in trying to work together, and that conditions are such that people can learn from these experiences. Thus, for example, allowing the group to "flounder around" for six meetings may be giving them a significant experience, but it is one from which the group's members learn little about group process; and what they do learn can seldom consciously be used to guide subsequent membership experience. Or, the trainer can see to it that the group is exposed to a great deal of information about groups, but the information may not be sufficiently related to the members' own deep experiencing for it to have meaning for their subsequent activities. The problems of maintaining a useful balance between feeling, thinking, and doing; between trainer, group, and individual control of behavior; between individual and group goals; between inferring principles from experience and applying known principles to guide new experience; between problem-solving directed toward stated goals and problem-solving related to the resolution of anxiety—all of these problems must be dealt with by the group under the supervision of the trainer.

The purpose of this chapter is to clarify what is involved in the laboratory method of training, and to formulate what appear to us to be basic assumptions and principles used by the trainer. We shall begin with the assumptions on which the laboratory method is based, and will then present a case study of a training group with some interpretations made by the trainer to guide his working with the group. We shall next indicate the sorts of changes produced by the training experience. Finally, we shall summarize the principles used by the trainer to guide the group at all times.

BASIC PRINCIPLES OF THE LABORATORY METHOD

1. The aim of training is (*a*) to help people learn how to behave in groups in such a way that the groups solve the problems for which they were assembed and (*b*) to insure that individuals have a meaningful, rewarding, and need-meeting experience. When both these conditions are present simultaneously the individual is challenged and rewarded for creativity and insights, and the decisions reached by the group are wiser than those any one person could reach by himself. Thus, we might say briefly that the aim of training is simultaneously to help other groups become more effective instruments for social action, on the one hand, and, on the other, to help individuals to grow and learn.

2. In order to accomplish this aim, the trainer ideally should work with the actual groups whose efficiency is to be improved. This would mean that he serve as a roving, "nomadic" consultant, and it would require the dedication of parts of group meetings to training. Actually, however, this is impractical: there are too many groups and too few trainers; furthermore, many of the groups most in need of training either would not acknowledge the

fact, or if they did, could not find the time or money to use the training consultant.

It is practical, however, to set up special training groups to which one or several members of the groups needing improvement could come. In this case, the aim of training is to help some members learn how to train their own groups. This is a difficult job because it means that these members must learn not only how to contribute more effectively as group members but also how consciously to influence the underlying psychological conditions and assumptions on which their group is operating. To do this beneficially means that they must not only be able to diagnose the existing situation in their group; they must also have an image of more desirable conditions and know how to work toward them. Fortunately most groups can accept help if it is given unobtrusively and with the interests of the group at heart, and the member-trainer is likely to find others in his group working with him. If he does not find that his efforts are actually helpful, the chances are that his motives for helping the group are mixed up with less desirable motives—to cut down the designated leader, or to promote some particular course of action, or to satisfy personal needs in ways which disturb the group. It follows that the member of the training group, then, must learn not only about group operation but also about himself—or at least about those aspects of himself which affect his interactions in the group.

3. It is because of this last requirement that training is sometimes thought of as a type of therapy. Conceived in this way, the theory of training would be primarily a theory about the ways in which people can be released from the neuroses which block their operation in groups. Emphasis would be placed on interpersonal relations and the group would be used both to provide a range of personalities for each member to interact with and as a supportive instrument to reinforce the individual's efforts to change —as, for example, in Alcoholics Anonymous. The reader will see that the laboratory method to be spelled out here requires enough understanding of the therapeutic method that conditions harmful to mental health and emotional growth can be avoided; but the laboratory method tends to conceive of training as a learning experience rather than a therapy experience, and the necessary

understandings are drawn from a much wider range of sciences. The laboratory method uses interpersonal interaction and group supportiveness, but it places these within the context of a group consciously trying to solve problems rather than dealing with them without relation to problem-solving.

4. The image of "effective operation," which produces wise decisions and individual growth, is an image of a desired state of affairs continuously prevailing. This image is characterized in different ways by different schools of thought about training. Some folks think of it as "democratic"; some prefer the term "group-centered," "co-operative," or "healthy." If we were to choose a single term, it would be "reality-based." Group operation is sound and therefore effective when it is "in contact with reality." This means such things as these: the immediate tasks of the group are within its competence, with the potentials and opportunities it has; the responsibilities the group assumes are proper to its position in the community or institution; the activities of the group represent direct working toward its goals, rather than indirect ways of building fantasies or attacking concealed enemies; the kind of participation required from members is well enough defined that all know how to participate, and the ones who have something to offer do participate; the tasks of the group are such that everyone there has a reason for being there—or else the composition of the group is determined by the kinds of resources needed for the defined task.

Since the group itself changes through learning, and since the nature of its problems changes continually, it follows that the image we are describing cannot be put in terms of some particular style of leadership, some particular level of peacefulness or avoidance of conflict, some one pitch of morale or enthusiasm. To maintain contact with things as they are requires adaptability, change, and flexibility of operation. It requires the continuous exercise of choice among alternative behaviors.

5. The means by which the group maintains contact with reality through the exercise of choice is determined by its method of operation. By "method" we mean a consistent way of approaching, thinking about, and determining its own behavior. Methods include reliance on the judgment of the leader, imitation of what

other groups have done in situations believed to be similar, analysis of the effects of past performance, and the like. In general, however, the only method man has for maintaining contact with reality is the scientific method, with its basic emphasis upon learning from the study of his own tested experience. In the case of a group, the experience most relied upon is that of the group itself, because so many of the realities to be taken into account are facts about the group as an on-going organism actively related to the larger community.

Labeling a method merely provides a name by which to call it. Labels tend to gather around themselves facts and feelings present in the situation in which the label was applied or is most used. The label "scientific method" evokes a variety of images: perhaps you see a scientist in a white coat squinting into a microscope, or maybe fifteen rats bumping into the walls of a maze, or possibly some character ringing the doorbell and than asking a lot of odd questions. In the case of a group, scientific method implies several important understandings: that the only way a group can discover its strengths and weaknesses is to tackle a defined problem and study what happens; that planning for group activities is a process of adding details as the group proceeds, rather than a process of producing detailed blueprints in advance; that whatever happens has perfectly natural causes, and that if we had enough of the "right kind" of relevant information we could explain it; that there is continuity throughout the life of a group, and one thing leads to another; that the *ultimate* test of an idea is what happens when it is put into effect, not whether it fits into a particular "ideology"; that the proper function of knowledge is to enable us to figure out a course of action in whose "rightness" we can have enough confidence to take action in such a way that its effect can be interpreted.

The method of learning in the training group is through conscious use of the experimental method under conditions "safe" enough that one can think objectively. And the problems to which it is applied are the problems the group is ready to deal with. Finally, the means by which the group learns about unrecognized factors that must be taken into account is through comparison of one situation with another. In particular, the group needs to contrast periods of work with periods of nonwork; periods of frustration with periods of high morale; periods having one kind of leadership with periods having some other kind. Thus, the factors that make a difference—in other words the "real" factors—are uncovered so they can be dealt with and understood.

6. The decision to regard training as a supervised experience in using the experimental method requires the assumption that at all times the group is working on some problem or is trying to overcome some barrier between itself and its goals. The "theory" which the training group learns is fundamentally a set of ideas about the sorts of conditions which imply various specific sorts of problems in a group. The "technology" which the training group learns is fundamentally a set of ideas about the ways of organizing group effort which will be useful to resolve such problems.

Initially, the training group is likely to think of problems in such terms as these: "The goals weren't clear"; "The leader was too autocratic"; "We didn't have enough time"; "We weren't interested in the topic." As training goes on, problems are more likely to be stated in such terms as these: "The needed roles were not defined well enough for us to know how to participate"; "The anxiety of the leader prevented his understanding what the members were trying to tell him"; "We did not know how the others felt, so our attempts to solve the stated problems were really ineffective efforts to share feelings"; "We engaged in academic debate because the real problem was too threatening," etc. Initially, the training group's ideas of technology pretty well collapse into this question: "What techniques can a group use and when should it use them?" As training goes on, the technological questions become: "What are the demands this problem makes on the group?" "Where are we going to find, or how are we going to develop, the skills needed to meet these demands?" "In what order should the various required activities be arranged for maximum participation and efficiency?"

Two general trends are noted: first, the tendency to move from superficial "interest" or "behavioral" (e.g., "he done wrong") definitions of group problems, which imply that everything is done consciously and intentionally by individuals, to definitions of problems in terms of basic feelings, motivations, conflicts, and anxieties which stand in the way of direct group goal achievement; second, a movement away from a tendency to act everything out, with no awareness of what the group is doing, to a tendency to think through the requirements of problems and then to create procedures most likely to meet these requirements.

The purpose of all experience during training is to contribute to the continuous development of greater awareness of what the group's problems are, what behaviors are required in the group to solve these problems, and how effort can be organized in such a way that individuals can present these required behaviors to the group.

7. During training, the group changes as a result of learning. The amount and kinds of change depend upon what is learned and how it is learned. A classroom group, for example, learns to talk more intelligently about social problems or about chemistry; it learns to solve objectively defined problems in arithmetic or composition with greater skill; and it learns to respond emotionally to many stimuli (e.g., in the arts) that previously left it unmoved. But it may remain just as dependent on the teacher for telling it what problems it is to study next, what skills it needs to develop, how it is to organize for study. In other words, the group may show little if any growth as a group, even though there may be considerable development of ease and satisfaction among the students if they have the chance to interact with each other rather than only with the teacher. In contrast, the training group shows very great growth and change because everything it learns rises out of its problems of operation and has implications for what it is to do differently.

It is for this reason that the trainer of the group may consider his major objective to be to "help the group grow." Among the signs of growth, of the development of power to use the experimental method, are: increasing self-direction; increasing efficiency of working; increasing ability to cope with frustration; increasing skill in avoiding realistically anticipated failure; increasing ability to channel spontaneously expressed emotion into work; increasing flexibility in designing plans to fit changed situations; increasing rapidity in recovering from emotionally destructive periods; increasing meeting of individual needs within group problem-solving activities; an increasing tendency to define group problems realistically and in fundamental or dynamic terms— e.g., in terms of what is "really" going on.

Halting of growth, or regression to earlier stages, is taken as evidence that the group has some problem of which it is probably not aware and on which it needs to work.

It is interesting that it is the group that grows. Individuals change their roles, their reactions, and their understandings, and the changes are organized around, and occur because of, their own individual needs. Individuals may arrive at quite different ways of explaining what is happening in the group, and they may change their ways of responding to each other. But they do not all change in the same direction or to the same extent. They develop, if anything, more rather than less individuality—because there is great freedom to try out new behaviors and attitudes. They learn how to act, each in his own way, to change the group situation to give themselves more opportunity to *be* themselves. In the process, they discover a great deal about the "selves" they are—or, more accurately, the selves they *can* be in a supportive but demanding situation.

The growth of a group requires a much wider range of contributions than any one person can supply. Needed contributions at the skill level include such things as setting the problem, clarifying ideas, finding common assumptions behind several ideas, summarizing, stimulating interest, compromising, suggesting hypotheses, generalizing, etc. These contributions must be made under a variety of emotional conditions: when the group feels dependent, aggressive, hostile, peaceful, withdrawn, uneasy, "warm," under pressure, sociable. Furthermore, these contributions must be made to a variety of topics: the styles of leadership, the nature of interpersonal identification, the concept of work, the idea of productivity. Any one person will find that he has competence with respect to certain skills under particular emotional conditions and with respect to a particular range of topics. Although topic and skill demands have some effect on participation, the most important determining factor is the emotional state of the group. Some people participate most easily when the group is dependent on the leader, or when it is fighting the leader, or when everyone is angry or when peace descends. Others may be made anxious or even become immobilized under each of these conditions. Yet the group as a whole works under all these conditions, works through a wide range of problems. And with each "working-through," the group develops greater strength, greater ability to tolerate frustration, and to progress along the various other dimensions of growth listed above.

8. Group growth, although not directly related to the growth of each individual, is, however, in the last analysis, dependent upon the kinds of people in the group. The basic emotional dynamics of the group is a working-out of the changing strains in the network of relationships among the members and trainer. For example, if everyone in the group were thoroughly content to be forever dependent on the trainer for all decisions, the trainer would find it very difficult to teach the group much about the nature of dependency, its uses, forms, and causes. Training is much easier when some people in the group are satisfied with being dependent and others react against the feeling of dependency. Under these conditions the trainer can help the group see that some of its conflict centers around the finding of an appropriate balance between dependency and resistance to dependency, and activities can be set up to discover or test ideas about the effects and control of dependency relationships. The curriculum of the training group is ultimately determined and limited by the composition of the group.

Thus each group "writes its own history." These histories are not entirely unique because most of us were raised in similar cultures. we subscribe to many of the same ideals and are troubled by many of the same value conflicts, even though we may react differently to these conflicts. It is a fairly safe prediction that at some time or another, and to some extent, every training group will get into the culturally induced problems of dependence versus independence, individuality versus conformity, freedom of expression versus inhibition of emotion, competition versus cooperation.

The problem of composing a group for the most effective training is not a simple one. The ability of the trainer is far more often the limiting factor than is the composition of the group. Probably the only reason to keep someone out of this kind of training program would be that he needs therapy instead. In other words, some individuals are not ready for such an experience, and no good is served by putting them through it. The more critical problem is to secure a neat balance among the various kinds of temperaments or emotional predispositions or character structures.

9. All of the above discussion implies that the trainer deals with the group as a whole. The trainer is concerned about whether processes going on in the group are growth-producing in the various senses indicated above. He believes that each individual has a great opportunity to learn things that are necessary and meaningful for him to learn, and he notices changes—sometimes very remarkable changes—in the performance of individuals in the group. In general, what the trainer using the laboratory method does not know (at least in 1953) is, from some standpoints, the most important thing of all: does change in individual performance represent merely an intelligent adaptation to the changes in the group as a whole, or does it mean a whole new integration of personality such that the individual will inevitably perform differently from now on? Follow-up studies to date indicate that both possibilities exist.

Thus, some individuals become "good group members" because that is expected, and because they have to make some changes in order to continue to participate in the group. But when they return to their "back home" groups, the power of adaptation remains, and they rapidly adjust to the prevailing conditions: it is as if they had not had the training experience at all. Fortunately, these individuals are rare. On the other hand, there are people whose apparent learnings and changes during training seem to carry over into subsequent group experience. Instead of adjusting to the norms of the group (no matter what the norms are) they make a two-way adaptation in which they both fit into the group and change it at the same time.

It seems reasonable to suppose that the training will be transferred to new situations to the extent that:

1. The individual has a realistic understanding of what is happening, particularly to him, during training.

2. This understanding is related by him to a wide variety of past experiences—that is, it gives him insights which enable him to understand other experiences he has had.

3. The individual experiences a substantial reduction of anxiety about the roles he plays and thus develops a greater feeling of adequacy.

4. The individual achieves commitment to a valid image of the kinds of processes characteristic of effective group functioning.

It seems clear that the laboratory method of training should be backed up by a program of individual (or possibly small group) interviewing, to give greater opportunity for each person to understand and study his own reactions to the group experience. A study now in progress should tell us whether this deduction is correct.

Up to this point, we have tried to give some characterization of the laboratory method of training—how it conceives the job of training, and the principles on which it operates. We wish now to present, rather briefly, a case study of one training group so that the reader can see what actually goes on; and then we will try to point out principles by which the trainer can continuously guide his own participation.

THE LABORATORY METHOD IN OPERATION: A CASE STUDY

This is a brief presentation of some of the events transpiring during a training course offered to graduate students. The course consisted of ten three-hour weekly meetings[2] with the trainer and, in addition, probably a like amount of time spent outside the meetings in informal groups discussing the class events. The class contained 25 people (the usual class contains 12–18 people), of widely different ages and experience. The trainer, here referred to as Jim,[3] had an assistant, Jane,[4] who participated little during the

2. More commonly, such groups have met every day for three weeks, as at the National Training Laboratory, Bethel, Maine.

3. For other news of Jim (he calls himself "Tom," here) see the National Training Laboratory in Group Development, *Bulletin No. 3* (1948), pp. 16–34. This gives "Jim's" perceptions of his first training group. For another group trained by Jim (Tom), see Stuart Chase, *Roads to Agreement* (New York: Harper & Bros., 1951), pp. 88–92.

4. Jane was Dr. Dorothy Stock, a project director in the Human Dynamics Laboratory.

meetings but helped Jim analyze and plan between meetings. This particular case is cited because it represented the most conscious effort so far to put the principles enunciated in this chapter into practice. Interpretations are put in italics to distinguish them from the descriptive comments.

MEETING I

Jim took the first 15 minutes to have people put their names on large cards and to make the usual remarks about objectives and method. (*Jim did not expect the remarks to mean much at this point, but he wished to satisfy initial expectations and to anticipate some of the feelings he knew would arise from time to time.*) The group had nothing to say when Jim was finished and he went on to suggest an activity to start with. (*They could not tell what the remarks were going to mean in terms of operation, and they did not know Jim and each other well enough to risk questions. They accepted the ritual and were not disturbed.*)

The suggested activity involved forming three subgroups, working for 14 minutes, re-forming new subgroups, working another 14 minutes, and then, for the third time, forming new subgroups. Jim gave them a question to discuss: What problems do you think we will encounter in attempting to use the experimental method? He also suggested that they might wish to contrast their experiences in the three subgroups. (*Jim knew that to get acquainted involves working together, not talking about yourself when it is not clear what sort of thing should be revealed. He gave the group members a question so that they would have some common starting point and goal for talking together. He posed the question in terms of difficulties in order to make possible expression of any negative feelings people might have. He put them in subgroups but did not participate himself so that they could talk more freely, and so that they would have an experience on their own, albeit a protected one. He had them move through three subgroups so that they would have the experience of getting acquainted three different times under somewhat different conditions. The 14-minute period was chosen as being long enough to avoid the frustration of not talking and short enough to prevent serious work on the assigned problems. He felt that neither of these would be desired at this point in the group's history: frustration would not be instructive, and the problem was not "real" enough to justify serious effort.*)

The subgroups fell to work with ease. While they were talking, Jim circulated around and tried to decide what differences the people would probably be aware of (and able to discuss) among their first, second, and third groups. When the whole group got together, they were polled as to how they would rank the three subgroups with respect to a number of kinds of feelings. (*Jim wanted some objective data on the blackboard so that there would always be a clear content to deal with if the group wished to use it; he also wanted the polling to occur so the members could see the extent to which others felt the same way they did; he further wanted to start right in using data and showing that such data can be interpreted usefully.*) The members thought their first subgroup stayed most closely to the assigned problem, was most aware of Jim's presence in the room, and was the one in which they felt most self-conscious. The discussion in the last group was seen as more personal, more oriented to problems of how the group was doing, was least "groupy," and for this group the time passed slowest.

Jim said the group could discuss anything of interest to them about their experiences in the three groups, and that the data on the board might help suggest hypotheses about group operation. The discussion was "free" (*much "freer" than under such instructions as "Discuss anything you want to"*); the data were referred to several times when the discussion needed a fresh topic, and the group made some effort to draw conclusions from the data. The greatest amount of feeling, however, expressed concern about the freedom with which one should express feeling, whether an individual can "be himself," how far he must knuckle under to the group, and notions about the effects of expressed hostility on other people. Jim stayed out of the discussion except to clarify some rather vague statements from time to time; he also came in at one point to "protect" an individual whose comments, he felt, would turn the group against that individual. (*The "protection" took the form of indicating to the group how to react to the remarks, rather than of talking at all about the individual who made them.*)

Most of the discussion was quite satisfying to the people, and the content was pretty much of their own choosing. The trainer, however, made all the decisions required to set up the activities. (*He had decided that the group should get into activity to provide an ex-*

perience to discuss, rather than that it should spend all its time—probably fruitlessly—talking about possible activities.)

The last hour was devoted to answering a self-perception questionnaire to help Jim's research program.

The first hour of the second meeting was set up as a "free" discussion, going on with the things the group had started at the end of the last meeting. The trainer stayed out, so that the group could get a clearer image of its strengths and weaknesses—an accurate image of itself. (*Jim usually saw himself as providing definitions within which the group could work, but not as influencing how the group worked, since that was the basic thing to be discovered and studied.*) The problems of individuality and freedom of expression were the centers of group concern. *The discussion also showed a wish on the part of some to "go deeper" in revealing their concerns, coupled with a tendency to cover up if anyone pushed them about these concerns.*

Jim gave everyone a questionnaire to fill out to get reactions to the "free" discussion, and again the answers were polled and listed on the board. There was a short discussion of the reactions, and most interest settled on the "roles people played" during the discussion: the blocker, conciliator, nonparticipant, etc. (*This seemed to confirm Jim's belief that during the first meeting or two, the major concern of people in training groups is to find a comfortable and socially approved role they can play; or, to put it more clearly, to find out how they can participate and what kinds of participation will be rewarded.*)

The last 30 minutes was spent in the subgroups' trying to use the data on the board in order to plan an activity for the next group meeting. The subgroups did not finish their plans, but Jim stopped them five minutes before the end of the period to have them report progress to each other. All the groups were concerned with the effects of different kinds of member roles. In addition, each plan showed some level of concern about group leadership—a new element that had not arisen explicitly in the total group. (*Jim felt that the group was not anxious about his leadership because they were working well under it; so he interpreted the concern to indicate recognition of the fact that member roles cannot be defined until assumptions about leadership and authority have been clarified.*)

MEETING III

Jim and Jane did a great deal of thinking before the third meeting. They had observed that one of the subgroups was a cohesive group of minority-group members whose culture was decidedly authoritarian and competitive. Jane had prepared an analysis of the research questionnaire given at the first meeting, and it was evident that there was a definite split in the group about whether individuals should feel free to express aggression and compete with each other and the leader, or whether everyone should work for harmony and avoid expressing strong feelings. (*It was felt that this fundamental difference in emotional orientation would have to be settled before people could participate in any very gratifying way; and that until it could be settled, the group would go round and round on the question. It was also felt that the group could not yet tackle so threatening a problem, and that the concern over kinds of member roles was an off-target way of edging into the problem.*) Jane and Jim saw two alternatives: first, they could encourage the group to think that the problem really was one of "how to define the role of the group member"; and this would logically result in a long list of "characteristics of the good group member." Second, some means might be found to so reduce the threat connected with this problem that it could safely be recognized and dealt with. In view of the fact that the conflict evidently was, at least in part, a conflict between subcultures within the total group, the trainers decided to reduce the threat by helping the group discover that people behave the way they do, not only because of their personalities (*which is the belief that made the problem threatening*) but also because of the cultures in which they grow up (*and they cannot be blamed for them*). It was further decided to try to help the group see that the problem was one of group standards—a concern of the total group—rather than a problem primarily for each individual to deal with on his own (*in order to reduce the threat further*).

Accordingly, Jim pointed out at the beginning of the third meeting that the group had three plans from the earlier activity of the three subgroups, and it now had the problem of combining these plans or of creating a single new one. He suggested that the processes involved in reaching the final plan were well worth study, and that he had a scheme for simultaneously arriving at a single plan and also studying some of the member roles involved in so doing. He outlined his proposal, and the group agreed to try it. (*What else could they do? It should be noted that the group had not openly recognized its deeper problem; it was concerned with member roles seen at the level of how people act.*)

Jim's proposed activity involved several steps; first, the three planning subgroups would meet long enough to sharpen their plans and get them clearly in mind. Second, two members from each of the subgroups would represent their subgroups in a conference to decide on the best plan for the total group while the rest of the subgroup members would observe, presumably from the standpoint of their own groups. In addition, Jim selected from each subgroup a person with some experience in group observation to be part of a three-man team to observe, presumably without subgroup bias. Third, Jim gave out questionnaires after the conference to enable the three subgroups, the observers, and the participants to indicate some of their reactions to the conference. Fourth, the answers worked out by the three subgroups were put on the board as the basis of discussion, with the observers and participants also contributing their opinions at will.

The plan was carried out. The conference discussion was vigorous and much feeling was expressed. The two representatives from the "minority" subcommittee fought hard to get their plan accepted without change. The representatives from another subgroup pushed for compromise; those from the third committee were not clear on the details of the plan their subgroup had proposed, and they tried to find common elements in the three plans. All the rest of the group responded openly to the various expressions of aggression and the efforts to compromise.

With the observations of the three subgroups summarized on the board, the whole group then spent the remaining hour in a rather penetrating sharing of feelings and ideas about the conference. There were some short flights into abstract questions (e.g., "What is 'structure' and how is it determined?"). Two people had been seen as "leaders" during the six-man conference. One of them was dominating, and drove for acceptance of his group's plan; the other was much more gentle, and tried to clarify feelings and discover areas of agreement. Jim entered into the dis-

cussion actively in an effort to interpret some of the things the
group saw. Thus it was seen that the two leaders were leaders
because each validly represented a side of the conflict within the
total group between competition and dominance versus co-operation and sharing. In effect, these two were spokesmen for different
sides of the group's feeling. It was seen, further, that these two
"leaders" also were much reinforced by the very different positions taken by their own subgroups in this matter. And it was
clear that people behaved the way they did not just because of
their personalities but also because of their loyalty to other groups
and to the ways of working in these other groups.

There was no resolution of the basic problem which had arisen
implicitly in so many different forms. However, the realization
that a problem existed was expressed in many individual statements.

(*The trainers felt that the meeting resulted in a greatly increased freedom
to express significant individual concerns, and, along with this feeling, that
there was a considerable increase in cohesiveness or groupness. People had
expressed their own concerns and had obtained reactions from the group; the
group was achieving more meaning for the members as a field in which
individual needs might be met.*)

MEETING IV

Because the trainers did not know the extent to which the previous discussion had prepared the group to deal with its basic
problem (of competition versus co-operation), they decided to
start the group with a continuation of the discussion from the last
meeting. The group talked for an hour in a more or less desultory
fashion, and except for a few comments, never reached the level
of penetration of the last meeting. (*The feeling aroused by the six-
man "conference" had been drained off during the week.*) Toward the
end of the first hour, Jim suggested that the group list the questions it now had in mind. Twelve questions were suggested, and
all but two were requests for advice about how to keep a group
working, how to minimize the effects of conflicting loyalties to
other groups, what to do when things get "emotional," etc.

During the break for coffee, the trainers had a whispered consultation, and decided to take the calculated risk of confronting

the group with the problem of its basic conflict. Accordingly, after the break, Jim openly said that he and Jane had been in consultation and that they had decided to suggest that Jane begin the new session by giving some impressions of the preceding discussion. (*It was decided to have Jane do this because if the group was not ready for the interpretation it would be likely temporarily to reject the interpreter along with the interpretation; and to reject Jim at this point would hurt the group too much, since it had not yet developed enough natural leadership to carry on alone.*) Jane pointed out what was clearly evident in the questions written on the board: that the group was seeking some means to control individual participation so that its conflict could not come out into the open; the group was anxious about the conflict, and was hunting for techniques to handle it rather than trying to understand and resolve it. Jim later added the opinion that techniques might be resorted to in some kinds of groups, but that in the training group the goal is understanding and resolution. The question was: "How ready was the group at this point to approach its conflict directly?"

(*This confrontation by means of an apparently reasonable interpretation of data on the blackboard in front of them could not be denied. But it could be resisted; and this would be shown by the discussion's going off onto other topics, by discussing the bases of interpretation, or by asking the trainer to tell them what to do next or even to give his judgment about how freely emotion should be openly expressed. The trainers felt that it must be left completely up to the group to decide whether, or how deeply, to go into the problem which they could no longer overlook. Therefore, the trainers stayed out of the ensuing discussion until the very end.*)

The first comments following the interpretation were individually concerned denials that anyone ever had hostile feelings, confessions of fear of expressing one's self freely, requests to return to the problem of the leader's role, and the like. (*In effect, the group experienced a mild shock, and the discussion had, for a few minutes, an every-man-for-himself quality.*) The group, then, under the emerging leadership of one or two people, began to ask what activity it could plan to study these emotional phenomena in an effort to understand them. Several ideas were suggested, and then Jim was asked point-blank to be a resource person and suggest an activity. Jim hesitated, and then said that if this question had been put to him because of the group's emotional dependency he did not want to answer it; but if the question merely meant that the group now was emotionally committed to the goal of working on the problem, then he would be happy to offer suggestions—he then offered three alternative suggestions for activity. After some discussion, the group decided on one of them, and laid plans for beginning work on it at the next meeting.

(*The trainers felt pleased with the meeting. They saw that the group had not run away from the problem, that the decision had been its own, and that the group's own leadership had begun to emerge. The trainers believed what they had seen, but still had some question as to the depth of the commitment and the extent to which the group had made it in order to avoid the pressure of the "authoritative" interpretation.*)

MEETING V

Jim opened the meeting by asking someone to recall for the group what the plan was. (*This was a test of commitment: If the plan had been made merely to escape the stress caused by the interpretation, then it was likely that no one would remember the plan very accurately. If, on the other hand, the plan had been an object of concern in its own right, then the group would remember it and forge ahead to complete its details and put it into operation.*)

The plan was quickly recalled by several members of the group, and at Jim's question as to what further details needed to be decided to put the plan in operation, the group quickly made several decisions. The plan was to break into five subgroups and have each subgroup decide on an "emotional role" to be played by one of the members. Each subgroup would then select one of its number and coach him on how to play the role. The roles decided on in the various subgroups included: a stereotypic "non-directive" person; a hostile person with feelings of always being "left out"; a person who cannot stand conflict and tries to conciliate; an assertive, unconflicted "strong" personality; and a person who believes in rationality "no matter what."

The five role-players discussed the question of how many more meetings the training group would have (beyond the minimum scheduled meetings). The scene was quite hilarious at points, and everyone had a good time. The scene went on for twenty minutes, and three of the players obviously enjoyed their own expression of very aggressive feelings.

After the coffee break, Jim took over, very much as a teacher might, to guide the group through the analysis of the emotional phenomena they had seen. (*Jim felt that the analysis of emotional dynamics is potentially dangerous because of possible exploitation for so many individual needs; he was determined that the analysis be objective and not become the vehicle for expressing feelings against others.*) He explained that talking about the emotional expressions of individuals should be done with some safeguards, that the roles might or might not represent the "real person" acting these, and that it was better to assume that it was all acting guided by the briefings given in the subgroups. Jim then went to the board and listed the following headings: "What We Saw" and "Speculative Interpretations." He then asked who the group wanted to start with; they named a person, and the analysis began. Jim carefully maintained a clear distinction between "fact" and "guess," and kept the discussion on each person going until the group had produced several alternative interpretations. (*This was done to make it impossible for the group to think they had really identified the role and the person.*) Then the role-player was asked to react to the group's speculations: he could reject all of them, support one or more, or add other ideas of his own. (*This was done primarily to allow the role-players to work through any uncomfortable feelings the group diagnosis may have produced—they could have the last word in a designedly open field.*)

This meeting was highly gratifying to all concerned. Individuals got out of it a good deal of relief for their own anxieties—at least as related to the training group situation—and the group as a whole felt "strong" and ready for anything. People stayed around for half an hour after the meeting, talking excitedly in small groups, and the typical feeling was probably best expressed by one person in response to the comment, "Gee, we didn't make any plans for next time!" The reply was: "We don't need to!"

MEETING VI

During the week between meetings, Jim did little thinking about the group. He had shared in the general feeling of strength and relief, which may have been heightened for him because of his recognition that he had taken a chance in confronting the group during Meeting IV. In effect, there were forces in the situation and in Jim that made him tend to overestimate the strength of the group: with part of his being, Jim wanted to believe that the group was now full grown, capable of solving all their problems on their own and without his help. On the other hand, Jim also knew that this belief was not realistic; that it could not be realistic. And, Jim wanted to believe that the group needed his help. If they did not need his help, then he would have no role, no place in the group, and, at a time when the group has become cohesive and rewarding, it is bitter to feel not needed. These attitudes, and Jim's real ambivalence of feelings about the group, are, of course, "unprofessional"; they are reflections of problems in Jim. Jim lost sight of his job as trainer and became concerned about himself, and this stood in the way of his being objective and helpful to the group.

Meeting VI, then, presents the picture of a group trying to identify a new problem to work on, and for which to plan activity, at the same time that they are struggling with the anxieties communicated by their leader; and, because they are the leader's anxieties, he is unable to help them—they have to operate in the face of confused emotions about their leadership. One can see that the problem for the group would have to be the nature of leadership and the relations between leader and group. (This is a legitimate problem, and one that nearly all training groups need to deal with. But it is unnecessarily difficult to study the problem when the question of leadership revolves around the trainer. It is much better to have the problem arise in terms of conflict within the group, rather than between the group and the trainer. When the conflict arises out of the efforts to establish and develop the group's natural leadership, the trainer can help by clarifying feelings well enough that the problem can be seen and worked out before the emotional intensity and frustration become so great as to disrupt work. Much uncontrolled frustration and depression present the group with a major problem, and any way out will be sought—even having a wild party. This is all very interesting and absorbing, but it makes practically no contribution to the goals of training.)

Jim opened the meeting by telling the group that it appeared to have completed (to the extent that it needed to, at this time) the working out of the anxiety problems associated with the expression of feelings. He went on to suggest that the group had presumably developed considerable strength in the process, but that it would have to wait to see what happened to be really sure of this. He then proposed that the group's task now was to plan its next activity; and he said he felt that the group could do this pretty much on its own, with his participation only as a resource person.

(*Jim's comments, and the way he made them, communicated to the group the double feelings both that Jim had confidence in them and that he did not have; that he would help them, but only on his own terms. It should be noted, too, that the task of the group, to plan a new direction based on a new analysis of problems—and following a very successful day which they could hardly repeat—was a larger task than any so far tackled by the group alone; and everyone knew it.*)

The group discussed plans in an unfocused and desultory fashion for about an hour. Many insightful contributions were made, but they were not picked up and reacted to. There was growing bewilderment and increasingly strong efforts by individuals to help the group; as these efforts increased and failed, uneasiness and frustration grew.

(*The group was struggling with the experience of an emotionally confused and ambiguous relationship with the trainer. They did not know whether they were being rejected or not, and for the first 20 minutes of the discussion there was no awareness even that there was a problem of this sort. There was probably some resistance to admitting the possibility. It is probable that a clear rejection by the leader, particularly if he had then walked out, would have been easier to deal with.*)

The break for coffee was an explosion of the total group into smaller fragments. (*There was a great load of feeling to share, but it could not be shared in the total group.*) During the break, Jim tried to collect his wits. He could see quite clearly what had happened. At the reality level, he saw that his judgment had not been mistaken: he had correctly judged the group's emotional unity resulting from the last meeting. But he had been completely blind to the fact that they did not have the skills required for complex problem-solving without his help. He put it to himself that he had gotten into the trap of confusing the emotional conditions present for growth with the ability to perform; he had felt the motivation and overlooked the lack of ability; the group did not have any secure, consciously applicable set of agreements on how to operate by themselves, and there was no independent natural leadership ready to take over. Many individuals were trying to fill the vacuum produced by Jim's abdication, but until the group accepted the fact of his abdication they could not accept the efforts to fill the vacuum. And Jim had not clearly abdicated.

After the coffee break, Jim suddenly came in strongly in an effort "to help the group understand what was going on." What the group perceived was an unaccountable change in Jim's role, and a violation of the definition he himself had given. (*The problem began to be acted out as a difference of opinion between those who had tried to take responsibility earlier and now felt that responsibility was being withdrawn from them by Jim, and those who wanted Jim to "take over" and pull them out of the difficulty. Neither group was happy about this and because of Jim's ambiguity and, now, his inconsistency, the problem could not be discussed.*) Several approaches, which probably would have been useful if there had not been the underlying unresolved problem of the group's relationship to Jim, were attempted. Thus, at one point, the group listed hypotheses on the board to account for their troubles, without a word about leadership. From time to time individuals would try to test one or another hypothesis, or to suggest procedures by which the group could test them. There were one or two efforts to state the problem directly in the form: "We don't know whether to trust Jim or not because he is inconsistent." At this point, Jim explained his incorrect diagnosis, but this added fuel to the anger of those who still felt that had they been given a little more time and less interference by Jim, they could have led the group out of its difficulty.

(*It seems clear that Jim's second diagnosis was correct. The strong efforts of individuals to provide leadership, and even the depth of the group's frustration showed that it wanted to tackle the problem, rather than to run away from it; this also showed that the group had high expectations for itself. On the other hand, the fact that the group could not make use of some very good suggestions indicates that the group had little technical competence as a group in analyzing problems and building on contributions; they could not use work as the way out of frustration. The development of the needed competence was blocked by the fact that the emotional confusion was in the area of leadership. And the lack of competence was what made Jim's behavior and attitudes such critically aggravating factors.*)

MEETING VII

Jim opened the meeting with the suggestion that probably a lot of "outside conversations" had gone on since the last meeting, and possibly it would help the group to form subgroups and exchange ideas. He called this quite frankly a "fishing expedition." (*The trainers were now convinced that the group would not be able to move until there had been a sharing of feelings among the members so that individual feeling, differently mobilized in each person, could be found acceptable, and, through this, the group's anxieties reduced to the point where work could begin.*) The group accepted the suggestion, and five subgroups formed. Discussions seemed subdued. Each subgroup reported to the total group, and each report showed a different way of reacting to the group's problems. The differences in the reports were closely related to differences in the personnel of the subgroups. The reports consisted of:

1. An analysis of the problems of last time.
2. A statement of principles so far learned plus suggestions of problems to be investigated.
3. A list of questions apparently related to the problem of control of the group.
4. A plea for help.
5. A listing of member "roles" needed for the group to progress.

(*Behind these reports were various assumptions about how to perceive the group's difficulties. Thus, report 1 assumes that the trouble is in the nature of the interaction among members, group, and trainer; report 2 assumes that the trouble is lack of ability to apply knowledge; report 3 assumes the problem to be one of leadership; report 4 assumes that the group is too "weak" to solve its problems; and report 5 assumes that the problem is that individuals do not know how to behave. All of the reports had some element of truth in them, but none really got down to the basic problem: the need for sharing feeling, reducing anxiety, and resolving the emotional ambiguities in the relationship between group and trainer.*)

The reports were given in a "dead-pan" manner, and there were no reactions to them. The fishing expedition was a failure. Presumably the same factors which had prevented the emergence of natural leadership among individuals were also working to prevent any subgroup from making a bid for leadership.

After desultory conversation in the group, Jim decided to try to get the group into contact with reality. He pointed out that one thing many of the remarks seemed to be saying is that the group is in a state of confusion; he asked whether everyone felt that to be true. There was general agreement, shown in nodding of heads and other gestures of recognition. The group did not pick this up, so, a few minutes later, Jim plunged in again, reminded them of the agreement about confusion, and said that the way out of confusion was through clarification: what were the questions needing to be clarified? Several questions were asked, and Jim wrote them on the board. Out of six questions, five dealt with Jim's role, and his hopes, consistencies, and feelings about the group.

Jim felt that the group, concerned over its mixed feelings with regard to its own leadership, was projecting the entire problem onto Jim as the symbol of leadership. However, he also felt that to some extent the questions were realistic, since Jim's troublesome behavior had precipitated (but not created) the present circumstances. Jim, therefore, decided to answer the questions. He spoke primarily of his conception of his role of trainer, and tried to define it as something different from the role of leader, so as to once and for all open the way for the group's leadership to emerge. Jim also explained why he had shifted roles during the last meeting. At this point Jim's anxieties were back under control, and the communication was very relieving to the group. There was a feeling that the relationship between Jim and the group was now patched up. (*Probably if this could have happened at the middle of the last meeting, it would have been completely effective. By now, however, there was the additional anxiety problem of the relationships between each individual and the group—anxieties which arose in response to the frustration the individuals had experienced in trying unsuccessfully to fill the leadership vacuum.*)

Jim's comments cleared the way for an unconflicted competition for leadership. He had said in effect that he did not wish to be leader, and that he would support the group's efforts to provide its own leadership. Individuals and, later on, cliques began to make strong efforts to get various plans accepted in the group.

None of these sorties was successful; each would gather momentum until the plan was revealed clearly enough that action could be taken. Then it would die, and the group would start talking about its need for control, for more enlightened membership behavior, for a definition of its long-range objectives. At one point toward the end of the meeting, the group was swept by a contagion of self-doubt, and there was some effort to pretend that the whole experience to date had been a failure. Jim tried to get behind one plan, and his support was no more successful than anyone else's had been.

(*It seems probable that a rather interesting shift had occurred in the form of the problem. At first, the problem had been felt as a competition for leadership, imbedded in anxieties about taking over responsibility, in a situation whose requirements for the taking of responsibility were not clear. Now, following Jim's comments, it became a tug of war between the desire to work and the desire to do something else, the nature of which was not at all clear to the group. The conflict was between those who were ready to work, to go ahead to make plans and carry them through, and those who were not ready for work. This appears to mean that Jim's comments had "freed" those individuals whose anxieties had mobilized around the question of leadership; but those whose anxieties were mobilized around feelings of personal inadequacy, or around their relationships to the group as a whole, still had this higher-priority problem to resolve. And, since these latter types of problems took a different form in each person, it was not possible to bring them into group awareness and give them clear definition.*)

In talking about it afterward, Jim and Jane decided that the group would not be able to go to work until there had been enough sharing of feeling for individuals to recognize that others had the same sense of discomfort that they did, the same problems of relating to the total group. (*If people could discover that these feelings were shared, they would then feel that the group was behind them in their efforts to work problems through. It seemed to Jim and Jane that the problem of definition of member role, which had been shelved while the group devoted almost two meetings to the problem of their fears of emotional expression, had now returned full force under the provocation of the more specific difficulties about leadership.*)

The trainers were undecided as to how to get this sharing of feeling to occur. They had used the fishing expedition in a vain hope that the subgroups would provide the needed permissive situation. They could see that no individual by himself could change the situation to one in which the need could be met—after all, many people had tried without success. The trainers finally felt that the best solution was to have a planning committee that would meet outside the group, returning to it with enough feeling of adequacy that its members could work in concert to keep the group working on a task. The task would provide enough clarity of purpose and definition of member role that people would be able to participate; and, if the need for sharing feeling really existed, it could occur. But no such committee had been provided for.

MEETING VIII

The day after Meeting VII, Tom, one of the members of the group, called on Jim. He said that he was very worried about the group, and that a lot of other members were, too; that they were engaging in endless inconclusive conversations in the dormitories and coffee shops; that possibly a group on the outside, if they knew Jim was behind them, might be able to come up with a plan which could be presented to the total group; and that such a "committee" could also work for the plan and increase its chances of success. However, Tom expressed considerable anxiety that this might seem, to the rest of the group, to be an unwarranted attempt at imposition by a minority. Jim told Tom to go ahead, although he also agreed that people's anxieties over their own roles might well be projected into the charge that the outside group was trying to "run things." Tom was troubled at the thought of leading such an expedition, but after finding that Jim was able to accept his hostility (expressed under the guise of reporting to Jim a couple of scurrilous and false rumors about him), he felt better about going ahead.

Tom opened the eighth meeting with a long, sober, introspective analysis of the feelings members had had in and out of the group since the trouble began. This was not easy for Tom, and he communicated a good deal of anxiety about the report he was making. The guilt felt by the committee in operating apart from the total group was clearly communicated. The germ of an idea for a plan was also presented, but not as something the committee felt strongly about.

The first reactions to Tom's report were highly individualistic. They ranged from deep resentment to gratitude, from wishing to deal with the report to wishing to ignore it completely. The members of Tom's committee operated very effectively and securely to keep the group pointed toward either of two tasks:

a) reacting to the statements of feeling that had been presented, or
b) working toward the development of a plan for action

(*Jim felt that the particular comments made by individuals represented their ways of reacting to their confrontation with reality; in other words, Tom's comments were recognized as valid, even though there were differences among individuals in their readiness to deal with awareness. If this were true, Jim felt, the group would need to break into more permissive subgroups so that individuals would have a better chance to work through the problems that this awareness had brought.*)

One member of the committee suggested that the group break into subgroups. No reason was given, although the committee's rather vague plan had involved breaking into subgroups. The suggestion was taken up immediately. There then remained the problem of deciding what the subgroup task would be. This was settled in a very few minutes in a way which took account of three major suggestions made by the group: one subgroup to work on goals, another on methodology, and a third on how to integrate subgroup thinking into the total group.

(*At this point, Jim knew that the group would pull itself out of its frustration. The fact that the decision could be made so readily showed that Tom's report had, as hoped, restored the feeling of "togetherness," that anxieties about feelings were now reduced by the recognition that individuals "were not alone." The fact that the question of what to discuss could be settled so quickly showed that it was a relatively unimportant question— the topic was the excuse, not the goal, for doing what everyone felt needed to be done. The fact that the subgroups, for the first time, had different tasks and that these were along the lines of expressed interest showed the extent to which the group was willing to accept individual differences, and that this probably meant an acceptance of the group's own natural leadership.*)

The groups promptly settled down to their tasks, allowing

themselves half an hour. The discussion was sober, and participation was well distributed. The groups kept to their work, with little digression into individual emotional expression. (*This worried Jim and led him to wonder if the groups were not really fleeing from the need to work through individual problems; but it soon became apparent from the wide range of suggestions in each group that individual emotionality was being integrated into work, rather than evaded. It also became apparent that it was not so necessary to deal directly with individual's anxieties (as would be done in therapy) as to re-establish for each individual the feeling of place and "belongingness" in the group. This was best done through co-operation in work rather than through expressions of individually centered emotion*).

The subgroups worked for the full half-hour. Each subgroup kept track of the time, and each subgroup, without prodding, took the initiative in preparing, as a group, its report. Coffee was ready by the time the first subgroup had completed its task; it broke up for coffee, but the others kept working until they felt satisfied with their reports. (*These actions were felt by Jim to indicate that the subgroups were demonstrating a high degree of maturity, as groups. Jim wondered what would happen when the reports were presented. If the breaking into subgroups had been done in the spirit of running away from the frustrations of the total group, Jim expected evidence of intersubgroup hostility to appear in the reporting; if, however, the subgroups formed out of an understood and direct need of the total group, Jim would expect the reports to be straightforward, objective, and useful to the total group. The sense of responsibility shown by the subgroups toward the total group was reassuring and led Jim to feel that the total group would be able to incorporate and assimilate this strength into its own operation.*)

The subgroup reports showed a high quality of thinking, and enough comprehensiveness to indicate that everyone in the subgroup had contributed, and that they had worked together effectively to clarify each other's thinking. The group was pleased with the reports, which seemed to be providing a consensus rather than provoking argument. It was as if the group was speaking in three different voices through the subgroups, rather than listening in parliamentary fashion to the reports of three working committees.

One of the reports outlined a four-step plan for next action, and this was accepted as a good plan. The first step was to ask Jim for his analysis of the growth of the group; next, to study this interpretation as the basis for making the principles of group operation more explicit; next, to set up some "back home" situations in which to test the principles; and, finally, to review various techniques of group work and discuss the sorts of situations in which they would be useful.

During the last few minutes, the group was reminded of the questionnaires (a repeat of the one used the first meeting) to be taken next time. The group quickly decided to come a half-hour early so as not to take too much time from the meeting.

The group took time to compare its feelings now with its feelings at the beginning of the meeting. The initial feelings of anxiety seemed very far away and, to some extent, unaccountable, as if the group was trying to forget the emotional travail as quickly as possible. The present feeling of well-being and adequacy was shared by all and could not be missed.

(*Looking back on the day, Jim and Jane felt that Tom's subgroup had been largely responsible for the remarkable recovery of the group. They analyzed the effects of the subgroup as follows:*

1. *It relieved some of the anxieties other subgroups had felt in meeting outside the total group, even though some resentment was stirred up in people who had consciously repressed, in the interests of "group unity," the impulse to report the deliberations of "their" subgroups.*

2. *It spoke for the feelings of most individuals in the group. The introspective analysis of feeling, and the anxieties that went with the analysis, rang a bell for most of the group. They recognized Tom's feelings as their own, and they identified with his anxieties in bringing these feelings out into the open. As the group listened in almost breathless silence, they knew that they, through Tom, were sharing with each other.*

3. *The members of the subgroup acted as a team to provide the leadership which the total group had needed so sorely.*

4. *The leadership was provided in such a way that anxieties over natural leadership were reduced rather than increased. The team gave the others a model— it removed the last doubts that members could provide acceptable leadership to the group.*

5. *It is possible, also, that in some inexplicit and subconscious way the total group recognized that all the members would have to have some of the same quality of experience that the members of Tom's subgroup had had. The ease*

*with which the subgroup members assumed leadership promised a reward for
others who would follow in their footsteps. And the contributions of Tom's
committee very much reduced the ground that subsequent subgroups would have
to cover.*

*Jim decided that to all intents and purposes the course was now over. In
trying to guess what would happen next, he conceded that there would be
much interest in his report next time, but he felt it unlikely that the group
would "pick it up" and discuss it very much. Jim asked himself what possibilities remained for the group:*

a)　It had satisfactorily dealt with the major group problem of the last three weeks.

b)　It had no demands (e.g., for action) from the "outside" that it had to meet.

*c)　The most likely possibility seemed to be that it could now become an instrument
for individual need-meeting. The individual needs would be mobilized by the
fact that the network of interpersonal relationships involved a feeling of
"closeness" among members—an opportunity for intimacy, perhaps; and this
would be a problem for some and a challenge to others.*

*Jim felt that the interest in his interpretations—really a request for him to
"tell all"—was made possible by this new feeling of closeness; that it was
an act through which Jim, in giving up to the group his special knowledge
or secrets, would now become one of them, a member on equal terms with
the others. But Jim also felt that the present well-being of the group would
make possible considerable objectivity in thinking about their past experience; and that they were in a position to assimilate and understand the
meaning of many ideas which previously would have eluded them. But the
question was, would they be motivated to learn?*

MEETING IX

Some people arrived a half-hour early, as planned. Others arrived at the usual time, and a few were late. They filled in the research questionnaire—the same one used during the first meeting.

The group was eager to get started listening to Jim's interpretations, and impatience was felt by some toward the slowpokes. Jim
and Jane had had their material dittoed in two documents: one, a
descriptive log of the meetings; the other, their interpretations.
The group decided to read the log first, and then have Jim hit the
high spots of the interpretations. Then, they could read the detailed interpretations with a better idea of the major themes to
look for.

When they had completed their reading, Jim gave a 20-minute, off-the-cuff set of impressions. He organized his statements around the theme of group growth, and tried to indicate the way in which the various events contributed to the development of the group. He was candid about his part in the difficulties during Meetings VI and VII, but he focused on their growth-stimulating aspects rather than on the feelings of discouragement. (*From the comments that followed, Jim judged that the notion that a group can grow even while frustrated and discouraged was a new revelation to some and of resentful contention for others. The questions asked of Jim were not taken up by other members, and this confirmed Jim's hunch that the completion of his report might usher in a period of essentially individually oriented need-meeting.*)

The coffee break took longer than usual, and discussion was happy and animated. A few individuals compared notes with others; they were concerned with reactions of which Jim's report had reminded them; two other knots of people seemed to be discussing existentialism and dog raising.

There was much good-humored resistance to coming back to the meeting table for the last half-hour. There was certainly no sense of urgent business to be done. The group was not in the mood to work; equally, it was not in the mood to undertake the slight amount of work required to agree explicitly not to work. What the members did, then, was to listen for about twenty minutes to a rather abstract conversation by four members. But eventually there arose the realization that this was no good either: they were being denied the gratifications of the coffee buzz groups and were not getting the satisfactions of group accomplishment. Two private conversations were going on quietly. (*The fact that the "pairers" felt that the group would permit this has special significance as evidence of the close interpersonal feeling in the group.*)

One person called for clarification of goals so that all could participate, and the group fell into a review of the next steps of the plan—presumably to be carried out next time. Jim pointed out that the effort to arrive at "principles" would be unrewarding except in so far as individuals could clarify ideas important to themselves. He also said that he believed that probably each individual had one or two questions he would like to have cleared up at the next (and last) meeting, and he suggested that the group begin the next meeting by compiling these questions, and then talk directly about them. No decision was reached regarding Jim's suggestions.

(*Jim felt that he, as trainer, probably should have called the group's attention to the fact that the last half-hour's work was not really work. But then he felt, why bother? He had rather enjoyed, as a new member, participating in the group's enjoyment of itself.*)

During the week preceding the tenth (and last) meeting, each individual began to try to adjust in his own fashion to the ending of the group. One person called a meeting to study one of Jim's articles; presumably those who attended wanted to prepare themselves to make the most of their last opportunity to learn from Jim. Another began reading everything he could in an effort to understand the rather dramatic changes that had occurred in his relations with some teen-age groups he was supervising; he also found an opportunity to tell Jim about these changes. Rumors came back to Jim that a movement was under way to request an eleventh meeting—and possibly more.

(*It seemed to Jim that the character of the group's outside activities had changed. Previously, individuals had banded together in unfocused bull-sessions for the purpose of dealing with rather diffuse feelings. Now, there was a direction in the activities, and the direction depended upon the individual. It was as if each person was trying, in a work-oriented way, to do whatever he had to do to adjust to the termination of the group. Jim felt that many individuals would have different wishes about how time should be used at the last meeting.*

When Jim thought in terms of the group as a whole, he felt that certain points were relevant, even though he was not altogether clear as to how these fitted together: first, the group had no compelling emotional conflict or anxiety which they would be motivated to deal with. Second, the group could not accept "just doing nothing" (e.g., turn the meeting into a social one) because this would be a serious violation of its concept of itself as a group that "grows." To not work would be too threatening. Third, although the group seemed secure and adequate, there would still be a wish to avoid the difficulties of a completely unstructured or ambiguously defined situation; the individuals would probably desire to work on their last day, but not to be frustrated by the work. This seemed to indicate reflective work rather than work on group process. Fourth, reflective work was also in line with the group's expressed wish to formulate principles. In other words, although the group had achieved emotional "closure" at the end of Meeting VIII, it still had to sort out its thoughts before it could achieve a sense of intellectual completion. Fifth, there was a feeling of interpersonal warmth in the group, a strong sense that individuals (whatever their personal motives might be) do "speak for the group." Sixth, Jim felt that there was little or no anxiety about leadership in the group: any leadership that could help to get the job done would be acceptable.)

MEETING X

Jim opened the final meeting. He said that probably there were various different things that people wished to see done before the course was over. He suggested that these wishes could be the basis of an agenda; he then asked the group for them, and wrote the different requests on the board.

There were eight requests, and they fell into three categories:

1. Reporting on the research and on a meeting some members had had the previous night.
2. Sharing ideas about what the experience had meant to them.
3. Clarifying further ideas about emotionality, work, growth, and applications of these ideas to other groups.

The categories were quickly agreed to. Jim felt that if the reports came first they might contribute information useful for the subsequent discussion, and he arranged the categories accordingly. (*He also felt, but did not say, that the group could use the individual reports to help discover how to delimit the discussion of principles.*)

The first report, on the research, was "followed up" into implications for what sort of leader would be most effective for what sort of group. The second report, on the previous night's meeting of 11 members of the group, dwelt mostly on the process problems encountered and solved by the subgroup. It was reassuring to the class. The success of the subgroup, rather than being a threat to the others, was shared by the others—it was their success, too. To get ready for reporting on "what the experience meant to me," Jim suggested that people write their reports first, and then select the one or two most interesting points to tell the group. He also said he would like the written statements for his own use in studying the group. Assent was expressed by a few people, and paper was passed out. The writing went on for 20 minutes; then Jim called a halt. (*The group's hard working on this self-analytic task reinforced Jim's feeling that members would have a heightened concern over themselves and would behave individualistically in seeking their conclusions from the experience.*)

The writing done, the group decided to "go around the table" to hear from each person—provided it did not take longer than 15 or 20 minutes. The group seemed "uninvolved"—neither eager nor denying. The reports began. The third speaker said the experience was a failure. (No reply beyond a murmuring.) Another speaker said his whole pattern of behavior had changed. (No reply.) Ideas, conclusions, unresolved questions—all were expressed; and without replies. There was attentiveness without tension, receptiveness without reaction, thoughtfulness without expression. It was as if each person were listening, not to someone else, but to himself; no shocks, no surprises, but quiet, steady interest, as in listening to music. The speakers were objective and controlled, but they also expressed feeling about what they were reporting—no confessions, no testimonials, no effort to "have the last word," no saying of one thing but meaning another, simply sober, shared introspection.

The coffee break lasted 20 minutes, and was spent in quiet conversation.

Toward the end of the break, Jim and two others sat down at the table. The others remained in conversation a few minutes longer. Then, as if a signal had been given, they all quickly sat down. Picking from among the topics on the board, Jim suggested that the most useful to start with might be "The Signs and Symptoms of a Group at Work." Ten different suggestions were made, and it was seen that these formed a pattern. The group saw that "work" could be toward stated "achievement" goals or on unstated but shared problems of their own processes. Forty-five minutes later the discussion shifted from the subject of group phenomena to the problem of leader-behavior in increasing the efficiency of group operation. A central theme of the entire discussion—of the group's life together—was the relationship between emotion and work. The meeting ended on time with a statement by Jim summarizing the last topic discussed and also stating some of his convictions about the relationships between group and leader self-confidence.

Jim had been actively participating, and had given freely and easily of his ideas. Discussion drew many illustrations from the life of the group together. The period was one of very high-level work, and retained the quality of internal communication: the feeling that every speaker somehow was speaking for all. According to comments later, many members achieved a feeling of "closure"—things "fell into place"; and there was considerable consciousness of the fact that much of the meaningfulness of the discussion came from the long experience together, and from the readiness and need for final understanding.

GROWTH PHASES AND TRAINING

This case study presents three major phases, and the ways of working in each phase reveal different degrees of fidelity to the principles on which the laboratory method is based.

The first phase, Meetings I through V, shows a conscious and successful application of training principles. The group developed a number of skills, worked through a basic and universal emotional problem, and had considerable awareness of what it was doing most of the time. The experiences were reflected on and reasonably well understood. Presumably the learning would have implications for succeeding participation in other groups. There was, on the whole, sufficient clarity in the situation that there could be maintained a balance between emotion and reflection such that these two levels of experiencing could be integrated (e.g., could interact with each other to produce meaningful, unconflicted understanding).

The second phase, Meetings VI through VIII, presents a different picture. It was a successful growth experience, but an ineffective training experience. The failure of training stems from the fact that the group was not sufficiently able to clarify to itself what was going on. The situation was too confused for cause-and-effect relationships to emerge in consciousness, and the emotional problems were so disturbing that calm reflection was impossible. The group was preoccupied with its own emotionality, it was unable to make use of individual insights, and it was swept from time to time by waves of emotional contagion.

During Meeting VIII, the group made a spectacular recovery from the frustrations of Meetings VI and VII. This was the wish of the group, and it succeeded—and this is also the meaning of the meeting: a working out of frustration. But the group was probably little aware of what was going on. One notes, for example, that the subgroup reports, which were felt to represent high-level thinking, did not offer any analysis. Principles, yes, but these were things the experience reminded them of—not pinpointed diagnostic understandings of emotional dynamics. And t e content of the reports was lost for the most part in the feeling oι atification that swept through the group as it listened.

Fr ι the experiences of the second phase, one may doubt that much as learned that could later guide the operation of the members subsequent groups.

The third hase, Meetings IX and X, would, one might suppose, represent he golden opportunity for objective thinking and consolidation ot ideas—for thinking back over the preceding experience and seeing it "whole"; or for sober analysis of the differences between this training situation and other, more typical group situations.

Meeting X pretty well satisfies these expectations. It would be rated as a valuable day of training.

Meeting IX appears to have made little contribution to training. Jim's report was enjoyed as an assurance to the group that Jim was now a member, that the group had not wasted its time during Meetings VI and VII, that what happened to the group was understandable and not uncommon. In effect, it probably contributed to the group's concept of itself as a mature group, but not to the understanding of dynamics of group operation.

It should be noted that other evaluations of this case study could be made from other points of view. It is possible that many trainers would regard the second phase not as the worst but as the best, because of the intensity of feeling and the consequently greater possibilities of emotional (and subconscious) reorganization within individuals. A therapist called in during the second phase might well have turned it to good account. And even within the framework of the method as we have presented it, the training would have been much better in the second phase if there had been individual counseling available outside the group. Such possibilities of supportive training-help need more consideration and experimental study.

WHAT DID THEY LEARN?

The target of training is, of course, the individual members of the group. The final criterion of successful training is that the people significantly improve their performance in subsequent groups. To appraise this would require careful observation of their behavior in these other groups both before and after training. In the case presented here, the graduate students in the group did not come as representatives of particular groups in need of help. They were primarily concerned with the course as a sort of professional and research training: to fit them for foreseen but generally undefined co-operative working situations.

We have three kinds of evidence to consider in assessing the training in this group. First, there were noticeable changes in the way some people participated. These changes were generally toward better control and the channeling of disruptive impulses into work—a change toward constructive rather than destructive expression of emotion. In addition, noticeable changes in skill occurred: there were attempts to apply the skills of diagnosis, decision-making, and the like at more appropriate times. Second, the research questionnaires filled out during the first and ninth meetings (actually a sorting of 90 items of self-descriptions of role in groups) make possible a rather precise estimate of change in the way individuals felt they related themselves to the group. The particular questionnaire in this study was designed to show rather basic aspects of emotional orientation to the group and to its problems of reconciling work and emotional needs. Third, there were the written statements prepared by each member during the tenth meeting. These statements give evidence of the extent to which the members thought they had changed. The members were free to write on any aspects of change they wished, and this has the advantage of showing what each person thought was important; it has, however, the disadvantage of not allowing systematic comparisons with respect to any specific changes.

The trainers studied the data rather carefully and feel that the following estimates of change during training are reasonably accurate, and that if they are in error the direction of error is toward overconservativeness. In other words, the following judgments probably underestimate the effects of training rather than overstate them.

Here is the way the trainers see it:

Of 23 people from whom data were collected (out of 25 in the group):

7 people changed their behavior in the group, were aware of changes in their behavior, and had a good understanding of their participation in the group.

3 additional people changed their behavior in the group and were aware of the changes, but did not demonstrate any very adequate understanding of why these changes had occurred or what they meant for future participation.

4 additional people changed their behaviors in the group to some extent, indicated no awareness of these changes, but demonstrated considerable insight into the principles of group operation and individual participation.

The trainers felt that the training had been effective for these fourteen people, and that the first seven had profited most markedly.

8 people showed little change, and little awareness of change; the principles they learned were stated academically: they were not "internalized" enough, presumably, to guide future participation. The changes were in the direction of talking about group process a bit more glibly, but not toward better participation.

1 person, mostly nonparticipant, ended the course full of concern over one general problem involved in his own participation. He appeared to have learned very little and to have had his anxieties aroused, although not to a disruptive level of intensity.

The trainers felt that these nine people had had the least "readiness" for the experience, had learned least, and changed least; and they certainly had participated least.

Analysis of the research questionnaires generally confirmed the impressions that the members and trainers had of the changes in members. The correlation of pre-training and post-training questionnaires is higher—showing less change—for the last nine than for the first fourteen people classified above. The nine who did not profit so much tended to be more "rigid." They tended to be disturbed by emotional expression, and they tended to be "out of step" with the greater aggressiveness and outgoingness characteristic of the rest of the group. They tended to be more resistant and in two cases there was some threat involved in acknowledging their need for training.

Of the nine who got least out of the experience, the trainers felt that five would have profited greatly from individual counseling along with the training in the group; and that the three who changed but did not know it might have achieved awareness through such "outside interviews."

It is interesting to note that the course was very differently reacted to by different members. For three or four of them it appeared to serve as a rather limited but effectives therapy. Their friends and colleagues noted that these people expressed more warmth and spontaneity in their relationships: it was as if they had gained in acceptance of themselves and others. On the other hand, the eight "academicians" reacted to the experience pretty much in classroom terms: as a cognitive experience but not one with much emotional pull or meaning for them.

HOW THE TRAINER OPERATES

The role of the trainer is central. It requires considerable intellectual activity at all times to know how to stay out of the discussion at some points and how to come in at others. The trainer understands his job when in each situation he can consciously formulate several alternative things he might do, and can self-confidently select one as the most appropriate. In addition, he then must study the effects of the alternative selected as a key to further insights about the state of affairs in the group. The goal of the trainer is "to work himself out of a job" through helping the group take over as many of his initial roles as possible.

There are, however, two kinds of functions which probably become more firmly located in the trainer as time goes on. One of these is the provision of emotional support to the efforts of the group to experiment and learn. The group is able clearly to distinguish friendly encouragement to its own development of strength from efforts to take over or "do it for" the group. There is no sense in withdrawing friendly encouragement unless the trainer thinks the group ought to spend the rest of its time working through the feelings of being rejected by the person who is supposed to help them. Under proper training conditions, the group will tell the trainer when it feels that he is being too active; but the group finds it extremely difficult to tell him when he is being nonsupportive.

I make a point of this because it seems to me that a great deal of malpractice at the present time is due to the trainer's inability to distinguish feelings from actions. Some trainers do not know how to withdraw from action without also rejecting the group. Along with this confusion usually goes some feeling of guilt in the trainer's mind at doing *anything* for the group. He feels, somehow, that to be helpful he must show that he has no faith in the group; otherwise, he suspects his own motives. The realistic faith of the trainer is that the group will make the most out of any situation he helps set up; but there is also the understanding that no group can make much out of confused situations—unless they are set up consciously as objects for study and reflection.

Besides the function of continual encouragement to the group's efforts to develop competence and understanding, the trainer has a second function, which probably becomes more pronounced as the group grows. This is the teaching function. The trainer is the purveyor to the group of a set of scientifically based understandings about experimental method as applied to group problem-solving. In addition, he must teach the group many concepts about group process that are necessary for understanding. As the group works through vital experiences together it is more and more able to assimilate information and ideas from the social sciences, and it has more and more need for conceptualizing its own experience. The trainer who does not know how to supply needed conceptual resources should learn to do so; no good is served by pretending that important concepts, developed through years of scientific study, will be germinated spontaneously by a group in the space of a few meetings.

The problem of functions served by the trainer is also the problem of desired versus undesired qualities of dependency. The trainer must learn to distinguish among the various aspects and conditions of dependency. Acceptance of certain forms of dependency on him is part and parcel of the dynamics of training, because the group's trust in the trainer is actually the source of his ability to train. In every situation, some aspects of the trainer's relation to the group involve its dependency upon him, and he must accept some of this dependency as legitimate and desirable. There are other aspects that are acceptable initially but will disappear as the group develops its own resources. Finally, there are some kinds of dependency to which the group can resort under stress as one of several ways of avoiding the responsibilities that it must take on. Even these efforts toward greater dependency should not be fought by the trainer; rather, he should help the group to see what they are doing and then encourage them to find more growth-producing ways of dealing with such situations.

Let us now try to spell out more specifically the central targets of the trainer's conscious concern during group meetings.[5]

1. *The balance between work and emotion.*—At all times the trainer is interested in the "way things are going." His basic characterization is in terms of the balance between "work" and "emotionality." He is continually comparing conditions in the group with his model of work. Group work can be seen and felt. It can also be recognized by a variety of criteria. Thus, people, when the group is working, listen to each other. The comments of each individual show that he heard and understood the previous comments, and that he understood from them what the speaker meant, not what he wanted to imagine the speaker meant. Further, people seem to know how to contribute the sort of comment which is needed. In other words, there is a clear understanding of the member role, even though it may not have been discussed. Also, there is a sense of "getting some place," a sense of purpose and movement. The goal may or may not be defined; at times it would be very difficult for the group to put its purpose in words. But there is a shared feeling about the need for the discussion, and an acceptance by everyone of that need—whatever it is. When the group is working, individuals feel free to say what they want

5. The reader is again reminded that different trainers formulate the bases of their operation in different ways.

to; they do not want to say things that are off the subject, and they freely say whatever they think is pertinent. There is a sense of leisure and relaxation, coupled with the kind of excitement that goes with significant experiences when the group is working.

The trainer knows that groups do not achieve this kind of work immediately, but he and the members themselves can tell when the group is moving toward this quality of experience and when it is moving away from it.

The trainer assumes that the reasons why the group falls short of this image is that it has problems which stand in the way and which it cannot understand explicitly, even though it may be aware of its strong feelings about them. The trainer assumes that the group is always working on some problem concerning the relationship of its members, of defining goals or roles, of dealing with individual needs, or trying to avoid anxieties or other pains that go with new insights, etc.

The signs of lost effort include: trivial conversation, apathy, unusual politeness, incoherence, too much regard for the feelings of others, too rapid talking, talking at cross purposes, individually oriented confessions, hostility greater than the situation calls for, efforts to find out what the leader wants, making long lists on the blackboard, looking up past history of the group—and a host of other symptoms of avoidance, resistance, disorganization, attack, and disintegration.

2. *The trainer helps set conditions.*—The trainer distinguishes between "doing" and "thinking" activities. It is understood that the group is to plan and carry out activities and to reflect upon the results. During the planning and reflecting stages, the trainer intervenes to test the realism and feasibility of plans, and the validity and implications of conclusions. He serves as a resource person to make the planning and reflecting effective. But in the carrying out of a plan—such as role-playing several styles of leadership, or having working subgroups, or interviewing each other, or having "free discussion"—the leader does not intervene. The purpose of these activities is to provide information about the group's strengths and weaknesses, or to share feeling more directly, or to give individuals greater scope to "act out" feelings by providing temporary escape from the difficulties of having to try

to be a group member. In connection with the "doing" activities, the trainer is concerned that the purpose of the activity be clear enough that the information, recorded during the activity or obtained by testimony of observers and participants immediately afterward, can be interpreted. In these "acting out" or "doing" activities, nonwork conditions can be looked at safely because, after all, the activities were planned to demonstrate nonwork conditions; the hostility or dependence or other expressed feelings required by the activity were under control even though they may have been expressed in an excessive manner.

The trainer is likely to be most active during the shift from "doing" to "thinking," and vice versa. Thus, for example, when work orientation gets lost during a thinking activity—and the group knows instinctively when it happens—there begins to be a push for action. The trainer tries at this point to get planning which will make the difference between an escape into doing as compared to an orderly retreat into doing for the sake of providing useful diagnostic information.

On the other hand, when the group has been acting out its conflicts through an unfocused bull-session, anxieties have been mounting; the group may hope that by continuing to flounder it will somehow come up with a resolution of its emotional problems (which are responsible for the ambiguity and, therefore, the floundering) but it knows that usually it will not. Under these conditions, the trainer may call for a thinking period to look back at "what we have been doing." The purpose, of course, is to provide a structured work task which can pull the group back together, and to work toward the development of competence and readiness to deal with anxiety. And the work task is to diagnose the problem.

The point is, simply, that the trainer is aware of two fundamentally different sorts of activity, and is concerned to get a strategic alternation of these two types.

3. *The trainer speaks to the group.*—His remarks about individuals are confined to behavior presented by design during "acting out" periods, when their purpose is to demonstrate interpersonal dynamics. The trainer, during work periods, is constantly pulling the group together by seeing all problems as group problems.

Thus, the behavior of a deviate individual is per se no problem; the problem is that the group does not know how to respond to particular types of communications. Anger or bullying of individuals is seen not as a response to the individual, but as a response to the members' own anxieties, set off by the more or less accidental behavior of the deviate. In the same way, during a work situation, deviate behavior that is disturbing must nonetheless be seen as "speaking for the group." Otherwise, why is the group upset by it? Thus, even the most obtrusive individual behavior is seen by the trainer as arising out of the group situation that all helped create, and as important only because of the feelings it mobilizes in the group as a whole.

4. *The trainer helps the group understand.*—The steering of the group into needed activities can be done through two kinds of interpretation: one is in terms of learning theory; the other is in terms of psychiatric theory. Both are based on diagnosis of the state of relationship between work and emotionality in the group.

Learning theory is useful for planning: e.g., "We have just been formulating a lot of ideas about how the leader influences the group, and it now seems to me that the logical next step is to set up a situation in which we can see these behaviors and find out if they have the effects we think they will." The concepts here are that ideas need to be assimilated through the experiences of applying them; that learning is a kind of inquiring based on problem-solving models.

Psychiatric theory is useful for diagnosis: e.g., "We seem generally agreed that we saw Richard and Henry as leaders, that they were in a sense spokesmen for the group; but they appeared to be in competition with each other, which suggests that the group as a whole has mixed feelings about the problem." The concepts here are not so much concerned with the way in which learning takes place as with describing the dynamics of the situation.

Either type of interpretation can be used at certain times. The most successful type is usually not recognized by the group as an interpretation at all. This happens when the group sees that the trainer is merely summarizing several contributions which have already been made; he is building onto the group's own sensitivities, the group is "ready" for the interpretation, and the interpretation calls little attention to itself. The kind of diagnosis that is noticed as such is the one for which the group is not "ready." The objection frequently voiced against diagnosis or interpretation is probably an objection to poor timing, or to the unconscious hostility that a person whose timing is poor would presumably have.

Another method of steering the group—particularly in early stages when it has not yet developed a rationale for interpretation, or agreements on procedure, or a sharing of feeling about leadership, etc.—is simply to suggest what seems appropriate and to ask for permission to give it a try.

5. *The trainer helps the group "grow."*—The trainer may believe he sees what needs to be done next, or the diagnosis which should be made. How shall he decide whether to speak up? There are several general policies that need to be considered.

The first notion is that an insight achieved by the trainer at a particular time may occur to someone else at the same time, so perhaps the trainer should wait.

The second notion is that the trainer should enter the discussion only when he knows what he is doing and why: this cuts down an astonishing number of impulses to talk.

The third notion is that the trainer must forever be helping the group to take such responsibility for itself as it is ready for, and this means standing aside enough to let the group experiment with new skills, including ones for which they have in the past looked to the trainer.

The fourth notion is that the training value of the experience must be protected. For example, if the group is all set to role-play a scene and several individuals start a big argument over "whether role-playing is valid," the trainer has to decide whether the resistance to role-playing means that the plan to role-play needs further discussion, or whether to go ahead on the grounds that the factors expressed as resistance to role-playing will come out much better in the scene itself. Usually the latter is the case, and the subsequent discussion adds insight in a way that dealing with the resistance directly could not. The trainer's suggestion to "wait and see" often enables the group to move into action and collect data rather than to spend its time endlessly and fruitlessly in "planning." In the same vein are the unrealistic requests for certainty: the group can be delayed indefinitely because it is not "really sure" that it wants to move. In such a case it can be pointed out that nobody can be sure until the results are in.

6. *The trainer knows his limitations.*—Every trainer has certain blind spots or certain emotional conditions in which he cannot help the group. In such cases he can explain what is called for and ask if someone will take a shot at it. Thus, when a group gets into a discussion whose real purpose, hidden or explicit, is to clarify feelings about leadership, a trainer who cannot help getting defensive under such conditions can simply state that for private reasons he feels incompetent to help and that perhaps the group had better name a chairman pro tem. Of course, if the group has already developed its natural leadership, no explanation of trainer silence is necessary unless asked for.

7. *The trainer does not try to be a "member."*—The trainer needs to realize that he is not a group member. His job is to deal with the group, not with individuals. Thus, for example, a good deal of member behavior originates in the need to find a position in the group and to deal with feelings about certain members. This should not be the source of the trainer's behavior. He does not need to establish his position because it is defined from the very start, and he does not need to be concerned over his relationship to individuals because he is stimulated only by conditions within the total group. He must be sufficiently free of personal entanglements to respond to the interactions between members, but his behavior is expressed toward the whole group.

When the trainer himself enters into debate, he is in the difficult position of trying to support a position as a group member and trying to help the group respond to the conflict which he himself is helping to produce. In effect he is trying to be a protagonist in and a commentator on the battle at one and the same time. This is an impossible position, and it is inevitably the difficulty trainers with "messages" get into. The job of the trainer is to help the group deal with the problems it encounters, but he should not be seen as part of the problems.

The rigor with which this criterion is applied diminishes as the group grows. Particularly after the group's own leadership has emerged, the trainer is seen primarily as a consultant rather than a leader, and he may now safely enjoy *some* of the gratifications of membership in the group.

A SUMMARY STATEMENT

Perhaps the simplest way to recapitulate the principles and major features of the laboratory method of training would be to quote the remarks with which Jim intends to begin his next training group:

"We begin here as a collection of individuals. Perhaps a few of us know some things about each other, but by and large we do not know each other's attitudes, skills, beliefs, purposes, etc., with regard to questions of leadership and participation in groups.

"During our time together we shall change from a collection to a group. We shall do this as a result of our efforts to solve problems together. The problems we shall work on will be the things we feel are problems; in other words, they will have to do with difficulties we encounter. As we work through our own problems of operation we will grow as a group; to the extent that in this process we understand what is going on we will have a learning experience which should lead to more effective participation in other groups.

"As trainer to the group, my job will be three fold: first, to help the group have significant experiences together; second, to help the group understand what is happening during these experiences; and third, to help the group relate these ideas about its own experience to a general methodology for group problem-solving.

"Practically all my remarks will be addressed to the group and will be about the group—as if it were a single, albeit complex, organism. At first, I shall make definite suggestions to, and demands on, the group for certain types of activities. As the group learns to use the methodology of group problem-solving, it will begin to make these demands on itself. Basically, however, the demands we make will all serve two purposes: first, to keep the group in contact with reality, through collecting and interpreting information about its performance; and, second, to safeguard conditions in such a way that valid conclusions can be drawn from our experiences and that people will know in general how to participate when they wish to.

"Our theorizing will tend to be mostly about the processes of group work. We shall live our own history, but we can expect to have to deal with problems of freedom versus inhibition of emotional expression, the individual versus the group, natural versus designated leadership, and conflicts, possibly, between the subcultures we represent. In working through these problems, we shall learn to use two sets of concepts:

a) concepts of relationships between emotional and work processes

b) concepts of experimental method as applied to problem-solving by the group

"*In our working through these matters, I shall not tell anyone what to do, but I shall continually help the group see what needs to be done.* It will be up to each person to decide whether, how, and when to participate in the work of the group. He may share with the group his problems of participation to the extent that he wishes to. I hope that people will experiment with their own roles, and that each person will take the opportunity to test the sort of contributions he can make under various conditions.

"Many of you will feel a need to discuss your own participation and the meaning of your experience either with one of the trainers or with other members of the group. Such discussion can make a valuable contribution to your maximum utilization of this training experience."

More details about techniques for holding meetings which may be useful to trainers are given on pages 180–217. Chapters 7 and 8 present background for the understanding of some commonly observed difficulties of trainees. Pages 349–56 indicate conditions for resolving conflict between training and "back home" groups. The group case study, pages 322–26, is taken from a training group and illuminates the kind of decision process in which the trainer is continually involved. Some kinds of anxieties of which trainers need to be aware are described on pages 313–22. The discussion of steering the group through control of the trainer's role, pages 59–62, and of diagnosis and interpretation, pages 53–59, is directly applicable to the training situation.

CHAPTER 6

The effective meeting is planned according to the same principles that are central in all technologies for organizing human effort. In addition, a variety of techniques, useful for particular purposes, are available. The aim is to create a psychologically effective sequence of activities through which the specific aims of the meeting will be achieved.

DISTINCTIVE FEATURES

The authority of leadership in the public meeting is delegated by the audience through the act of attending, and it is reinforced by the expectancy that whoever calls the meeting will take charge. The primary target of change is either knowledge, attitudes, or readiness for action by the audience; secondary targets may be conditions to be changed, actions to be taken, memberships or finances to be secured for the host organization. The role of the audience is indicated by the leadership at the meetings, and the method of control is through the direction of activities planned in advance. The relationship of the meeting to other groups is generally through actions of individuals in the audience who may be persuaded to try to influence organizations to which they belong.

Effective Meetings: Principles and Procedures

Basic Principles of Social Technology

The aim of science is to describe nature and its laws. The aim of technology is to state policies by which man can control nature for stated ends. Technology is the set of ideas man uses in acting out his needs and in satisfying his purposes. As science develops and nature is understood better, technology also changes.

Thus in the days when it was "science" to assume that the gods who affect men also control stars, the technology of predicting the success of men's enterprises was based on interpreting the movements of stars. As science changed, and men and stars were seen to be independent in their actions, the technology also changed.

At the present time, science in the field of human relations and social action has developed a great deal further than have our technologies for affecting action in valid ways. The preceding parts of this book attempt to show the sort of technologies toward which science in these areas is leading us. We have discussed technological considerations with respect to community action, in-service training, classroom instruction, administration and management, and human relations training. These are, in effect, technologies in five areas of application of the science of human dynamics, by which we mean a coherent body of relevant principles drawn from hitherto "different" social sciences. Are these technologies different? In what respects are they alike? Is there a basic technology of social action?

There are certain principles which appear to be common to these technologies and, we suspect, to all technologies of social action and learning. It is our purpose to formulate four basic principles, which we think are clearly entitled to first place among all technologies of social action.

PRINCIPLE 1: THE PRINCIPLE OF EXTERNAL DEMAND

In a group, the behavior of each person affects and is affected by the behaviors of the others. The power of a group depends upon the extent to which the mutual influencing of members' behaviors is helpful. For members to facilitate each other's efforts, they must share some of the same ideas and feelings about the goal and about what is required to reach the goal. For effective co-operation among members, the most important feeling to be shared is that of "a job to be done."

The development of this feeling usually signals a change from vague longing to acceptance of demands or requirements that the group is prepared to meet. It is as if some "outsider" (the problem) had to be dealt with on its *own* terms—the actions to be taken are seen to stem from the nature of the problem itself rather than from the whim of the leader, the urgings of a consultant, or the wish to identify with action taken elsewhere. In other words, the conditions to be changed are formulated and possible actions are discussed objectively as though they existed apart from the members of the group—even though the problem could not exist if the members of the group had not had private feelings and concerns about it.

What we mean by saying that "a group has formulated a set of purposes," is that it has defined and accepted a set of demands which it will try to meet. It is in this sense that purposes are "externalized" as demands.

Basically, there are three ways in which demands can be externalized:

1. Orders from a "higher" authority which has power to reward and punish. Demands of this sort are "pressures," and the group has to devote energy and time to change its way of operation in order to meet these pressures. These pressures may be seen as reasonable or not. They are "reasonable" if the group "sees where they come from"—in other words, if they are seen as arising out of the requirements of the "situation."

2. Changed conditions in the environment, which call for adjustment by the group. The university budget cut, which affects each department; the burning down of Farmer Smith's silo; the passing of tax legislation; the rising cost of material and labor—all these things are not seen as being caused by the group, but the group has to take them into account in its own planning and operation. Such "outside" factors make themselves known as difficulties in maintaining the established way of doing things.

3. Projection of internal needs as a set of external relations to be changed. One is uncomfortable and he does something about it. To do something in any rational way requires that one think about why he is uncomfortable and what things he can change so that he will feel better. This is the classic concept of need-meeting.

Groups do the same thing. The typical citizen improvement group meets to "improve the community." The goal is stated very broadly to provide a large enough umbrella for many different people. The process of narrowing purposes and defining specific jobs is basically the problem of focusing feeling and diagnosing what changes can be made to provide greatest relief and satisfaction. Meeting of need has the quality both of learning and of taking action, because changes and insights happen within one's self (learning) and because these changes and insights are stimulated by what one does in relation to the environment (action).

In the applications presented so far, the "external demands" are of various sorts:

In classroom learning, the external demands are the requirements of a learning activity. The work of the group is to carry through activities in which their experiences will result in "significant" learning. But you do not plan significant learning, you plan activity. The teacher makes the demand that the class participate in such activities. The more effective the teaching situation, the more the response of the class is to the activity demand rather than the teacher demand, since only the former is educative.

In the laboratory training group, the external demand is the required roles that must be produced by the group. The trainer's job is to clarify "what is needed" to get out of confusion, to have useful shared experience, and the like. The group's job is to figure out how to supply "what is needed," and in this process, its members learn not only how to diagnose needs but also the experimental method as applied to groups participating in social action, a variety of skills of leadership and membership, and, probably, some useful insights about themselves as personalities.

In the management situation, the external demand is the pressures from above and from below. Any order from above has to be considered and dealt with simply because it came from above. An appropriate order represents to subordinates a kind of external demand which they can easily identify with their own purposes as well.

In the in-service training program, the external demand is the changing of the faculty's perception of its place in the community through improvement of instruction. The all-school program, which provides the basis for controlling intergroup competition (of the training groups) and channeling it constructively, is primarily one through which the school acts interdependently with other groups in the community. The community becomes a vast consumer-audience which, however, cannot sit entirely on the side lines. Members of the community work with the school; thus there is some "reality" of relationship between school and community. One is not free to think anything he wishes without any check on the process. Professional "improvement" is the legitimate basis for improved school "position" within the family of community groups.

In the community action situation, the external demand is the obligation to take action to improve one's community. It is the feeling of pressure to "get something done" which causes action to start on one's doorstep: problems at home are understood and can be worked on. The demands are seen as arising from objective problems: one works on housing, education, job opportunity —not on race relations or ideologies per se. These latter problems are dealt with as factors affecting the former, but they cannot be dealt with alone and by themselves through processes of co-operation.

In all of the above situations, there are, of course, many kinds of external demands at work. We have merely attempted to show the unique or most characteristic demand for each application area.

The meaning of the "principle of external demands" as part of a technology of social learning and action is that provision must be made to facilitate:

1. The formulation of group purposes in such a way that they are felt as demands from the outside made on the group as a whole.
2. The development of group leadership and control in its most basic terms: as the means through which the group co-ordinates individual effort to meet the external demands.

PRINCIPLE 2: THE PRINCIPLE OF RESPONSIBILITY
ASSIGNED TO GROUPS

For human beings to be able to co-ordinate their efforts, they must know "what to expect" from each other. The things we expect from each other as a result of discussion and agreement are the "responsibilities" of particular individuals. That is, each individual is responsible for doing something—for carrying out action of some particular type under some set of conditions; in other words, "responsibility" is for implementing policy. Since creativity and initiative are required, there must be sufficient freedom and autonomy for the individual so that he can act. Thus goes the orthodox argument.

So long as the work gets done satisfactorily, the above set of concepts—which may be summed up in the admonition, "Find the right man for the job, be sure he knows what's wanted, and then turn him loose"—are adequate. When, however, the work is not getting done properly, we discover that there are certain difficulties in operating with these concepts.

The most serious difficulty is that individual actions are seldom actions of single individuals; they are, rather, interactions or co-actions of two or more people. Most acts of problem-solving in social spheres are acts of communication; and what breaks down, typically, is the process of communication. If the process of communication conformed to the simple model of A talking while B listens, followed by B talking while A listens, then we might be able to see action as simply the exercise of responsibility by individuals. The fact is, however, that what A says depends on how B listens; A gets continual feedback of cues from B, and A modifies his message as he interprets B's cues. Communication, then, is more fruitfully viewed as a process within a group; in this case consisting of at least A and B.

In broad terms, the social action and implementation of policy is dependent on group standards of performance and quality, and it is through these standards that the particular capabilities of each individual for resistance, objectivity, creativity, and determination are selected and reinforced. This leads us to the conclusion that responsibilities are in fact located in groups, wherever they may be represented on a table of organization.

A second argument for the principle that responsibilities should be assigned to groups rather than to individuals is that, under these conditions, the job is defined as including a range of social interaction with peers, and this means that there is enhanced opportunity for meeting "unofficial" but highly motivating needs of individuals. The range of needs that can be met in a co-operative work situation is considerably greater than the range possible in a solitary repetitive task situation.

A third argument is that groups, under proper conditions of leadership, will make wiser decisions about matters within their competence than will any individual.

The principle of responsibility assigned to groups stands for the following included ideas:

1. Demands are felt to be on the group as a whole, rather than on one individual, although one individual may have the special role of speaking *for* the group to others.
2. The group meets the external demand through defining its meaning to the members, diagnosing and formulating problems, deciding how to tackle the problems, assigning special functions to the individuals who carry them through, and the like. In other words, the group *co-operates* to meet external demands.
3. The data required for operation by the group come from its own experience, not from the experience of only one person or from the experience of some other group. Working co-operatively is a matter of taking the relevant social facts into account. It is necessary to consider facts about the operation not just of one's self but of others, and this concern implies responsibility for all the group.
4. For a group to be "responsible" means that it is responsible *to* somebody, as well as *for* something. The responsible group has an audience which is concerned with its performance, and which is likely to be associated in the group's mind with the external demands. It is to this "audience" that the group reports its progress, and it is to this audience that the group probably looks for such outside support as it needs.
5. Individuals do, of course, have responsibilities. But these are not for implementing policy or for problem-solving action per se. The responsibility of each individual is for his own co-operation and participation to further the progress of the group toward its goals. He

acts with reference to the group both when he is physically present in group discussion and when he is acting "on his own" outside the group.

PRINCIPLE 3: THE PRINCIPLE OF INDIVIDUAL CHALLENGE IN THE LEAST-SIZED GROUP

The central assumption of this principle is that the quality of performance depends on how one is motivated to perform, and that it is possible to compose groups in such a way that motivation is high. Such groups are the "*smallest groups in which it is possible to have represented at a functional level all the social and achievement skills required for the particular required activity.*"[1]

In general, the way to increase motivation is to help people find a wider range of "rewards" for working. This is done by defining roles in such a way that each person is, and feels he is, necessary to the group; each person has opportunity to grow on the job; each person feels secure and able to do his job.

1. All too often people know that if they just "sit tight," someone else will do their job. The way to avoid this is to avoid overlapping of functions and duplications of roles.

2. All too often people find it hard to break into a discussion, and so they withdraw. Thus they miss out on the testing of ideas so essential to learning. The solution to this is to have the group as small as possible, so that each person can have more of the group's time.

3. A small group also makes the nonparticipant more visible, and may lead him, when he does not know what the problem is, to inquire of the others so that he can see how to break in.

4. In a small group each person tends to feel a greater share of the responsibility for meeting the demand. This means that he also expects a greater percentage of whatever approval or punishment follows from the group effort.

5. A small group also can operate at a level of greater intimacy, and this means greater involvement of the members in the process of the group, and a wider range of possible need-meeting, extending into the personal domain.

6. A small group can work more informally because it does not

1. H. A. Thelen, "Group Dynamics in Instruction: The Principle of Least Group Size," *School Review* (March, 1949), p. 142.

have to make all rules and purposes explicit: people communicate more easily. This means greater relaxation, greater tolerance of individual effort, better morale, and more freedom to experiment.

7. The small group, as a subdivision of a larger group, also is likely to help its members adapt to the larger group. This is the place for tussling with the problems that cannot be discussed in the larger group; and such discussion should do much to help the larger group.

In general, if groups are composed in such a way that each person can have a larger "place" he will tend to try to move into this place. In effect, he accepts the challenge. The administrative and leadership problem is to see how to compose groups in such a way that the "place" people need is also the "place" people will have if they accept the work challenge.

PRINCIPLE 4: THE PRINCIPLE OF STEERING BY CONSEQUENCES

Our first three principles recognize the nature of a problem, the nature of interdependence of effort, and the importance that the meanings of work have for individuals. Thus are represented the social-objective, group, and individual "levels" of human effort.

Our basic assumption so far is that the purpose of a technology is to set conditions such that what happens is what is wanted and needed. We get co-operation by setting up a situation in which co-operation is the natural and effective thing to do—we never demand co-operation. We get individual motivation by setting up a situation such that individuals want to strive—we do not tell them to strive. We get good leadership by setting up situations in such a way that the group as a whole is challenged—under these conditions leadership will be forthcoming.

The technologist is a person who sets conditions. He manipulates the situation, but he does not manipulate people. A successful technologist manipulates the objective situation in such a way that people find it to their advantage to act in the way the technologist believes they should in order to meet their needs. An unsuccessful technologist manipulates the situation, finds that individuals do not know what to do or else simply reject the situation; he then tries to put on pressure, set up a system of rewards and punishments that are really not part of the job, etc.

Now actually what we are looking for is a technology that proceeds at all times with the best possible guesses and which provides for its own corrections in each situation. It is not a "correction" to make the monstrous or undignified seem respectable; a "correction" rather extends the scope of legitimate motivation and the reward to the individual for participating.

The principle by which this continuous correction or "steering" is accomplished is the Principle of Steering by Consequences. It might be called the Principle of Feedback, but I have chosen to use language which implies that conscious thought is involved in steering a group.

The principle includes at least the following associated ideas:

1. Most goals are reached by a sequence of identifiable acts, and each is the result of a process of weighing and selecting among alternatives.
2. Since the acts are related as a sequence in time, it follows that each act changes the situation in which the next act is performed.
3. Thus, the consequences of each act need to be taken into account in determining the next act.

There are two interesting implications of this logic:

1. The effort should be to take each action in such a way that it yields a maximum of information about the situation (so the next act can be planned more wisely).
2. This in turn means that taking of action becomes an application of the experimental method (of action research—to which much attention is devoted in chapters 10 and 11).

The meaning of this principle in a technology of social action and learning is that:

1. Jobs should be divided into small units so that problem-solving is actually a defined sequence of identifiable subactions.

2. The purpose of each subaction must be clearly seen, so that its consequences can be appraised (as to the extent to which it satisfies its purposes).

3. Deliberation is required following each act and before deciding on the next.

4. Part of taking action is planning on how to collect the data

required to evaluate the action, and how to use these data when they are in.

5. The entire range of consequences should be taken into account following each act. The range is implied in the above three principles: What do the consequences of this act tell us about the nature of our problem or of the external demands? What are the consequences in terms of our own division of functions and our definition of group responsibility? How do people now feel with regard to the challenge of the next step, their readiness to undertake it, their feelings of confidence about it, their possibilities of reward for trying?

6. The actions of a group have consequences for other groups as well. Consequences ramify like the spreading circular ripples on a pond. This means that other groups need to be classified according to a communication schedule: To what groups should what sort of experience be reported? And what groups are in a position, in view of their purposes, to collect useful information for my group?

Back of these principles is a deep commitment to what seem to be the scientific facts in the case: that men are interdependent. The only sense in which one acts alone is physical: some things are done in private. But the group mediates between the individual and the world of life and experience. A man's ideas of what is, what is good, what is possible, what is allowable, what is desirable—are all partly determined by the groups to which he belongs.

This whole book attempts to answer the question: How can we take account of the facts of social interdependence to live better lives? I should say that this is the major problem being formulated in politics—institutional, domestic, and international— since 1914. The principles discussed above are shorthand ways of summarizing some of the cores of ideas which are elaborated over and over in this book.

We believe that we cannot change facts: men work hardest to meet their own needs; a group which is new gets easily confused about its job; there are some kinds of decisions that a group simply has to make for itself. What we can do is to accept these things as true about ourselves, and then organize ourselves in such a way that we work *with* rather than against nature. If men work to meet their needs, then we should figure out how to set up situations in such a way that that is possible. If a new group gets confused easily, then we should pay careful attention to making facts and problems clear, small enough to be attacked, and un-confused by extraneous expression of anxiety that has nothing to do with the job. If there are some decisions the group has to make for itself, then the first task is to try to recognize such occasions when they arise.

These, then, are the technological goals.

Techniques for Better Operation

There are, to a person used only to the parliamentary, pro-gram-planning type of operation, an astonishing array of "new ways" in which groups can work. Role-playing, buzz groups, panels, problem census, listening teams, interviewing, polling, demonstrations, even silence periods—these terms have become part of the conversation of the group leader. And rightly so: in any art—and leadership is an art as well as a science—there is plenty of room for the creative use of new devices. We have prob-ably just begun to scratch the surface of the mine of useful ideas for working better in groups.

There is, however, a body of past experience from summer workshops and conferences, that leads me to put in a word of caution: a technique is in itself neither good nor bad, but it can be used effectively, with little consequence, or disastrously. Role-playing out of place can be gruesome; buzz grouping when there is nothing to talk about is downright embarrassing; discussion by a panel of "experts" who have had no experience relevant to the needs of the group is simply maddening; problem censuses before people feel able to formulate their "real problems" stick them with goals they will reject later; audience listening teams with no opportunity to report back get angry, and so on. I should say that these new techniques should not be assimilated as part of the orthodoxy of a new religion, and they should not stand for "group dynamics."

If you have a job to do and know what the job is, you are then ready to talk about techniques. The critical technical questions are:

1. What is the main thing this technique should accomplish?
2. Under what conditions does it work that way?
3. What are the other things it does, too, that may not be desirable?
4. What part of the technique is "given" and what things about it are modified in accordance with each particular situation?

We shall present these techniques in the form of a set of models or snapshots of groups in action. We shall then show some of the large number of modifications possible for adapting these basic models to special conditions or needs. And we shall use the discussion as an excuse also to make a number of observations about group behavior and leadership in general.

MODEL TECHNIQUE NO. 1: ROLE-PLAYING

To the best of my knowledge, the technique of role-playing, which children employ entirely spontaneously, was adapted to use of adults by Dr. J. L. Moreno, of the Psychodramatic Institute in New York. He worked out two quite different models, which he called "psychodrama" and "sociodrama." With each of these models, he developed a rather complete and detailed rationale and language. Psychodrama, according to Moreno, is a scheme for giving individual therapy through acting-out rather than talking-out procedures. It should only be used by a skilled and adequately trained therapist, and it has no place in this discussion.

Sociodrama, on the other hand, is one form of what has loosely become known as role-playing. In general, sociodrama is for the purpose of testing ideas in advance of putting them into effect in a "real" situation. It is, then, a means for *rehearsing* action and, through subsequent diagnosis of the action, identifying various factors that enter into the situation. Sociodrama is often used in this way in laboratory training groups.[2]

All the uses of role-playing have this in common:

1. The situation to be enacted is a dramatic one, with a begin-

2. Anyone interested in these dramatic devices would find it well worth his while to visit the Psychodramatic Institute during one of the public performances of psychodrama or sociodrama.

ning, middle, and end. It is not a sugar-coated panel discussion: there is a problematic situation, with suspense and point.

2. There is no script, written line by line. The skit is developed from a consideration of the nature of each of the characters in the scene, their attitudes toward each other, toward the problem, and toward various factors entering into the problem. In effect, then, the plot is what you get when people of different sorts are thrown into a situation together. It is dramatic to the extent that these people, in their different roles, come into conflict with each other or develop some other quality of personal relationship.

From here on, the basic scheme may be modified for a variety of purposes.

Purpose 1.—To "warm up" an audience; to get "involvement."

This is a complex business. It involves such things as: (*a*) "giving" everyone a chance to share feeling with the rest of the audience—which occurs when they experience the same dramatic reactions together, much as in a regular theater; (*b*) expressing a wide range of feelings about the problem involved, so that everyone will feel freer to express the way *he* feels; (*c*) obtaining everyone's immediate interest, without a good many boring preliminaries; (*d*) communicating problems directly rather than merely characterizing them in descriptive language; (*e*) providing everyone a common place from which to start, and a "safe," because fictional, situation to talk about.

All these ends can be accomplished through role-playing if it is carefully planned and developed for these purposes. Ordinarily it can be most useful in such situations as a group of citizens meeting to consider for the first time the problems of their community. In chapter 1 this use was discussed. The procedures usually include the following steps:

1. Since this activity comes first on a program (after a decent word or two of introduction), it must be prepared in advance, presumably by a planning committee.

2. After deciding on the objectives of the meeting, the committee considers a wide range of situations which are familiar in the everyday experience of the audience, and which show the problems or issues in a reasonably direct way. One, or preferably several members of the planning committee, take responsibility

from here on. They begin by getting from the other members suggestions of people who might enjoy role-playing.

3. The potential role-players are gathered, and the purposes of the program and its various parts are explained. They are then presented with suggestions for situations, and begin to add their own. They are encouraged to think in terms of the sort of part or character they would each like to play. After some discussion of this sort, they usually arrive at the definition of a situation they like.

4. The casting begins, usually with the group as a whole throwing in suggestions as to the attitudes and feelings of the various characters. (What would our "tough administrator" feel when someone came in with this request? How does he feel about his subordinates? What are his pet peeves, his enthusiasms, etc?) After a considerable number of "bright ideas" are in the open, people begin to see the roles they would like, and they also begin to nudge each other into them.

There needs to be some control over the casting process. People should not be chosen on the basis of friendship, or real-life position, or status. They should be chosen because the part is meaningful to them: they have confronted such situations often, and have genuine feelings about it. And people who cannot talk above a whisper, or who freeze in audience situations, or who want to act just to prove to themselves that they can, should not be invited to this meeting at all. The control over casting is, when necessary, the responsibility of the people setting up the scene. If possible they should be tactful; if not, they will have to be blunt. Such bluntness is usually acceptable as long as it is clear that the leader is talking out of concern for the job rather than out of personal anxiety.

5. The development of the skit begins. It is played through several times, and everyone makes suggestions to sharpen its impact. The temptation to load the scene with a "message" or with the point of view the planning committee may want the audience to adopt must be sternly resisted. This role-playing is for honest stimulation, not for persuasion.

6. The polishing-up process is completed. Here there are a variety of possible procedures. Some people like to establish an

order of speaking, and to decide what issues will be introduced when, and by whom. Others prefer not to decide such matters explicitly. A great deal depends upon the confidence and experience of the players. But it should be understood that this use of role-playing is a planned communication, worked up in detail and in advance; it is not a spontaneous let's-see-what-will-happen sort of activity. It may seem spontaneous, as any good play does, but this is the result of feeling the role as it is played, not the result of creating it fresh the first time. Because it is worked up by the participants themselves, it should suit their talents, and should have the kind of spontaneity we mean by the word "naturalness."

7. A day or two before the meeting, the skit should be rehearsed in the auditorium that will be used for the meeting, entrances and exits smoothed out, voice-carrying abilities tested, and the whole thing timed.

The exact forms which such skits can take are dictated by the specific circumstances in which they are used. For example, a three-day conference on school administration might be started with a few scenes in which an administrator is portrayed trying to "handle" a variety of typical problems. Possibly he could handle each situation twice, by method *A* and by method *B*, in which *A* is "typical" and *B* is "good," or in which both *A* and *B* have some "good" aspects and some "bad" aspects. Or, if a faculty steering committee wanted to launch the in-service program described in chapter 2, it might start with a classroom incident showing some teacher-pupil planning, and then follow this by scenes showing "students" from the class talking about it outside, the teacher talking about it to two other teachers, and one of the students telling his parents about it at supper.

Or, for a final and more difficult example, suppose a local League of Women Voters wants to present a program on taxation. It might start with a role-played skit of one of those family conferences in which the adolescent daughter wants a new party dress, which leads papa into giving a practical lesson on economics, from which the group gets into the business of taxation and looks for all the ways they pay taxes—and ends with the positive question of what all our taxes pay for. The difficulty of these scenes is that taxation is not in itself a dramatic subject: the drama has to come in the building up and reduction of conflict between the players, and the tax business is grafted on. But it still can make the point that we are affected by taxation, and that is a fair way to begin.[3]

This kind of role-playing is most effective when the problem is one which is controversial or threatening, so that it is hard to discuss. By simply portraying it as accurately as possible, it is possible to avoid the need to characterize it, and thus avoid as well the implied evaluations connoted in practically all use of language.

Purpose 2.—To help communicate a specific problem so people will have something "real" to talk about as the basis for discovering their own problems.

When a group of people are working toward better methods of dealing with various kinds of situations, it is almost inevitable that at some point they will get off into "experience swapping": "You know, I was in a situation like that last week. His secretary said he was out, but I didn't believe her, so I began making friends with her to prove I wasn't really out to hurt anyone, and then she. . . ." At this point, the chairman could say, "Why don't you show us, Mr. Brown? Anyone in the group look to you like the secretary you are talking about? Miss Jackson? Why not take her in the hall and give her enough facts to go on, and while you are doing that we can try to make some guesses as to what you will say and how she will answer you." Then they come back and, in effect, show the group what Mr. Brown is talking about— but they show it more as it actually might happen and less in the way Mr. Brown wants them to think it happened. It is more "real," and a much better starting point for insights, than the merely verbal description of the same events.

For setting a problem which is to be analyzed and discussed, one wants a spontaneous performance. The hesitations and embarrassments and fishing-for-words and windy excursions are all evidence to be considered in trying to understanding the dynamics of the situation. In fact, without these, the group may find it hard to get started in a discussion.

3. I am indebted to a local League group for this suggestion—they said it worked pretty well.

Following the scene sketched above, Mr. Brown should be given first innings because it was *his* experience, and he may feel that Miss Jackson did not do justice to it. It is only fair to let him tell how the *real* situation was actually far more successful, and how it was different from this scene. After that, the group will probably decide to discuss the scene anyway, not as Mr. Brown's actual experience, but as an event of interest in its own right. Thus it is removed from Brown's bailiwick, and he can enter into the discussion nondefensively. In the discussion, the kinds of questions most likely to be of value are such matters as: "Where did Mr. Brown seem to be making most headway, and least headway?" "How did the secretary, as portrayed by Miss Jackson, seem to react to his proposals?" "What assumptions did Mr. Brown seem to be making about the relationships between himself, the secretary, and her boss?"

Out of such questions, there emerges a variety of answers. And THIS is the real problem: to explain or reconcile or reduce the conflict implied by these different perceptions of the group. The next step should be the setting up of a variety of hypotheses to be studied and tested.

Another very similar use of role-playing to this, is in diagnosis of the problems the group is facing in its own operation as a group. Situations useful for this involve, usually, a leader (present or absent in the scene), members who do not get along, and several who do. For example, several teachers arrive at the night school building and find the door locked. They fall into discussion about the principal while waiting for him to appear and unlock the door.

In this situation, the attitudes of the members toward their leader will almost certainly be projected into the scene, as will some of the conflicts over leadership which the group may be having. The critical point in the discussion afterward is when somebody says: "I wonder if these 'teachers' weren't also saying some of the things we feel about our own leadership?" The most difficult problem in this diagnostic use of role-playing is to know how and when to make the transition from play-acting to the actual group. The most common mistake is for the leader to be too eager, putting everyone on the defensive by presenting an interpretation before the group is "ready" for it. The best suggestion is simply that if the group is "ready" someone else will think of the question all by himself.

Purpose 3.—To test various ways of dealing with a problem situation.

This is the commonest and, in many ways, the most generally successful use of role-playing. It is also closest in its details to sociodrama.

After a problem is defined, the group sets up a number of different portrayals of how it might be handled. Usually all the elements remain the same except for the central character who is trying to deal with the situation.

A good example of this use was in a foremen training institute. A question arose as to the difficulty of handling infractions of rules without jeopardizing good long-term relations with the men. The foremen had been forced to come to this "training session"; and were not at all sure they needed training. But when the foremen were invited to suggest a tough situation of this sort, they got a good deal of satisfaction out of posing the following problem:

"One of the best spray-painters in the division is caught smoking for the third time. There is a rule: 'Three times and you're out.' The man is a Negro, and tends to feel that white foremen are against him. He has a good record, except for the smoking, and is due for promotion soon. Everyone knows he should be promoted. You are the foreman. What would you do?"

One of the foremen was picked by the group to play the worker. Three others said they would show ways of dealing with the situation. Each of the foremen tried his luck. Two of them offered the man all sorts of fatherly advice and tried to appeal to his better nature. The third one fired him, and then explained what he would have to do to get back on the payroll, and how he might go about saving some of his past performance record if he did come back. The group finally saw that this was actually the only alternative they had.

A fourth man spoke up: he would like to show another way to handle such a scene. Invited to go ahead, he walked up to the "worker," grabbed him by the shirt front, said, "Smoking again!" smashed his cigar in his face and threw him out, to the accompaniment of obscenity and profanity on both sides. The group reacted vigorously and hilariously. Without attempting to explain the dynamics at this point, we can at least predict that from this point on the training session was not only not resisted, it was enthusiastically entered into. Both sides had been faced, and the reservations were gone.

In general, the chief procedures in this use of role-playing are:

1. Pick a typical, familiar, and problematic situation.
2. Demonstrate different ways of dealing with it, without trying to make one "bad" and another "good."
3. Prepare the audience to look for differences in the way the characters act (descriptive) and how they feel (inference, usually).
4. "Cut" each scene as soon as it has made its point or presented an adequate sample of behavior.
5. Discuss the scenes, writing on the blackboard the group's answers to the questions.
6. Check the various ideas as to how the characters felt against the testimony of the characters themselves.
7. Go from this point into discussion of the different assumptions on which action was based, or into generalizations that may be true of other situations "like" these, or into incidents in the history of the group that come to mind, or into possible explanations of why people react the way they were portrayed.

Purpose 4.—To develop "sensitivity."

It is possible to "plant" into a scene rather subtle factors which the group needs practice in working with.

For example: A surprising number of situations involve someone trying to get someone else to do something: give money, sign a petition, write a letter, serve on a board, buy a product or service, come to a meeting, pay a bill, etc. In a fair percentage of cases, the person being worked on does not comply. He gives reasons such as lack of time, lack of money, prior contribution of effort or of funds, or, possibly, lack of concern or interest. Often these actually are his reasons, but in many cases one may correctly feel that they are not his real reasons. It is thus important to learn to be sensitive to what the other fellow is really saying, underneath his excuses, and such sensitivity can be developed or aided by role-playing.

For a demonstration, pairs of people go out of the room to prepare scenes. In each scene, one person is trying to get the other to do something, and the other is resisting. In resisting, he is told to give one set of reasons but actually to be dead set against the proposal for some deeper, possibly irrational reason, such as lack of trust in the demander, jealousy of the demander's status, objections to the morals of the group the demander represents, basic unwillingness to give except as a means to personal power, some hidden but treasured slight stored up over the years, etc.

The discussion following these scenes needs to be handled with care because the group can say deeply anxiety-arousing things when it is hunting around for a "deep" interpretation. If the trainer gets satisfaction out of dissecting personalities, he should not try this technique. A good example of its proper use is given in connection with Meeting V, chapter 5.

It probably should be pointed out, to keep the record straight, that this kind of use should *not* give people the idea that they are going to be able to overcome deep resistances; it serves merely to help them understand better the dynamics of interpersonal relations.

Other uses of role-playing are legion:

1. In role-reversal, the scene is played twice, with the protagonists taking each other's roles the second time. Typical situations: conflict between worker and foreman, parent and child, white and Negro.

2. "Alter egos" may be provided as auxiliary characters who "reveal" private unexpressed thoughts of the actors. Typical situations: one man refuses to help another; this person feels fearful, hesitant, angry—but denies that he does.

3. "Consultants" may be provided to advise an actor as to what he should do next at various choice-points within the scene. Action is stopped or "frozen" while the actor discusses with his consultants. Typical situation: four consultants giving advice from four different points of view to a "leader" trying to run a difficult staff meeting.

4. The audience may be used as consultants who watch a scene, then form buzz groups to diagnose how the situation could have been played better. The "leader" is briefed by a representative from each of the consultant groups, and then replays the

scene trying consciously to take the suggestions into account. Typical situation: demonstration and training activity for a "leadership conference."

In conclusion, we should like to remind the reader that the chief precaution for handling discussion subsequent to role-playing sessions is always and forever to maintain the attitude that we have in front of us a sample of behavior to look at, but we are not competent to judge whether it is at all typical of the actual personalities of the role-players. Such speculations must be ruled out. And second, it is good policy to follow the group's lead in the discussion. If members get into a discussion of "deep" factors that may be involved, one can keep the discussion "safe" by turning it onto the question of: "What further evidence would one need to decide among these hunches?" If the group wants to discuss the scene at a seemingly superficial level, that is their privilege and probably is evidence that they are not yet ready to go deeper. Such evidence should be respected.[4]

MODEL TECHNIQUE NO. 2: BUZZ SESSIONS

The technique of "buzz groups" appears to have been invented by Dr. Donald Phillips at Michigan State University. The "Phillips 66" technique is one of breaking the large audience into small groups of six members each, having them introduce themselves to each other, and then talk for six minutes to find answers to some questions assigned to the whole audience. One of the six people acts as chairman and another as recorder; the latter reports back to the total group the deliberations of his buzz group.

There seems to be little reason for insisting that each group must contain exactly six people: this merely complicates setting up the groups. The time of six minutes also seems arbitrary: it should depend on how big or how interesting or intriguing the question is, how much people have to say about it, and how much digression they need, etc. In general, the simplest way to tell when the group discussion has gone on long enough is to ask several groups how much more time they need after they have gotten well started. An alternative is to wait until a drop in noise volume

4. The journal *Group Psychotherapy* (New York: Beacon Press) contains many articles about the uses of sociodrama and psychodrama.

shows either that the groups have nothing more to say or that they are now soberly trying to work on the problem (as distinguished from a sharing of off-the-cuff reactions). For working toward serious solutions, more formal working committees should be used, with planning for adequate resources.

The buzz-group technique has changed many meetings from passive listening seances into active, alert, and action-oriented sessions. The technique properly used can accomplish a great deal in moving the group toward purposive activity. It is highly flexible and easy to use. Let us describe the steps in a typical buzz-group situation, and then show some of the many ways the technique has been found useful.

1. First, the entire audience must be instructed very clearly about (*a*) what it is to discuss, and (*b*) what and how it is to report back to the total group.

a) The matter to be discussed should be something the audience needs and is ready to discuss. There is implied, then, a warming-up activity, such as role-playing, to get the audience "ready" to talk, and to give them some immediate experience as a point of departure for their discussion. The question may then be formulated in such terms as: What are all the things you see which might be done to improve our neighborhood? What additional examples of this sort of thing have happened to you? What might the leader do differently to improve the situation we just saw? What do you suggest as steps we must take to solve this problem? What questions shall we address to our resource person? Which of these suggested topics do you think, after preliminary discussion, is the most appropriate for us to start work on? What instructions would you like to give to our delegate before he goes to that council meeting? (It helps to write the questions on a large blackboard visible to all.)

b) The definition of the product to be brought back to the total group also can be varied: "Let's just see how many different ideas we can get from all the buzz groups"; or: Prepare one person from each group to be part of a panel to discuss in front of the group all the most important suggestions emerging from his buzz group; or: "Let's use the buzz groups as an opportunity for each person to try out his ideas in a small group, and then, if he would like to report the ideas to the total group, he will have his chance."

2. The audience is given good reasons for discussing in smaller groups. The best reason is probably the "real" one: "There are so many of us that it will be hard for us all to be heard." The audience, therefore, may properly be urged to work out a two-stage process in which everyone has his say to a few others, with each small group summarizing its findings and reporting them to the total group. Or it might be pointed out that for a controversial subject, it would probably be a good idea for each person to have a chance to rehearse his arguments in a small, informal group before presenting them to the total audience. Or again, it can be made clear that by dividing into thirty groups, thirty people can talk at a time instead of just one, which means thirty times as much discussion and, therefore, many more useful ideas.

3. If there are special roles, such as chairman or recorder for the buzz groups, the audience should be reminded of this by the director of the meeting.

4. The audience is then instructed in the most convenient way to break up into groups: for instance, everyone in the odd rows can stand up, turn his chair around to face the row behind, and then sit down. Then the audience can divide into groups of not more than eight or ten, and start discussing. The director acts with confidence as though this were the most natural thing in the world.

5. As the buzz groups begin, the director wanders around and listens to conversations from each group; he may decide that the question is not clear enough, and interrupt the proceedings long enough to restate the problem. He should also be sure that nobody is left out of a group unless he wants to be left out. But in general, the director should not participate in the buzz-group deliberations because the object is to get the *group* into discussion, not the director.

6. The director judges when the discussion is beginning to wear thin, or be repetitious, or lack interest. He may then call out a two-minute warning, and finally terminate the buzzing.

7. The total group is reconvened, and the reporting-back procedure is started.

This procedure implies the kinds of opportunities provided through buzz sessions. First, the groups are small, the people have been introduced, and the director is on the other side of the room. These factors combine to make possible a relatively free or candid expression of individual feeling, such as may be needed after an exciting or emotion-arousing presentation. When used for this purpose, adding a chairman and recorder vitiates some of the freedom by restoring these notes of formality; these roles may not be desirable.

Second, the fact that the buzz groups are unsupervised by the director or anyone else in charge means that they have to take responsibility for their own operation. In effect, leadership is transferred from the "officials" to the people themselves. This is desirable for such functions as deciding whát the meeting should talk about, letting each individual discover the extent to which he is intcrcstcd in proposcd actions, appraising thc organization's program, discussing recommendations, etc.

Thus the buzz group offers a natural and useful transition from the listening situation to the decision of each individual to act. It is an intermediate step in the movement of responsibility from the officials to the small groups to the individuals. It is this dynamic which causes meetings sometimes to change their whole action orientation as a result of the informal small-group discussions. What happens is that each individual suddenly finds that he has the role of an active participant at the meeting: his action later is merely further active participation required to get closure in the role begun in the buzz group.

Third, the fact that a lot of talking goes on at once means that surveys and polls can be taken very rapidly. The situation becomes one in which one person in each group (the recorder) interviews the other members and lists the different ideas or suggestions they have. The various recorder's lists, particularly if they are made by recording each different idea on a separate 3- by 5-inch card, can be quickly shuffled, classified, and reported back to the total meeting.

The fact that there is opportunity for a lot of talking in an informal setting also means that people have a chance to rehearse their ideas or practice skills in a reasonably nonthreatening situation. Thus buzz groups can be set up as practice sessions for recording, observing, leading, summarizing, etc.

With this much general overview of the procedures involved, we may now examine a number of suggestive uses of the technique.

Example 1.—To get a meeting started on significant problems, with the members assuming considerable responsibility.

A student club which was limping along with no very clear or significant objectives, invited Professor Thomas to tell them about "The Student's Role in Curriculum Decisions." Thomas guessed that this topic implied a wish for more active participation in determination of the graduate school program, and he decided to act on that hunch. The meeting was scheduled in an informal social room within one of the academic buildings.

Thomas arrived ten minutes early, and a few of the students were already occupying easy chairs and not talking to each other. Acting on impulse, Thomas took the bull by the horns. He walked over to the student nearest the door, introduced himself, and said: "Let's pull your chair over here. I want you to meet some more nice people." The move was made, and Thomas introduced the first student to the second and third. Then he said: "I understand that I am expected to open the meeting in fifteen or twenty minutes. When I do, I shall start by asking the group: 'What sort of things that students do probably have an influence on our graduate courses?' Why don't you three sort of discuss this question now so you'll have some good suggestions we can start with?"

The indefatigable Thomas then moved on to the next student and repeated the performance. By the time he got halfway around the room, setting up buzz groups as he went, most of the chairs were taken, so he then gave his instructions to all the others: to introduce themselves and get started on his question.

At 8:15 the groups were still going strong, so Thomas gave them another fifteen minutes, called the meeting to order, and asked his question. The answers came quick and fast. The meeting retained its steam to the very end, and its final outcome was a decision that each student would observe in the next several meetings of one of his classes the kinds of questions raised by students during discussion periods, and the kinds of answers given by the teacher. They would then compare notes at the next club meeting and try to see what sort of assumptions the teachers' answers seemed to imply about the needs of the students asking the questions.

Comment: Thomas, of course, had the advantage of being used to having students act on his suggestions, and this gave him confidence enough to experiment. The students, too, he could count on as being rather starved for social interaction—why else would they stick with an ineffectual club program? His hunch was that along with this starvation for social relations there would also be a feeling of lack of "place" in the graduate school; and that if this were so there might be a good deal of energy available for taking some sort of action.

This meeting revived the club for a period of several months. It then subsided into its former lethargy, presumably because its need was satisfied by the making of a gesture or because it lacked the leadership skill required to build on its own experiences. Several of the club members enrolled the following quarter in one of Thomas' classes.[5]

Example 2.—To set up the agenda for a meaningful learning experience.

One evening at 7:30 P.M., "Red" Fredericks phoned Mr. Garth at home. He explained that he was running a series of lectures for home economics teachers on eight successive Wednesday nights, and that the speaker for tonight, who was flying down from Minneapolis, had been grounded in Milwaukee, and would be at least an hour late. In the meanwhile, the teachers were pouring in; what should he do?

Garth told "Red" to tell the teachers just what had happened, and suggest to them that since they were all familiar with the problems the speaker was going to talk about, they might gather in small groups to formulate the questions around which they would like to have the speaker organize his presentation. "Red" doubted that it would work, in view of the inexperience of the teachers in such situations but, faced with the alternative of an hour of tedious waiting, tried it anyway. The only demurral actually offered by the teachers was that possibly the speaker would

5. This incident was reported to me by Professor Thomas and several students.

not like having questions made up for him. "Red" took a chance and said he was certain that this particular speaker would be delighted to be able to talk to questions he could be sure the audience cared about.

The buzz groups went to work in some embarrassment, but quickly warmed up, because the problems were familiar and challenging. The teachers exchanged some of their own experiences, and were quite reluctant to come back together to list their questions on the board. "Red" thought fast, and asked the groups simply to put the questions on cards and give them to him; thus they could keep on talking. By the time the speaker arrived, the questions had been sorted and arranged in a pile in order of their popularity, as shown by the number of groups asking each.

The speaker was delighted. He thumbed through the questions quickly, estimated the amount of time he could allot for each, and then proceeded to give an excellent performance, for he was sure of his audience's interest, and their responsiveness was most rewarding to him.[6]

Comment: Sometimes an airline and an act of God conspire to make clear the difference between speaker as "stimulator" and speaker as resource person.

Example 3.—To overcome a feeling of helplessness or apathy, and to redirect a group toward action.

Overcoming feelings of defeatism is something that one seldom can manage by himself, and yet which no one else can manage for him. We have seen the process occur many, many times during "buzz sessions" within large community meetings, and the meeting described at the end of chapter 1 shows this use of buzz sessions.

The people in the audience are first given a chance, through role-played problems, to acknowledge to themselves that the staged problems are theirs as well. This recognition is facilitated by the reactions of the rest of the audience; it is easier to admit things everyone else is admitting. The second part of the program gives the "facts," and this information acts in two ways:

1. It shows how large, serious, and difficult of solution the

6. Reported to me by both "Red" and Garth.

problems are—which may increase resentment and frustration; and

2. Because the problems become much more sharply defined, it increases a feeling of confidence in the possibility of doing something. In effect, the information shows the targets against which energy needs to be directed, and this knowledge makes more energy available to be directed.

The buzz sessions are given the question: What specific things can be done about the situation causing concern? After the chairs are rearranged and people have introduced themselves, the conversation becomes lively. The first subject of discussion almost invariably involves things people feel angry about, and not the assigned question. These things usually include community conditions (overcrowding), personal complaints ("How the neighbors' kids tear up my petunias"), and anecdotes ("How I tried to do something about it but nobody would help"). All this, and more besides, finds expression *before* the groups can start thinking constructively about specific behaviors or plans.

When they finally get going on what can be done, the list grows rapidly, with plenty of excursions into side issues. When the groups reconvene and share their lists with others, there is great social reinforcement and strengthening of the forward-looking attitude, and the reorientation from defeatism to optimistic determination is largely accomplished.

Comment: This illustration reveals the peculiar and unique usefulness of the buzz session: to provide opportunity to "blow off" enough steam that one can get to work—or, to be more precise about it, to give people a chance to reduce some of their anxieties so that they can direct energy into trying to better the situation.

The kind of transition described above would be most unlikely to occur under the guiding hand of the chairman and within the total group. But it is a kind of transition people in general try to make, for it is driven by the need for adequacy. The usual groupings which arise spontaneously after the boss dismisses a staff meeting, or following a meeting where the PTA chairman acted arbitrarily—these informal "gripe groups" help individuals meet needs to reduce their anxieties. Having a meaningful work question and knowing that a report is expected enables people in small groups to discipline their cathartic expression and rather rapidly turn energy into constructive channels.

Example 4.—To test a set of ideas, and to increase communication between speaker and audience.

A simple but effective illustration of buzz sessions in this connection is described by Stuart Chase in *Roads to Agreement.*[7] The audience of about 310 people was divided into six sections, and each section given an assignment *before* Chase began his lecture. The "external" demands were to improve *Roads to Agreement*, then being written, and to improve training methods used at Bethel and "back home" by the delegates. The six specific assignments were:

"Group 1 was to listen for implications in the lecture which might prove useful to Bethel.

"Group 2 was to listen for ideas which the speaker should elaborate later, things he had slurred over. . . .

"Group 3 was to listen for high points of the talk, and later emphasize them to the audience.

"Group 4 was to think about additional data for possible inclusion in Chase's book.

"Group 5 was to listen to his description of areas of human conflict and see what areas could be added.

"Group 6 was to concentrate on suggestions for making the book more readable. . . ."[8]

For these demands to be met, it was clear that Chase would have to make clear the purposes of the book, summarize its contents, and read the group a sample sufficiently long that they could get valid impressions of the style of the book. And it was clear that the audience would have to listen, not just give stereotypic responses.

After the speech, each of the six sections of the audience was divided further into three or four buzz groups to discuss its assignment. Spokesmen from all the buzz groups within each section met together to prepare a report for their section, and the six final reports were presented to the entire group. These six reports took as much time as Chase's initial speech.

7. New York: Harper & Bros., 1951, pp. 93–96.
8. *Ibid.*, p. 94.

Comment: Was the purpose really satisfied? Was communication increased between speaker and audience by reducing the subconscious resistances on both sides to communication? Chase says of his feelings during the lecture: "The audience gave me a different feeling from any I had ever encountered. The words did not bounce back as they often do from a bored or indifferent aggregation; they went home, but I was not entertaining anybody. The words went home but were turned around and examined before being taken in. The audience was listening as I never have been listened to from a platform—not agreeing, not disagreeing, neither hostile nor especially friendly, weighing and thinking."[9] And the audience, on questionnaires filled in after the meeting, indicated clearly a feeling that the experience had significance for them.

The usual speaker-audience situation is one in which the audience is trying to take from the speaker something of himself: his ideas or wisdom. Possession of these ideas, however, is what gives the speaker his prestige and power. To what extent this results in speakers not really wanting to "give," one cannot be sure. It is clear, however, that the situation recognizes only one direction of demand, from audience to speaker; the demands the speaker makes on the audience for respect, warmth, adulation, or audible approval are not explicitly facilitated and are often not even admitted.

The simplest way to change the speaker situation from one of conflict to one of at least partial co-operation is to arrange matters in such a way that speaker and audience together face a set of externalized demands. Thus an externalized demand could be to improve the speaker's speech—as if it were, as presented, a committee report to be modified by the whole meeting before final adoption. Another externalized demand could be to evaluate the group's present practices in view of a set of ideas presented by the speaker. In either case, speaker and audience have a reason and a way to collaborate, and this greatly facilitates communication.

9. *Ibid.*, pp. 94–95.

MODEL TECHNIQUE NO. 3: PANEL DISCUSSION

The panel discussion is a conversation among several people, held in front of a larger group. It is one of the most abused techniques; but it can be extremely effective—provided it is properly planned and guided. There are a variety of reasons why people might make use of a panel discussion. We shall list some of these reasons, good and bad, and discuss their implications. Then we shall try to suggest how to set up and use the panel discussion technique.

Reason 1.—"Let's have naturalness and spontaneity—it gets people more interested." This is the watchword on the radio round tables and panels. When a panel *does* have spontaneity and interest—which is rather seldom—it is because it is carefully planned and rehearsed.

The notion that a panel is easy to use because "all you have to do is get a few quick-on-the-draw speakers together" results merely in a number of quick-on-the-draw speakers sitting around and talking. They may or may not say anything worth hearing or relevant to the program topic. Not having any clear idea of what to talk about, they will probably end with experience-swapping or abstractions.

Naturalness and spontaneity are the result of careful organization of topics to be discussed, definition of the point of view or role of each of the panelists, and a moderator whose main job is to help the audience and the panel know at all times just what is being discussed and where it fits into the over-all discussion.

Reason 2.—A panel makes possible the discussion of the topic from several different points of view, and, when these get into conflict, the audience gets drawn into the discussion.

A panel provides for several different points of view only if the members *have* different points of view and if the moderator makes sure that each person in turn offers his comments on the same topic. As any mediator or leader knows, conflict growing out of different points of view usually disappears when the discussants agree to talk about particular cases; to maintain conflict usually means to maintain high-level abstraction.

The conflict—the struggle between giants—which was counted

on to get people worked up, also is likely to disappear for another reason: it is bad manners to fight in public. The panelists who get into violent dispute in front of the group may actually arouse the audience's interest, but the interest will be in the personalities of the protagonists, not in the merits of the argument.

If all that is wanted is a good conflict, why not just set up a well-planned debate, in which conflict is controlled and expected, and let it go at that?

Reason 3.—Dividing up the presentation makes it less of a burden on any one person.

This is correct, and the result is a series of short speeches. This is not a discussion, and is not a panel discussion, either.

Reason 4.—A panel discussion is a good way to start discussion from the floor.

This is true when the panel discussion is planned to open up issues, sharpen questions, present ideas in a stimulating and colorful way, etc. But the panel can also kill questioning. Here are some effective discussion-stopping techniques I have seen panels use (not usually on purpose):

1. Overwhelm the audience with its vast experience, prestige, subtlety, or cleverness.

2. Exhaust the topic, giving clear and satisfactory answers to all the questions likely to occur to anyone.

3. Bore the audience so thoroughly that anyone asking a question and thus starting the panel going again will be seen by the rest of the audience as a candidate for tarring and feathering.

4. Become so cozy with each other that the audience feel like intruders and wonder if they should not just tiptoe out.

Reason 5.—A panel of well-known speakers draws a bigger crowd than does a lecture by one man.

It depends on the man.

These considerations lead to the following suggestions for setting up a panel discussion:

1. Decide what the program is about, what it is hoped will be accomplished through the program, and what sequence of parts or activities will be needed to accomplish its purposes. After this

is done, the requirements the panel discussion is to meet will be evident.

2. Consider the range of kinds of people or roles required on the panel: a civic leader, a housewife, a welfare worker, a policeman, etc.

3. Decide who to invite to be on the panel in each category, and explore with them how they would fit in and what they think they could do to help. If the exploration is reassuring, invite them to serve. If not, invite them to suggest someone else "to take their place."

4. Get the panel together for a rehearsal, and let the moderator summarize the main outline of the discussion. The panel can discuss the outline, correct it, reorganize it, and block out in general each person's approach to each point. The panel members also can decide what, if any, signals to use to get the moderator to call on them.

5. Have the moderator prepare a final outline, which will then be duplicated and sent to the others on the panel. He should probably indicate the approximate distribution of time among the topics.

6. At the meeting, have the chairman introduce the moderator (if they are separate individuals), who in turn defines the problem the panel is to tackle and then introduces the others. As the discussion proceeds, the moderator restates the questions, makes sure the points agreed upon are made, and summarizes at the end of each section of discussion. The summary should probably end with a question or two (preferably written on a blackboard) that will stimulate the audience.

7. Summarize at the end in such a way that the audience is clear as to just where the panel is leaving the major problem.

8. Have the chairman introduce the next activity, which may be one or more of the following:

a) Invite questions from the floor to the panel, in a discussion led by the moderator; or

b) Divide into buzz groups to react to the questions and then report back; or

c) Divide into discussion groups for prolonged discussion. Each discussion group may take a few of the questions, and the audience can subdivide according to interest in the questions.

d) Ask for additional questions to be added to the list the panel identified, and then use a rapid voting procedure to discover the priority of interest in the questions—in effect this amounts to making up the agenda for the remaining discussion.

Example.—To open up a big problem.

The most successful panel discussion I have seen was planned by the steps outlined above. It had to do with neighborhood conservation, and the speakers represented each of the major types of organizations or agencies interested in this problem. The outline of topics was logical:

    a) What are the evidences that the neighborhood is deteriorating?
    b) What are the forces contributing to deterioration?
    c) What are the major ways to fight deterioration?
    d) Which of these ways are now being tried, and by whom?
    e) What specific things ought to be done right now, and later?

Not all the speakers contributed to all the questions. In so far as possible, they made their points by citing clear-cut illustrations from the experiences of their own agencies. The moderator stated each question, and tried to make it clear and challenging. He summarized frequently, and he sometimes made positive evaluations of the impact of the speaker's organization with respect to particular forms of action.

The next planned activity was to be buzz groupings, but the audience upset this by firing in questions and offering comments the minute the panel discussion was over. The moderator turned over some of the questions to other members of the audience whom he knew had relevant experience to contribute. For two questions, which were matters of fact the panel could not answer, the moderator asked if anyone in the audience knew the answer (and found people who did). The panel also participated in asking questions of each other and of the audience. The discussion shifted from audience to moderator to panel to audience; it became, toward the end, simply a free discussion with the moderator summarizing from time to time, and the people calling on each other.

The meeting ended forty minutes overtime when the moderator said it was almost time to go home. The chairman, capitalizing on the great interest of the group, suggested that a number of people might volunteer to become a committee to plan a follow-up meeting (which had not been anticipated). Twelve volunteers came forward, set a date for their meeting, and the chairman adjourned the session. It was another hour before everyone finally left.

Some other uses of panel discussion: panels can be used after presentations of buzz-group thinking to comment interpretatively on the various suggestions, highlighting the most significant suggestions, relating them to each other, and otherwise clarifying and organizing the ideas from all the groups. Even in an ordinary discussion situation, a panel of two observers can sometimes be used to summarize the discussion as a basis for helping the group see where to go next in the discussion. Or a panel of two or three resource people can be provided to be called on by the group at any point at which they need technical information.

MODEL TECHNIQUE NO. 4: THE GROUP INTERVIEW

This technique deserves more use than it currently gets. The group interview fits very well into problem-solving meetings of any sort; and it probably provides for the most effective use of resource people.

The group interview is simply a situation in which one person, the interviewer, asks questions of several others. He ordinarily has a list of questions developed by the group or by a planning committee, and he usually asks the same question of each interviewee in turn. A useful "house rule" for the interviewees is that they should respond to the questions only with ideas that have not already been given. To give all the interviewees equal visibility and status, the interviewer begins each round with a different interviewee.

Example.—Reporting buzz-group ideas.

The problem of presenting to the total group the results of discussion in fifteen buzz groups can be a time-consuming and boring process. Group interviewing is especially useful as a way of not only presenting the thinking of the buzz groups but also for organizing their reports and appraising the importance of their suggestions. It works like this:

The reporter from each of the buzz groups comes to the front and sits down. His job is to represent the *thinking* of his particular buzz group. The interviewer may use the list of questions assigned to the buzz groups (if there was one) as an interview schedule, or may simply ask each reporter for the most significant idea his group thought of. By a show of hands among the reporters, the popularity and acceptability of each idea can be tested. The more important ideas are written on the blackboard, both for future reference and to maintain a sense of constructive effort. Up to five questions can be handled with as many as twelve reporters without loss of interest among the larger group.

Other uses of group interviewing: Plans can be tested economically by interviewing a panel of selected people who are competent with respect to the plan under consideration; for example, a new personnel policy for use in a hospital can be examined by a panel composed of a doctor, a supervisor, a nurse, an aide, a service man, etc. Broad objectives such as "community improvement" can be broken down into component problems of the sort a club or class can deal with through the use of experts who thoroughly understand such problems, interviewed by a person who is thoroughly familiar with the resources of his group.

FURTHER NOTIONS FOR GROUP MEETINGS

Throughout this book there are numerous additional techniques suggested for a variety of other purposes. Chapter 11 is meant to help in the actual leading of discussion, as is also chapter 2. In general, we reiterate: the proper technique is one created to fit the requirements of the situation. The creative process is, however, helped by a background of knowledge and experience and ideas of what to look for, and images of what goes on, during discussion. The practical aim of this first part of the book has been to derive policies and principles for guiding operation in a variety of areas of social learning and action. These principles plus the concrete illustrations and models will, we hope, help equip the leader or planning committee with the analytical tools and insights they need.[10]

The chief omission of this chapter—and a critical one—is the recognition that a meeting is only one episode in the life of a group or community. Understanding the relevant social context of meetings is basic to proper diagnosis of objectives and to effective follow-up. The preceding five chapters develop a variety of contexts and show the kinds of backgrounds and motivations of which the planners of meetings ought to be aware. In addition, chairmen will find the content of chapters 10 and 11 pertinent to successful operation.

10. The reader is strongly urged to become familiar with *Adult Leadership*, a journal issued monthly by the Adult Education Association of the United States of America, 743 N. Wabash Ave., Chicago, Ill. Selected practical articles in this magazine could well be the subject of intensive study by small groups of leaders of all kinds of groups.

EXPLANATIONS: A PRELIMINARY NOTE

Behind every technology, every policy decision—indeed, every behavior—is a set of understandings of the nature of the processes one is dealing with. These understandings may be explicit or implicit, clear or vague, narrow in scope or comprehensive in insight. It is the purpose of Part II to present the range and kind of understandings that I believe are required for creative action.

Such a presentation involves a selection of ideas from the broad field of the social sciences, decisions about their effective organization, and policies for deciding in each case how "deep" to go. The central criterion I have used in making these judgments is the probable usefulness of the material for illumination and explanation of the technologies in Part I. It is my hope that the technologies will make the explanations more meaningful, and that the latter material will free the practitioner or technologist for experimentation leading to better technologies.

The development of Part II is based on several propositions: that the needs of individuals cause them to participate in groups; that the group as an organism exists to satisfy the purposes for which it was gathered together; that the group is influenced by the standards of the environing community and that actions taken by the group influence the community; and, finally, that through experiences in the groups of the community the individual develops and changes his pattern of needs. Thus the line of reasoning comes full circle.

More specifically, chapter 7 proposes that much of a person's behavior as a group member stems from his needs to work out his relationships to various groups and to resolve conflicts arising from the different approaches offered by different groups to the same problems of living. In chapter 8 we point out that the individual deals with these problems through processes of feel-

ing, thinking, and doing; and that the particular balance among these processes is characteristic of his personality and is learned through experiences with other people. In chapter 9 we look at the various sorts of realities with which experience deals and which we attempt to control through consciously applied methods. Chapter 10 explains the development of the group itself as a whole—a miniature society with its own standards of behavior, needs, and policies for controlling itself. In chapter 11 we discuss leadership as the means through which the group guides the creation of its culture, the attainment of its purposes, and the satisfaction of needs of individuals. We also examine some of the typical problems of leaders. In chapter 12 we attempt to make clear the notion that the operation of a group is not just a matter of the kinds of members and the competence of the leader; it is also a reflection of social conditions within the larger community. We indicate how groups contribute to the development of the community and to the state of intergroup relations.

Reference is made at appropriate points to earlier pages in which are explained or illustrated specific matters in further detail.

CHAPTER 7

We meet our needs as members of groups, and the ways we behave are the ways that we have learned in such groups. When confronted with alternative action possibilities, as in solving any genuine problem, the different possibilities are weighed partly in terms of their acceptability to our past groups—as we see them.

Social problem-solving requires the sorting out of "overlapping group memberships" and the selection of behavior in terms of the needs of the present "real" situation.

Membership: The Groups Within

It is a matter of common observation that individuals differ in their approach to people and problems—and to life in general. We use words like "optimistic," "cheerful," "suspicious," "wrapped up in himself," "driving," "lazy." We think of some people as being out-going, making friends easily, enjoying being with people and feeling free to make demands upon them. We may think of others as being withdrawn, reflective, finding it hard to ask or receive favors. These and many other characteristics of personality are developed through experiencing. The equipment or tendencies one inherits biologically and culturally are continually undergoing modification through communication and interaction with other people. The classic studies of the differences in personalities of identical twins reared in different family environments; the studies of the change in such a relatively stable property as the I.Q. as a result of changing the social environment; the fact that people can be redirected through therapy of various sorts—such studies support our belief that people may be affected in fundamental ways by the nature of their relationships with other people.

As observers and students of human behavior, we find certain directions of change or areas of concern which most people have in common. Thus most people want approval from others; they have a hunger for "belonging" to an identifiable group; they need to feel that they can be themselves—that they can express feelings spontaneously without fear of punishment. Various students of these problems cast the list of "needs" in different forms, but most students do act as if such needs exist. And in studying individual-group relationships, there is general agreement that part of an individual's energy during any meeting of persons goes into trying to meet these private needs as they exist in himself.

223

We believe that people learn the ways they can use to meet needs, and that they learn these ways through group experience. But the ways in which past groups, imaginary groups, and absent groups operate in influencing behavior need to be understood better than they are at present.

As one moves into detailed study of particular situations, it becomes clear that different things in a situation are seen as problems for different people. Thus, whatever kind of leadership a group has, there are likely to be some people who accept it and work with it, and there are likely to be some others who feel uncomfortable and who spend a good deal of energy "working on" it. These latter people may attack the leadership, may try to form cliques outside the group to act as pressure blocs, may withdraw from participation, and the like. We need explanations for these things—a way to understand them so that we can deal with them more effectively.

There is also the question of direction and growth. We know that groups and people may change as a result of working together; are there certain directions of change, certain goals toward which change tends? If there are, we need to understand these tendencies and take them into account. The more we can make use of them, the greater our results will be. When we work against "natural tendencies" we have to use much more energy to solve problems because we find everyone subconsciously resisting the ways of working. The final result of working against the group is that leadership has to use more policing, it has to give up its objectives, or it has to be sabotaged or overthrown.

To discuss and learn about these problems, we need to have concepts and ideas to work with. And we need to organize these concepts not as isolated ideas but as working tools which complement and supplement each other. I propose the concept of "membership" as one of the principal tools, central to thinking about the problems indicated above. The rest of this chapter will try to develop some of the meanings associated with this concept.

We shall begin with the classic picture of how social needs develop and how, through experience with other people, the individual learns to behave. We shall think of his characteristic tendencies toward certain patterns of behavior as his "personality." Next we shall consider how tensions are created within a person as a result of conflicting demands made on him by different groups in his past or present experience. In our speculations, we shall pursue this matter into the mind of the person, and will advance the thesis that much of the determination of individual behavior is through decisions reached by his own ad hoc "internal committee." Finally, we shall suggest the directions in which individuals and groups tend to change over a period of time. At this point we shall have the opportunity to summarize the rest of the material, and to see more clearly how these problems relate to each other.

THE CLASSIC PICTURE OF THE DEVELOPMENT OF PERSONALITY THROUGH SOCIAL EXPERIENCE

As a starting point we may begin with the baby. He is hungry, therefore restless. He makes a lot of motions, including vocal ones. Mother comes with the bottle. This happens many times, and he learns that yelling brings mother, even when he is not hungry, and that mothers are useful to reduce boredom, as well as to provide for material wants. He can do little for himself; he is dependent on others for nearly everything. He learns that every need-meeting activity involves a stronger person. He learns that this stronger person is not entirely reliable, that she may deny him at times, that she can even punish. He begins to work out ways of increasing the probability that this person will respond as he needs. Thus subconsciously he becomes a social strategist, and in many cases exerts real leadership (or even tyranny) over the household. The important thing for us to note is that even the simplest material problem of the baby has social overtones; co-operation is involved.

After a while, the human being learns to direct effort to provide and maintain the conditions under which his needs can be met; this becomes in itself a secondary or instrumental need, but it is just as real and more pervasive than most other needs. The problems of co-operation or competition, dependence or independence or interdependence arise as problems of ways of working to solve the problems of hunger, housing, group morale, etc. The attitudes, theories, and skills which one forms and uses to deal with people become, in effect, a world-view, and the key to prediction of one's behavior.

People differ in their availability for interaction. Strangers are mostly not available. As acquaintance deepens, the breadth and depth of communication possibilities increase. People who have significant usefulness for each other tend to hold many beliefs, attitudes, and notions in common. They are likely to subscribe to a set of common purposes; and the existence of shared purposes gives them the right to make demands on each other.

When two or more people have the sort of communality described above, we think of them as constituting a "group." The quality of a person's possible interactions, his gratifications and satisfactions, depends upon his position—central or peripheral—in the group. The extent of his affiliation determines his opportunity to meet needs, e.g., to compare ideas with other people, to be stimulated or challenged, to unleash energy of others in his own behalf. In any particular group, the quality of each individual's affiliation is known, not always consciously. The group learns to act as if it differentiated roles; it comes to expect, under certain conditions, that Joe will plunge in with new ideas, that Mary will be concerned about the nonparticipants, that Jack will be sensitive to the "democraticness" of procedures used, that Ida will waste time and block action, and so on.

The development of such expectancies operates to give the group the security of being able to anticipate and ward off interpersonal problems it cannot solve. When a member tries to change his pattern of behavior, he may meet resistance from the group because he is upsetting their ability to predict his behavior and to know how to respond to it.

The amount of motivation one has depends a good deal on the amount of reward one thinks one can get. The fellow who thinks that whatever he does will not influence the group may either become a nonparticipant or he may fight the group. To get the approval which reassures one and increases the desire to participate and tackle problems, one must know how the member role is defined—what will be judged relevant or irrelevant—and what standards of performance will be applied—what will be judged helpful or destructive. Just as groups develop expectations through which roles are stabilized, so they develop standards for judging quality and, eventually, for acceptance and rejection of members.

It is as if a set of agreements is reached in the group, and each member is party to these agreements, and controlled by them in his opportunities and his rewards. The group may respond to violation of the agreements either with punishment of the "criminal" or with reconsideration of the rules to see why they were broken. The latter method, itself reached by agreement, is the way the group can continue to exist in the face of changes external to itself but reflected by members. The former method, of punishment, is unhealthy, and, in the long run, self-defeating.

It is to the interests of all members continually to be ready to modify their agreements. The member behavior most significant in this adjustive process is expression of feeling. A member communicates his reactions to the group's expectancies for roles, its ways of working, and its values, by the emotion-carrying elements in his statements. Thus, in a training group recently, we found that over a course of fifteen meetings every other statement (on the average) had some recognizable feeling in it. Feelings represent the members' evaluation of the situation, and they have to be taken into account as data needed to understand and improve the situation.

The word "climate" is used to speak about the state of affairs in the group with respect to dealing with feelings. A "free" climate is characterized by two properties: first, there are agreed-upon limits to expression, but within these limits anything can be expressed without fear of reprisal. Second, there is analysis of expressed feelings as important contributions to be reflected upon and understood. The group in which there is freedom to fight but not to work is one in which anything can be said but nothing can be reflected upon. The climate is one of license, not of freedom. Individuals do not grow in such a group.

The most common feeling to be expressed and dealt with is aggression. Without aggression there is slavish dependence, "drifting with the tide." Every new gain in maturity has to be fought for, and every planned change requires aggression to carry it out. One of the most serious problems in thinking about socialization is the tendency to equate aggression with hostility, resulting in rejection or guilt about both.

The rules of operation one learns in a face-to-face group are the most real ones. These rules for working together and for expressing one's self become generalized in the individual's value-attitude system, and these rules plus his learned reactions to them describe his personality. Even when a person is alone, he tends to think and act in accordance with these learned agreements, the culture of the group. (The soliloquies of two executives [pages 103–8] imply numerous relationships among past experiences in groups, attitudes and values, and personality.)

Thus runs the classical picture of the development of social personality, of one's own way of life. The "group" is seen as the frame of reference and the environment in which the individual moves; and "membership" describes the quality of the relationship between the individual and the group. What, specifically do we mean by a "group" and by "membership"?

DEFINITIONS OF "GROUP" AND "MEMBERSHIP"

Man lives in a complex world. He relates himself in different ways under different conditions to various parts or aspects of his world. He differentiates among objects, both material and abstract in nature, and different objects have different meanings for him in various situations. The meanings people have for him and the way he relates to them are important objects of inquiry because men are interdependent; all men are involved somehow in everything man does.

In immediate experience, at any one time, only a relatively small number of people are involved with a person. We use the word "group" to indicate these people. Depending on the act and the situation, the group not only contains different people, but the relationships among them are different. And the variety of relationships among people involved together in a situation is so extensive that we have to conclude that "groupness" is a general impression, not a specific characteristic. It is not helpful to try to mark some amount or kind of "groupness" as typical of a "group," nor to say that any lesser amount of "groupness" may characterize a "collection" but not a "group." In other words, the dichotomy "group–not group" is of little value.

We form our impressions of "groupness" from a large number of specific properties of the collection. Here are some of the properties that people have in mind when they talk about "groups":

1. The membership can be defined. We know who is in the group, either by name or by definition of the kind of person who belongs. Thus we know the names of those at a party. This group is defined easily, its size is known to the member. On the other hand, in a national organization to which we pay dues, we may not know its size, but we have an image of the "sort" of person who belongs. And when we send in dues or run for office or take on any other responsibility on behalf of the association, this image of the other members affects our behavior.

2. The members think of themselves as constituting a group. There is a shared image of the collection; this image marks it off from other collections. To paraphrase an old quip, a group is a bunch of people who think they are a group.

3. There is a sense of shared purpose among members. The members can state some "reasons" for their being a group, and the reasons include a concept of something striven for, some advantage to be gained through mutual effort. (There is often a distinction between the reasons members give, and the reasons a student of the group might think were more important. In other words, there are not only consciously but also subconsciously understood aspects of the group *raison d'être*.)

4. There is a feeling of greater ease of communication among members than between members and nonmembers. There is a feeling of greater intimacy and of preference for others within the group.

5. One has a sense of approval or disapproval for himself and his actions, receiving feedback from others in the group. One takes this information into account in determining subsequent behavior.

6. One feels an obligation to respond to the behavior of others in the group. The embarrassment most people feel during a

silence in a group probably contains feelings of frustration at not knowing how to respond. (There may be some feeling of personal inadequacy—one cannot carry out his felt obligation to respond.)

7. A member has expectations for certain ways of behaving in the various situations in which the group finds itself. He is aware of performance standards, and of limits to expression; of criteria of relevance which he can use to control and direct his behavior in such a way that he can obtain reward for participating.

8. There are leadership policies and roles. There is a recognition of the need to co-ordinate effort efficiently, to maintain the conditions required for problem-solving. Policies are formed at some level of explicitness about how the group is to guide itself. There is agreement on what sort of authority will ultimately guide decision-making.

9. There emerges a status system, a hierarchy of worth of individuals to the group. In a mature group, this hierarchy is based on demonstrated ability to contribute to the group—to further its interests, either within it or in its behalf. In an immature group, this hierarchy may be based on such factors as social class, wealth, occupation, age, number of children, years of experience, etc. But the hierarchy exists, and members have clear ideas of where they fit along the scale.

Different students emphasize different dimensions from the list above; and the list can be written in different ways. Basically, we may think of "groupness" as an over-all impression of the extent of involvement people have with each other, of the ways they can interact with each other, and of the methods of control of behavior they accept for each other and for themselves. No two groups are alike in the various dimensions indicated above. There may be considerable "involvement" but very inadequate leadership. There may be a well-shared set of purposes unaccompanied by much differentiation among member roles. There are vast differences in the patterning of these dimensions in "autocratic," "democratic," and "lassez-faire" groups.

One can think of groups arising out of social conditions, such as contiguity or the need to solve problems; chapter 1 presents a perfect example. One may also think that groups arise out of the need for membership—out of the need to have people available for interaction, the need for feelings of significance and influence, the need for expressing feeling and getting the reactions of others to it as a way to self-understanding. The laboratory group (chapter 5) exemplifies these processes.

In any case, membership is the perception by the individual of the quality of his relationships to the group. The broadest concept of membership would be the individual's perceptions of his role in the human race. Membership is a feeling which integrates the individual's feelings and ideas about his participation with others.

If a person belonged only to one group, or if all groups were alike (making them one group in effect), then life would be much less complicated than it is at present. But what happens when an individual belongs simultaneously to several groups, and his behavior represents an acting-out of his memberships in two or more groups at the same time? For this is the state of affairs in our situation today, when our communities are divided, and the various groups which exist are heterogeneous.

TYPES OF REFERENCE GROUPS

What different sorts of groups are these, in which an individual may hold membership, and to which he may address his behavior?

First, of course, there is the actual group of people he is meeting with in a given time and place. This is the only group he can really interact with, test ideas, appraise himself, and learn from. Only in the actual group can one have new experience, new raw materials for reflection and challenge. In any actual group, however, there are differences in member role, and in the extent to which different people matter to each other. In any meeting, we tend to address our remarks to a few individuals, for these are the ones whose reactions we trust or are worried about. In a group of twenty people or so, the effective group for each of us is probably not much larger than eight. This effective group, different for each member, may change its composition from time to time; but whatever its composition, it represents to us the total group. We have the feeling that we can influence the total group through these people. They are, in a sense, gatekeepers to our influence and to the exertion of our rights of membership.

Second, there is the group we represent. We are sent as its official representative (or we think we are so sent), and it is expected of us that we shall speak for our group. We represent its wishes, its membership and power, its ideas about how to proceed. We fight for these things and, in so doing, we feel that we are fighting for our group. Thus we have vested interests.

A second origin of the vested interest is almost the opposite. We may quite unnecessarily defend our group with a sort of blind loyalty, and it is possible that the motivation for this stems from feelings of lack of membership. We are worried about our place in the group and we therefore defend the group to assure ourselves that we belong—that there is something there to defend.

In either case, however, the person reacts both to the actual group and to the vested interest group as it is carried about in his mind. If he is anxious about his membership in this group, the actual group may experience considerable difficulty in working with him. When a person comes as an appointed representative, he owes it to himself to find out what problems the group he represents consider only tentatively settled in their minds, what problems he is not to accept suggestions about, and, finally, what actions his group wants taken in case of head-on collision with the actual group.

A third type of group to which people refer their behavior might be characterized as the abstracted group or the "relic" group. This is a faceless group, which the individual probably could not identify at all accurately. The people, roles, and actions have dropped out of memory; all that is left is coercive belief. The public in the phrase "public opinion" is an abstracted group. So is the "community" for most people; so are the "nation," the "church," the "scientists," etc.

The most usual relic of the abstracted group is the value system, remembered long after times, places, circumstances, and individuals are forgotten. In our quest for authority and certainty we often carry over to the actual group the values and attitudes that made sense for some previous group; we hope that they will guide us out of the perplexities of the present group. When values abstracted from these forgotten groups or cultures come into conflict with the evaluative criteria of a current actual group, the former had better be examined carefully to see if there is enough similarity of circumstance that they can be accepted as the "absolutes" one wishes they were.

A fourth type of group under whose influence one may act in an actual group is the "hangover" group. Basically this is a group similar to the family in which one had membership problems and anxieties which are still not relieved. The unresolved anxieties arising from sibling rivalry in the family may rise again in any situation of working with peers. When this happens, a person reacts to his peers in the actual group as if they were brothers and sisters from long ago or far away. Many problems of leadership probably are not legitimately problems in the actual group but are hung-over problems from unsatisfied relationships with father or mother or priest or people in authority. Anxieties connected with an unsatisfied craving for leadership in one group may be translated into tremendous and inappropriate striving for or avoidance of leadership in another group. It is as if a person were always working out the same plot in all his memberships; as if he were in the inexorable grip of problems which would not let him go. Group therapists are particularly concerned with seeing how an actual group can help individuals understand these peripheral motivations in their behavior.

A fifth type is the fantasied or constructed group. It probably operates more when the individual is alone than when he is in an actual group. Still, even in an actual group, a person will sometimes withdraw into fantasies in which he is getting from a constructed group the responses he cannot get from an actual group. There are descriptions of the child, punished by the teacher, who then daydreams about how sorry everybody will be when he gets drowned rescuing the fair-haired daughter of the superintendent from the mill pond; one may also at such times have dreams of glory in which one receives ovations from large and conveniently vague crowds; destruction and death plots can also be used.

For our purposes, however, the most interesting constructed groups are those produced to give one emotional support. An imagined audience can be used to provide one with authority against the actual group—to help sustain a course of action which is unpopular (or which it is feared will be unpopular). If a person has read a lawbook he may develop for himself and the group the fantasy that he is now representing the "legal point of view." Consultants called into schools are often seduced into thinking they represent a group of gray-bearded professors of education. A member addressing the actual group or a teacher giving a lecture may be addressing some other group not actually present. "Talking over our heads" is a common way in which the audience recognizes this. They read into it snobbishness, exhibitionism, and the like; but it may merely be that the lecturer got his wires crossed and is using the platform to defend his thesis from the criticism of a lot of absent or even nonexistent critics.

In any case, when a person does not accept the actual group and address his behavior to it, he will use some other group or mixture of groups, even if they have to be specially constructed for the occasion. Such groups are clearly and consciously seen by some people; with others, these extra groups remain in the subconscious.

It will be our postulate that in any perplexing situation in the actual group, it is as if there were other groups overlapping. In other words, the problem for the member is partly one of dealing with conflict among or anxiety about his memberships. Behaviors that enhance membership in one group are felt to lead to rejection in other groups. Any choice of behavior thus is to some extent felt to be a choice among groups.

Roger Barker gives an excellent picture of the possible overlapping groups operating in a teaching situation:

Teachers must be highly sensitive to the changing demands of many relatively independent groups: their classes, their colleagues, their administrators, their communities. Because of their exposed and dependent position, the behavior of teachers is very sensitive to these simultaneously acting, but independent and often conflicting influences. Consider some concrete determinants of the teacher's behavior in the classroom. First of all, there is the classroom situation: the attitude of the pupils, the requirements of the lesson, and the teacher's intentions and ideals with respect to it. At the same time, the teacher's behavior is to some extent determined by the facts of the larger school administration: perhaps an uncertainty as to the attitude of the administration toward his work, a feeling of frustration, failure, and abuse because a colleague has received an "unwarranted" salary increase, or a feeling of futility over the small prospect of professional advancement. There is also the community situation which the teacher cannot escape and to which he is particularly sensitive: limitations upon his personal freedom in some political, social and economic spheres, and coercion in others.[1]

We seem to be on safe ground so far in recognizing that an individual is influenced by groups other than those "actually" present. This is another way of saying that people can be in conflict and can have anxieties about it—they can feel pressures and doubts—and that we look to previous social experience as somehow involved in these perplexities.

The technologies presented in Part I grapple with these problems. Thus, with respect to racial matters, the neighborhood group, chapter 1, provides a test of attitudes frequently formed in fantasied groups. The teacher in chapter 2 deals with roles of children which are maintained in actual peer and family groups. In chapter 3, the small training group bridges between vested interests of the teacher in his classroom and in his total faculty. A major problem of chapter 4 is to avoid overlapping of the demanding groups "above" and "below" with co-operating groups at the same level.

Accepting the notion that people do find themselves in situations which fall under the jurisdiction of overlapping groups, the next question follows: What goes on within the individual, and how is his behavior affected?

A TENTATIVE PICTURE OF THE EFFECT OF OVERLAPPING GROUPS ON BEHAVIOR

Our job at this point is to construct a bridge of explanation that will connect two sorts of information. On the one hand, we have the notion that in problematic situations an individual is under the influence of two or more groups whose requirements for membership are felt by him to be incompatible. On the other hand, we have generally accepted observations of the variety of ways in which an individual can behave when he is in doubt: he may "withdraw" from the situation, in which case he becomes nonparticipant so far as the business of the group is concerned;

[1] Roger G. Barker, "Difficulties of Communication between Educators and Psychologists: Some Speculations," *Journal of Educational Psychology*, September, 1942, pp. 416–26.

he may fight any of a number of possible targets as a means to defining limits more clearly—the leader, the group, himself, the problem, the possibilities of solution; he may become dependent in the sense that he gives up his own rights to take initiative and tries to find someone to follow; he may flee to a high level of generality or into telling stories, swapping experience, splitting hairs, or arguing procedures; etc. What we are looking for at this point is some way to predict from the nature of the pressures on a person in a perplexing situation what behavior he will present to the group. Or we may turn the question around and ask what information, from observations of a person's behavior, we can get about the pressures he is under.

The groups that overlap at any particular time are the ones which have meaning of some sort for us in the particular situation. They are groups with which we identify; we have some quality of membership in them. In each of these groups our behavior as members is different. You behave differently in a staff meeting than in your family. As a Scout leader your role is clearly distinguishable from your role as a fourth hand at bridge. We are, on different occasions, different people. And we are different in just the ways we have to be different to maintain the kind of membership we need in the various groups we are party to. When groups overlap in our minds we become, in effect, several different people at the same time.

There is a struggle within us among our various selves—the different people we are as members in each of the groups which somehow are felt to be pertinent to a given situation. In effect, our behavior is decided by what goes on around an internal "conference table." If we can bring all our selves to agreement, we proceed fairly directly and easily. If we cannot, our behavior depends upon the dynamics of the conference within. Thus if the "Scout Master" in us wants to give advice, the "psychologist" in us wants to reflect the other fellow's feeling, the "judge" in us wants to punish—if these others all stick to their line there is no decision, and we may have to withdraw momentarily from the group, or strike out at it, or find ourselves defending an ill-advised position reflecting that group pressure which is momentarily dominant within us.

The notions presented above may be summarized as follows:

cues in any actual situation remind us of groups in which we are anxious about our membership role. Our reactions to the present group become contaminated with anxieties about ourselves in relation to other groups. The different selves we have in those other groups come into conflict. The interaction among these selves decides how we shall behave—with confidence, hostility, ease, creativity. It is thus that internal conflict can be seen as conflict in membership roles, and that whatever decision is reached enhances membership in some groups at the expense of membership in others. The stress and strain of conflict becomes the pain of losing approval and affiliation and other need-satisfactions in some groups while gaining these things in other groups. The decision is likely to express our judgment of which changes in membership will be least painful or most rewarding.

This viewpoint has interesting implications. Thus as group members, we may see a person's opinions as more than merely a response to the "actual" situation; therefore, before accepting an opinion we would wish to test it against the facts of the actual situation. Or in therapy, for instance, when an individual is in conflict it might be profitable to inquire after the other people to whom the patient feels his behavior makes a difference. One can see, too, the problem presented to pupils when the climate differs from classroom to classroom, or from school to home.

This picture also points to the problems of heterogeneity among groups in our society. The wish for a society in which the major values (or requirements for membership in groups) are consistent is a wish for less conflict in people. A homogeneous society seems an impractical hope, and it would be undesirable in any case. But there is one important possibility which is the central thesis of this work: that in groups which customarily test ideas against the facts—of both ideas and feelings—people can learn ways to integrate these inner selves. They can learn to react to situations as they are; they can learn to use past experience for wisdom and guidance, without interference.

SOCIAL GOALS AND MEMBERSHIP

People live together, they need each other, they are influenced by each other—in short, they are interdependent. Interdependence is a mixture of dependence and independence. The quality of membership in the group defines the nature of the mixture; it decides the relative degrees of independence and dependence, and also the things for which a person depends on the group and the things for which the group depends on him. Membership is the right to influence; it is also the agreement to accept influence. Obviously, the more fully involved one is in group membership the greater are both the privileges and the responsibilities—the more meaningful and significant is the relationship. Full membership is a means to enable one to meet his needs more effectively (or change them to needs that can be met).

But the type of group makes a difference. Groups which are oriented toward the goals of their members and test all ideas against what they are trying to accomplish, tend to seek stability in the understanding of basic principles. Events are seen as representing the operation of understood "laws." Because these "laws" are understood, it is possible to predict what will happen next. With the ability to predict and anticipate comes freedom, by which we mean the possibilities of deciding behavior intelligently and to our advantage. Here all things can be tested and, if necessary, changed, even the requirements of membership. Membership is referred to the situation as it exists and to the authority of group experience.

It seems clear that there will be little conflict among memberships in such groups. When conflict does arise, one knows what to do because the group agreements include provision for testing and modifying the membership role. We shall refer to this type of group as "purpose-oriented."

On the other hand, some groups appear to be oriented toward the maintenance of preconceived ideas. Their basis of performance and stability is ritual, custom, and preservation of the power structure. Events are seen as unpredictable and as threatening, because new ways have to be found to deal with them, and there is no means for discovering new ways with confidence. Reliance is on a higher authority—sometimes mystically revealed. Judgments are not tested against the facts of group life. The group always has to guess because it not only does not have the relevant facts to go on, it does not even know the categories of facts it ought to have. Membership roles are rigidly defined and enforced through coercive expectations. All members are expected to accept a common ideology, and unorthodox views are resisted. Such rules as the group makes explicit to itself govern procedures rather than methods of working. We shall refer to this type of group as "procedure-oriented."

The individual whose major social training and experience is in the purpose-oriented group will be able to accommodate subsequently to the wide variety of groups in our heterogeneous society. Social training in the procedure-oriented type of group will tend to block effectiveness in subsequent group experience.

SOME COMMENTS ON THIS CHAPTER

Our basic objective is to understand how people work together, why difficulties arise, how to avoid or remove them. There are two very different aspects to the problem. One whole side of the matter stems from the facts about human relations—the conditions under which people can participate in social experiences, the nature of the participation, the immediate and long-range obstacles to it, and the values and costs of various patterns of participation. The other side of the matter is the fact that society is faced with such "objective" problems as housing, food distribution, lack of parking space, supervision of city officials, etc. In any real situation, both the human relations problems and the objective problems must be dealt with simultaneously.

This chapter has said nothing about "objective" problem-solving, and it has said nothing very directly translatable into action about human relations problem-solving. We have tried to show that the individual has a "place" in groups, that he fits into and is part of a larger social structure. We have also implied that the social structure to which he responds is the social structure as seen and experienced by the individual. This social structure is "subjective" in the sense that it differs for different people. From the concept of overlapping group memberships, we have pointed to a major source of the "human relations" problems in group operation. We have also implied that these problems of individuals do not arise from wilfulness, obstinacy, or stupidity per se, but are due to his experiences in a community. We can see that people can be awkward in handling these conflicts and the anxieties over

their conflicts, and as we go on we want to indicate some understandings that may be helpful in this regard. We have also implied that groups can operate in such a way that the individual is
not so often or deeply trapped by membership conflicts.

The reader may wonder just how literally the notion of an
"internal conference" is meant. What are these other selves, and
how do they interact? The answer is that this is a theory of functioning—it is *as if* some such process went on. It is by no means
meant to be a description of verified phenomena. Such a description, if made in psychological terms, would go heavily into impulses, their blockage, reinforcement, and control. In physiologi-
cal terms, it would go into the matter of the behavior of the
nervous system. It seems most helpful in this context to think of
the individual as a "black box." Knowing something about what
goes into it and about what comes out of it, we then try to guess
at the sort of thing going on inside. If we are successful, we can
use this information to predict what will come out from our
knowledge of what goes in, and vice versa. This particular concept of the internal conference appeals to me because I see public
behavior as coextensive with private behavior; and not radically
different from it. How much of public behavior is merely "acting
out" the things in one's mind? It seems to me that the relationship
between a person's thoughts and feelings and what he does in a
group is so close that we are entitled to think that the two sorts of
phenomena are fundamentally similar. In such a case either
could be modified by experience with the other; and I think this
happens.

To what extent do the matters discussed here belong to "consciousness" and to "unconsciousness" of the person? There may
be some feeling that the more "conscious" these things are, the
more readily they can be controlled and worked with. Clearly,
there are differences from one person to the next and from one
situation to the next. There may be some minimum level of conscious diagnosis that must go on before a person can proceed
effectively to deal with his problems of membership. Certainly
one of the major policies of trainers in human relations is to make
it possible for such inexplicitly understood factors to emerge into
consciousness so they can be dealt with at a more overt level.

Another basic question: To what extent is behavior a matter of "free choice" by the individual, and to what extent is it determined by such factors as his membership in groups? We do not expect to settle this question, but we are certainly investigating it in various ways throughout this work. At the present stage of the discussion, we should like to call attention to two sorts of relevant observations. The first is that it is possible to generalize about how people will behave. For example, if we know that Tony is the son of an Italian immigrant who worked in a vineyard in Italy and now lives in the "Italian" section of a large city, we might expect from this alone that Tony will be caught between the transplanted Italian society and the urban American society. We expect him to have difficulties in moving from one to the other, or of maintaining loyalty and relationships to both. If he is an adolescent, we expect him to be torn in his choice of friendships, and to be very sensitive to "stereotypic" remarks made by his "American" friends. Simply because of his membership conflicts, we may expect such things as extra self-assertiveness, defensiveness or rebelliousness directed at the Italian group, efforts to copy the mannerisms of some "American" adolescent, and the like. The fact that such expectations are generally held by the people with whom he comes in contact will tend to make them come true. Much work on caste and class characteristics of various ethnic groups in American society has led to many generalizations of this sort. We may as well accept the fact that there is to some extent a cultural determinism in individual behavior.

On the other hand, we may observe a second adolescent, Gino, ostensibly from the identical cultural situation, who seems to function in a way vastly different from Tony. The latter becomes "Americanized" with very little apparent conflict, and gets along well in other groups; Gino seems to get caught in a shadowland of dubious fringe groups, projects his troubles on everyone else, and becomes a victim for every demagogue who comes along. This, too, can be predicted, but to do so requires a great deal more information about the relationships between the parents and the children, about such biological matters as energy output, and about such psychological matters as his fantasies and the subjective meanings for him of his experience. The latter type of information is protected by custom. We tend to feel that it is an "invasion of privacy" to try to find out these things.

The matter at present can be left somewhat as follows: Behavioral norms or expectancies for groups of people exist. To assert that any particular individual does, must, or should act in accordance with these norms is to engage in a kind of stereotyping which may be harmful because it prevents our seeing and reacting to the individual as he "really" is. But knowledge of norms and personality dynamics should not be resented, because we all use them intuitively. The problem is to learn our facts more accurately, and then to train ourselves to use such knowledge more appropriately. At most, all that can be predicted in advance is the existence of certain tendencies to react to types of situations (described in general terms) in certain types of ways. A specific reaction usually cannot be predicted accurately except by an observer or member of the group, and then only in the moment just before the behavior occurs.

The conclusion to the question of free will versus determinism is thus that there are broadly stated limits within which individuals can be seen to operate; but there is room within these limits for unpredicted, original, self-expressive behavior. A person can be himself, self-determining and creative, but to be so he must understand and accept his memberships in a variety of groups.

This chapter begins with the individual as the locus of tendencies to behave in the host of social groups in which he is involved. Several chapters hence, after considering many more factors and concepts, we will complete the circle by returning to the individual as the means for building communities. We will at that point try to show that the fact of overlapping memberships is not merely a source of problems for the individual, but also offers the most promising possibilities for building the kind of world we want.

CHAPTER 8

Awareness and interpretation of our own feelings in a situation is the starting point for defining the problems we have to solve. Thinking about the problem is a process of rehearsing possible actions in our minds. The "best" solution is based on all the necessary data in the problematic situation, and it represents the application of open-minded experimental attitudes.

A problem is "solved" when serenity of feeling returns and new insights have been fitted into our scheme of things. Both we and the situation undergo changes, and these changes give rise to new problems.

Integration: Evaluating and Acting

INTRODUCTION

We have suggested that in any given situation, a person may find himself confronted with problems of divided loyalty, expectations about how to behave that are carried over from some past group but which he fears are not appropriate in the present group, anxieties about himself in similar situations in the past, and the like. In other words, the person is played upon by many forces which are mobilized by cues in the present situation.

These ideas deal essentially with the *structure* of the pressures to which one is subject. But these concepts do not give us much insight into what the individual will do, what changes will occur, and how these changes are going to be brought about. Concepts of this sort refer to "process"; processes result in change of structure, and without ideas of structure we have no way of describing such changes.

The primary concept needed for an understanding of behaving as a process is that of purpose. We do not "understand" behavior until we can assign it a purpose, conscious or unconscious. The purpose we have talked about so far is to resolve conflicts in one's memberships and to reduce anxieties associated with these conflicts. We are postulating the idea that when a person has such anxieties about his membership, he will behave in a way which, from his point of view, will reduce these anxieties—either by testing them and finding them unnecessary, or by learning to live with them, or by sharing them with others, or in some other way.

A second concept needed for a consideration of the process of change is that of problem-solving. Whenever a structure needs to be altered, there must be some reason why it has not already automatically changed and this ordinarily involves the notion of an obstacle that must be overcome. The obstacle must be diagnosed; plans for overcoming it must be laid, alternatives weighed, action

245

taken and continuously tested as the process of change continues. This series of steps, when rigorously undertaken, is "action research"; in all problematic situations similar steps go on with more or less consciousness and formality. This abstract series of steps provides us with a model with which to compare actual behavior. It is a model deriving from a conception of behavior as purposive, rather than as a simple set of conditioned responses to situations over which no control is possible.

From observation of people, one soon learns that there are vast differences among individuals and among groups with regard to the extent to which problem-solving is conscious, and therefore with regard to the possibility of learning problem-solving methods and applying them with increasing efficiency and productivity.

Some people and groups are conscious of objective barriers only, and try to deal with them as if there were no other problems involved. The notion that a research worker in social science is himself not involved as a person is in accord with this pathetic fallacy; the very choice of a problem for research necessarily signifies his involvement in the situation. The notion that the group observer can "stay out" of the group's activity is equally mistaken. On the other hand, some people and groups seem almost entirely concerned with anxiety problems, with their own selves. One hears people insisting that a group must develop "as a group" before it can be expected to deal with objective problems. The main outcome of such efforts is probably to increase anxiety further by making everyone self-conscious.

These lopsided approaches differ in the types or aspects of group process to which attention is given. Those who try to deal with group problem-solving as if its content were entirely objective tend to pay attention to the "logical" processes of interpreting information. They typically make the mistake of confusing the formal steps, which in our culture we accept as the ways to demonstrate or prove already known theses, with the steps through which a group has to go in its own sometimes blundering way in order to arrive at the conclusions or decisions. What is forgotten, typically, is that feelings exist, have to be taken into account, and actually are the bases in experience for knowing which steps the group must take and in what order.

On the other hand, those who see problem-solving primarily as the development of "groupness," or as the solving of interpersonal problems among the members, tend to pay considerable attention to "permissiveness" and expression of feeling. They get feeling "out in the open" and shared—and this is certainly helpful. But it is not enough. There is no way to know how to proceed unless there are objective requirements to serve as the basis for testing and interpreting feeling. A clear example is the so-called "race problem." No community has ever yet solved the problem of interracial anxiety by approaching it directly; what is required, rather, is a type of experience through which people learn to deal with the anxieties surrounding their notions of "race." But this experience has to be provided with regard to problems such as housing, employment, wage levels, educational opportunity, hospital care, and other objectively defined concerns. It is only in these objective problems that unequivocal facts can be obtained and therefore that the success or failure of policy can be demonstrated clearly. The use of this principle is demonstrated in chapter 1.

We shall begin in this chapter with the postulate that the fundamental problems people have to solve arise from membership conflicts and anxieties. We shall then approach the processes of solution with our model of problem-solving: diagnosis, interpretation, planning, acting, obtaining feedback, modifying plans and actions, and so on. We shall look at these steps as processes of feeling, thinking, and acting. We shall be concerned with the balance among these processes, and the control of this balance. And we shall use the term "integration" to describe the effectiveness and appropriateness of the principles by which a person or group appears to control this balance of processes.

FEELING

Feeling is a state of affairs within a person or group, evoked by situations or parts of situations. Feelings cannot be expressed by words; we can talk *about* them, but we cannot talk *them*. On the other hand, we can communicate to others how we feel. We do it partly through the nonspecific content of our talk—not through the idea we wish to express but through the way we express it: the tone of voice, the inflections, the tempo of speech. We also use formal elements of speech: the elaborateness of our phrases, the shock we convey through bluntness, the associations of feelings with which people invest particular words, etc. In general, any departure of our behavior from what people think a problem requires is likely to be interpreted as an indication of feelings. Such indications we may refer to as the "affect" of statements.

Feelings are, of course, communicated by many behaviors other than speech. Speaking happens to be particularly useful to communicate them, perhaps because the tiny muscles of the vocal cords are extremely sensitive to changes in tension within the body and respond in audible ways that are detectable. But posture, expression, gesturing—all these movements, and particularly the involuntary ones, communicate to others how we feel. Or at least they communicate the fact that our feelings have changed.

In a group, we note many ways in which people respond to such communication. A change of seating from one meeting to the next often confirms our impressions of change of friendship feelings among members. Verbal responses may include attacking, reassuring, changing the subject, or asking for clarification. Responses may be further expressions of the same feeling, or of some other feeling. They may somehow take account of the mood of the group as a whole during a fairly long period, or they may seem to arise from a single comment by one person.

In general, an expression of feeling engenders further feeling in others, and their responses are actually stimulated by their own feelings. Thus when a person attacks: "I just don't think we are getting anywhere; I don't know what we are trying to do, and I don't think anyone else does either," his action may evoke different feelings among the various members of his group. One person responds as if this were an attack on the group or on the leader; he feels defensive. Another person may respond to the feeling of frustration which he hears in the statement; he may add to it: "Amen, brother." Or he may respond to the feeling of frustration with some diagnostic comment: "It seems to me that we are all pretty frustrated at the moment." Another person may counterattack: "I'd like to refer you to the purposes we stated and wrote on the board at the last meeting." Still another, who has been actively participating, may feel discouraged and fall silent. These responses give us some clues as to the way in which feelings affect the group. Fundamentally, expressed feelings are responded to as if they were evaluations. Different people may view such expressions as evaluative of different things: the leader, the group, the problem, the activity, the speaker, other individuals, other groups.

Feelings themselves are nonspecific; they are involuntary, overall responses. They signal to us that we like or dislike the way things are going; that we anticipate success or failure; that we are comfortable or uncomfortable; that we feel relaxed and adequate or tense and inadequate in the situation; that we sense danger or haven; that we are in conflict or at peace; that we have anxiety or are undisturbed. If we are unaware of these signals, if we do not know how we feel, we tend to "act out" the feelings; in one way or another we express them to the group. If they arise primarily from the events in the life of the actual group, such expression is probably helpful. But if they arise from other sources, not in the experience of the rest of the group, then a direct expression may be troublesome.

For example, if the group has learned that I become aggressive whenever the goals of the group are unclear, then they can use my expression of aggressive feelings as a barometer to indicate the possibility that further goal clarification may be needed. On the other hand, if my aggression during a particular meeting is due to the fact that earlier in the day I had an argument during which I handled myself badly, the group, not knowing the source of my anger, will be at a loss to know how to respond to it. It then constitutes an additional and unnecessary problem for the group to deal with.

When we are aware of our feelings, we may respond to them in three ways. One way is to deny them, to pretend they do not exist or to attribute them to others. Thus people who cannot accept their own feelings of hostility are likely to say that *they* are not hostile but that everyone else is. This is called projection. It is a subconscious rationalization of one's own feelings which he dare not acknowledge in consciousness: "If everyone is hostile to me then I am justified in being hostile myself, even though I deny to you that I feel hostile." If a person does not have open this projective way of accepting feelings he refuses to acknowledge, he is likely to feel anxious and probably guilty. He may withdraw, lash out at others, change the subject, etc. None of these devices are helpful to the group.

A second way to deal with our awareness of how we feel is to accept the fact that we feel as we do and then try to interpret this fact as a guide to action. Thus a person who recognizes that he feels hostile may try to explain to himself why this is so. Through watching what is happening to the group each time he has these hostile feelings he may discover that he feels this way every time a particular person speaks, or whenever a stereotypic statement is made about his religious group, or whenever the group loses its sense of direction. He may then decide to report to the group the results of his insight: that he is unclear about the direction in which the group is going, or that he wonders whether particular kinds of statements are realistic, etc.

A first way of reacting to one's feeling is to "act it out"; the second is to interpret it and report his diagnosis of group malfunctioning to be corrected. The third way is somewhere between the first two. It is to report objectively how one feels. Thus he might say in a reasonably pleasant but sincere way: "I feel unhappy at the turn our discussion has taken." Such statements invite others to indicate whether they share the feeling; if they do, it may be worth taking time for everyone to help diagnose the group experiences causing this "unhappiness." Often sharing the knowledge that we all feel anxious by itself reduces anxiety enough to let the group move ahead.

Common knowledge of generally shared feelings in the group is extremely important information. It is essential to get and interpret this information if the group is to select its activities in a way that is maximally productive. But feelings do not have to be ascertained and interpreted every hour on the hour. As long as everyone who has a contribution to make is making it, as new ideas are coming up, as people are listening to each other and building on each other's ideas—there is no need to be concerned about feelings. High morale is readily shared. But when things go sour, when the discussion drags, when there is little feeling of growth of insight, when there is much unnecessary dependence on the leader, then ascertaining the feelings which are shared may give the data needed to rectify the situation.

It should be evident that the unbridled, disorderly, acting-out of feeling is by itself of little value. Catharsis alone does not help.

THINKING AND ACTING

We do not respond to everything about us. We take action only on the things about which we have feelings. Of course, if we like our feelings, we will want to maintain the situation, rather than change it. But when our feelings are painful—more painful than the discomfort of taking action—we are likely to move if we can see something to do. The demagogue operates in essentially this type of situation: he shows people the easy way out of the uncomfortableness of their feelings. The more persuasive he is in discounting what is really involved in the action—its long-range costs, for example—the greater the danger in following him.

There is a more healthy basis for taking action: this is to search for greater reward rather than to search for the avoidance of discomfort. Training groups frequently operate in this way. During their periods of high morale and productiveness, individuals feel more rewarded for participation, and the group goal becomes identified with having more such periods. To reach this goal, the group members must analyze the differences between the desired situation and the more usual one of lower efficiency. If they can recognize this difference, they can then alter their policies of operation in an effort to reach the goal. In more general terms: the nature of group goals involves a state of being which has been experienced and of which the group wants more. If a group has never experienced a really productive period, there is no assurance that the goal of productiveness is appropriate or attainable. The basis for confidence in goals is the group's own experience, not the promises of a leader whose ways of knowing are not available to the group.

In general, a diagnosis of our feelings with regard to our problem is the starting point for intelligent behavior. Knowledge of the sorts of situations which gave rise in the past to the feelings in question is helpful in making the diagnosis. This is an intellectual operation. It involves comparing the facts about a present situation with the facts about other experienced situations, with an eye to seeing the similarities and differences between the two.

Following diagnosis, in the problem-solving process, there comes a fascinating process of rehearsal of action. Planning action is in many ways similar to the writing of a play. The kinds of roles needed—characterizations—must be considered; the plot line— the strategic sequence of required action—becomes clearer; the dialogue is written and tested for validity against the group's intuitions from past experience. The conversation is likely to move from the hypothetical level ("If such and such were to occur, one could then do such and such") to the level of immediate readiness for action ("I think we ought to start by doing so and so").

Emotionally, at least, the problem is solved at the point where people can see what the next step is going to be. Action is the acting out of that which has been rehearsed in the mind. While action is being taken, additional feelings arise, and the next step is planned in response to the new definition of the problem that has thus become possible. Problems are never really solved in any conclusive or absolute sense. They are merely reformulated in such a way that action can be taken. In the process, however, the environment gets changed and attitudes are altered.

In this view, thinking is vicarious anticipatory action. People react to the imagined action with feeling, and at the point where there is a sufficient shared feeling of confidence in the group, action can be taken. This confidence emerges when people can visualize clearly what is to be done, and when they feel it is the "right" thing to do. For confidence to be highest, the group sets up criteria which the action is to satisfy and then considers a number of alternative plans, selecting the one that meets the criteria best. And the more "operational" the plan—the more easily translatable into imagined action—the easier it is to visualize and test it against the criteria. Acting out alternative plans through role-playing (spontaneous dramatic situations which contain the elements of the problem to be solved) is often helpful in appraising a suggested course of action. Guidance may be obtained from various sources—accepted practices, analysis in terms of values involved, use of experts, dry runs—all these may be used to help examine proposed plans for action.

During this group job of planning action, what sort of thinking is the individual member doing? Fundamentally, he is trying to work out existing membership problems and, probably, attempting to influence the group in such a way that additional membership problems do not arise for him. Thus he has a vested interest in the direction of action upon which the group decides. He knows that after all the talking is over, he will be committed to do something, to play some role, and he prefers that this action be congenial and rewarding to himself.

The group member, then, is thinking about the strategy for solving the problem, but, at the same time, he is concerned that the strategy selected should make sense in terms of his own needs. He must be realistically concerned with such problems as the amount of frustration he will probably encounter in relation to the amount he can tolerate easily, the perceptions he thinks others will have of him if he undertakes the particular job suggested, the future opportunities which will be opened to him by participation in action, etc. By and large, members do not discuss such problems with the group, not wishing to expose their membership problems to others. In a sense, then, each member has his own "hidden agenda" in a meeting.

We see now the importance of the objective problem facing the group. With all members having their own hidden agendas to work on, there must be some sort of reality outside the group, some purpose over and above the concerns of each individual to which attention can be directed. The objective problem makes communication possible, it gives people something about which to share feeling, it gives them a focus which is not more favorable toward one individual than another. Without it there would be no basis for differentiating roles, for settling leadership competition, for organizing effort. There would be no criteria for testing ideas, and the group would end in nothing but a series of divisive moves for individual power.

During discussion of the objective problem, members project their own general concerns onto the outside reality. A person concerned about himself in relation to leadership in the group may be the one to ask who is going to be in charge of the project. One who is divided in loyalty between this group and another one may be the one to inquire about the philosophical assumptions behind the action to be taken—particularly with regard to the ethics of the situation. A member who is worried about lack of time may be the one to insist on a careful analysis of the job requirements for getting the proposed action accomplished. One with a problem of "feeling left out" all the time may ask what communication must be provided for among workers while they are taking action. All these are important and useful questions, growing out of the sensitivity of individual members to the particular factors which they emphasize during problem-solving. But these individual motivations are not the real concern of the group, which is to interpret queries within the body of decisions that need to be made. By the time answers have been found to some questions, others have been tabled, and still others determined to be irrelevant, each individual should not only feel secure in going along but should also have a clear idea of his role and where he fits into the process.

The ingredients of problem-solving are the processes through which members try to deal with their problems, which, of course, include their involvements in the objective problems. With the large array of member-concerns to be expressed and dealt with, it is clear that there must be some means of controlling contributions and, particularly, the timing of contributions. The more complete an image the group has of the structure of a problem, of the wide range of types of ideas required, the more readily it can control the offering of the various contributions. It is worth paying explicit attention in a group to developing a common "frame of reference" or "set" toward problem-solving. We shall see that the control of contributions in such a way that they add up efficiently into a group product is the function of leadership, and we shall have more to say about that later.

But for the time being, let me point out that the group operates as if it had some set of ideas about how to solve problems, about the larger purposes it is to achieve. The work is done by individuals, but within the framework of agreements and understandings about the nature of problem-solving. And let us also note two further points about this agreed-upon approach to problem-solving: first, that this becomes the code or set of beliefs the group lives by, and it gets incorporated into the individual's ideas of what the group stands for; and second, the more thoroughly this code is understood by the individual the more responsibility he can take for self-discipline, for making his contributions in a way that helps the group most directly but at the same time gives him maximum opportunity to meet his own needs.

INTEGRATION

In the last chapter I referred to integration as a state of affairs in which one's various "selves" were in harmony and mutually reinforcing. Under such conditions, committment to action is greatest, and the action itself is most direct. We might refer to this as structural integration.

The processes by which membership problems can be solved involves the achievement of structural integration. In this section we shall examine the relationships between the two major types of process—evaluation and action; we shall see that these both occur in sequence or combination, and we shall consider the nature of the relationships between them as likely to lead toward or away from structural integration. Thus, some behaviors, involving a particular combination of evaluation and action, may result in better integration; other behaviors may lead in the opposite direction.

From the standpoint of our model of problem-solving, ideally, at least, every "unpleasant" feeling would lead to the need for action; and every action undertaken would result in a new evaluation of the changed situation. The relationships between acting and evaluating would be seen as sequential and as guided by the need to reduce anxiety over overlapping memberships. In this ideal picture, a very small feeling could result in a new act which would engender more feelings and actions. One would be busy indeed!

Actually, the tension associated with "unpleasant" feelings has to be sufficiently great and sufficiently recognized that the person is "ready" to do something to reduce it. Some people appear to be able to tolerate a good deal of tension before they take action; others seem to translate most feelings of discomfort directly into action. Some people seem to have to carry a planned action through to completion before they allow themselves to be aware of the feelings produced during action; others appear to start modifying their action as soon as it starts, using the feelings discovered in the process of acting as the basis for steering their behavior. Then again, there are those whose tensions toward action appear to be reduced simply through the mental rehearsal stage; their need to know that they can handle situations is satisfied by the visualization of a possible plan of action. There are also those who need actually to take every planned action as a way, perhaps, of convincing themselves of their own adequacy; and these people may resist any plan which makes unusual demands on them.

The feeling of adequacy, that a person may live serenely in the various groups he belongs to, is probably an expression of confidence that he can find the action-channels he needs to reduce anxieties should they arise. He feels sure that he will not be "trapped" in intergroup or membership problems, and thus need not fear participation in the host of varieties of social relationships. There is only one way in which such adequacy can be learned and accepted: through finding out from experience that these self-attitudes are realistic. Action is an individual's means of testing his own attitudes about himself. Only action evokes responses by others, and only action (or public behavior) has consequences that can be appraised.

From the standpoint of the group member, participation is experimentation. He decides more or less consciously which behaviors to submit to the group, and pays attention to the feelings engendered in himself by the responses the group makes. One of the usual conclusions to be drawn from the experiment is a notion of "place," of the quality of membership in the actual group. In this sense, every group we operate in is a laboratory in which we test ideas about ourselves and our relationships to others.

There are two extreme modes of experimentation by group

members, corresponding roughly to inductive and deductive methods. These methods are most clearly recognizable in the early life of the group. One is to "dive in": to make comments testing the leadership's permissiveness, the boundaries to expression of ideas and feelings. The member in effect tries out the roles he would like best, to see if he can establish himself in them. The second extreme method is to sit back and watch what happens to the fellows who dive in. From the way the leadership responds to them, one learns how to relate to leadership. The active people are watched closely. If a conflict develops over methods of leadership, the watcher identifies with both protagonists, for they are apt to represent different sides of his own confusion or ambivalence.

The two methods are likely to be used by different types of members. We expect rash behavior from aggressive and counterdependent people—people who cannot tolerate the idea that they must depend on anyone. We expect the "safer" method to be employed by more dependent people. Dependency and counterdependency, of course, are learned from previous experience; they reflect the qualities of membership which one has developed as most suitable to meet needs in other groups.

These differences in approach illustrate differences in the principles with which people appear to operate in their search for integration of experience. The watcher tends to be critical. He responds to the actions of others. He tends, often, to have his greatest facility with data that others have produced and "processed" for him. His evaluations are primarily of the feelings expressed by others, and he may actually be more aware of them than of his own feelings—or at least he "feels" safer in reacting to others' feelings than to his own. He may deny his own feelings because he cannot accept them, and may be "blocked" until the permissiveness of the group is so well established that he need not fear punishment or reprisal for his feelings. The "plunger" makes less subtle evaluations—he accepts opposition at first hand—and takes action more easily. He represents the opposite situation to the watcher: a person who is relatively more sensitive to and aware of his own feelings than the feelings of others.

The kind of member experimentation which is of greatest help to the group stems from an easy relationship to the problem and to the people in the group. Such a member is not anxious, and seems to act spontaneously rather than compulsively (like the plungers) or with inhibition (like the watchers). His spontaneity reflects an "inner freedom" which comes from acceptance of the limits, on the one hand, and lack of fear of his own feelings, on the other. One might expect a considerable amount of self-discipline in the spontaneous person: the problem-solving methods are understood so fully that behavior is automatically relevant to problem-solving and therefore can be expressed easily. With this sort of self-discipline, action-channels are available, and he does not get "tied up" within himself as a result of frustration. His energy goes to the problem rather than being expended internally in fantasies, bottled emotions, and monumental evasions of feelings and inhibitions of impulses.

Thus various people appear to follow different principles of experiencing and reacting. These different principles result at any given time in a particular kind and quality of integration, each with characteristic amounts of spontaneity, peace, ease, inhibition, anxiety, or tension. With each pattern of integration, there is a characteristic evaluation-action pattern, and its characteristics become the foundations of the ability to solve problems. These patterns are made known to the observer as different ways of conducting the experimental inquiry through which the member solves his membership problems, within the framework of the objective problem-solving of the group.

ADAPTATION

Social learnings are determined by the social aspects of experiencing. The face-to-face group is the most effective laboratory for social learning because there is immediate response to one's behavior, and cause-effect relations are therefore readily established. In every group, there are agreements and rules. And there is also a group-sanctioned set of explanations about why these rules are necessary, under what conditions they hold in force, and how they may be changed.

From the standpoint of the individual's need to grow and develop, two questions need to be asked: Does life under these rules have enough scope for me to experiment? How valid are our explanations of the rules? If there is sufficient opportunity and validity, then living in the group increases the possibilities of adaptation in other situations, of meeting life as it comes. If there is not sufficient scope, or if the group explanations are unsound— as when authoritarian dictates are sought and accepted without question—then experience in the group is teaching the individual things that will make his adaptations in other situations more difficult.

The "purpose-oriented" group referred to in the preceding chapter is likely to be an environment in which means to adaptation can be learned. The "procedure-oriented" group has false bases for adaptation; it teaches a rationale which, when it is tried in other groups, will result in frustration and member conflict.

The purpose-oriented group is one which is realistically in touch with the situation; the procedure-oriented group is not. Being "in touch" means producing behaviors appropriate to the demands of a situation; and this requires accurate appraisal of the elements that can be changed by means available to the group and of the limitations that, for the time being at least, have to be accepted.

Adaptation is thus both an individual and a group affair. The individual adapts to the group—accepting some things and changing others. But *through* this adaptation—not apart from it— the individual also adapts to the larger world for which his group provides the necessary experience.

The concepts of thinking, acting, and feeling, and of integration and adaptation, were basic tools used in designing the technologies in Part I. Throughout the case study in chapter 5, these concepts are used explicitly and openly by the group as an aid to its training. The skill of the teacher in planning classroom activities that will meet the needs of his children depends upon his recognition of these processes going on within the children. The success of the neighborhood groups in chapter 1 and the productive working groups in chapter 4 is determined by the extent of their vested interest in purpose rather than in procedure. The ability to guess correctly the balance between evaluative and acting responses of audiences is fundamental to the strategic use of the techniques of chapter 6.

These considerations are important because they are a part of the realities with which a group must deal—in one way or another.

CHAPTER 9

A group is influenced by and must take account of the laws of nature, the laws and customs of groups in the community, the unique way of life of the group itself, and the meanings and needs of its individual members.

This is a highly complex process and it requires continuous awareness of the relationships between achievement and process problems.

Reality: Factors in the Problem-Situation

INTRODUCTION

The basic principle for the guidance of human behavior is the "reality principle." This principle states that there are facts which need to be taken into account; there is a prior reality—a set of existing conditions independent of the will of a person or group—within which one must operate. When a person tries to act as if these conditions do not exist, or as if they were different than they are, his action is aggravating to the problem-situation rather than constructive; it makes bigger problems out of little ones; it jeopardizes immediate goal achievement; and, through thwarting the potential for individual and group growth, it may curtail long-range possibilities.

In practice, the meaning of the reality principle is that some possible behaviors and actions are "appropriate" and "realistic"; others are not. One way to describe the task of a group is "the production of behavior appropriate to the situation." It is clear that to pursue the matter further, we must know how to define the situation, the factors one must know immediately to take action, and the factors which can safely be left to discover themselves as action unfolds.

"Appropriate behavior" is achieved through the exercise of choice, and this is done by selecting from among possible alternatives. The exercise of choice is creative with regard to formulating alternatives; it is judgmental with regard to the selection of a particular alternative that is most appropriate—i.e., most capable of realization in the existing situation.

Some choice-points are crucial. In these the consequences of choosing one alternative rather than another may be long-range and conclusive, because the range of alternatives for future choices is drastically reduced by the specific action undertaken. On the other hand, there are choices in which the particular alternative selected is of little importance, where all that is required is that some decision be made. An example of this is the selection of a person to be chairman in a meeting of a mature group. If all the alternatives satisfy the best criteria the group can formulate, then it makes little difference which of these alternatives is selected. Certainly the history of the group will depend upon the choice made, but no group can do more than make the best choice it can at the time.

As a rule, effective group operation and productivity is possible only when the group is aware of its crucial choice-points, is creative in formulating alternatives, and is able to select with confidence one alternative as most appropriate.

In this chapter, we wish to consider the realities of the group-in-a-situation. We wish first to see what sort of ideas have to be taken into account; to do this we shall consider several different sorts of "realities." We shall pay some attention to thinking about the extent to which each sort of reality is coercive, and the extent to which it can be changed. We then wish to consider the variety of changes necessary in situations, and to point out the kinds of things groups have to make choices about and take action on.

TYPES OF REALITIES

We have considerable confidence, in the absence of any contradictory experience, that things dropped will fall; that the sun will rise at the prescribed time; that dry coal will burn if heated to its kindling temperature in a proper supply of air; that an airplane will rise faster if it takes off into the wind rather than with the wind. We accept such statements as "facts," presumably proof against human tampering or vested interest. They are also generalizations, not depending for their truth upon some special combination of circumstances. They are also bases of prediction as to what I can safely expect: that if I do so and so, such and such consequences will follow. And finally, they can be tested and found "true" by people of different races, creeds, political beliefs, and intelligence.

Although these statements are made by men, we tend to act as if men only "discovered" the laws, and we attribute the laws to the nature of the physical world, not to the nature of men. We also think of these statements as being able to "stand alone"; they require very little in the way of supporting assumptions. Possibly they refer to situations so deeply understood and familiar that the supporting assumptions can be taken for granted. Thus we regard the physical world as one vast self-consistent system: the universe. All parts of this system work on the same principles, so that study of any one part helps us understand better the operation of the whole.

This physical world extends, in our thinking at least, some distance into the organic biological world. Physiology, for example, is the study of physical and chemical aspects of living beings. Those aspects of life in which we feel most certain of our understanding are the ones to which we can apply the concepts of physical science. Where such concepts cannot be used, biological science employs the idea of probability. Probability statements are true for groups, but cannot be used to make certain predictions about any individual or event. We can know, for example, that 25 per cent of the offspring of a blue-eyed father and one type of brown-eyed mother will have blue eyes. But we cannot relate blue eyes to birth-order, sex, month of conception, or any other characteristic which distinguishes one child from another. All we can really say is that so far as any particular child is concerned, he has one chance in four of having blue eyes. In the same way, the actuarial tables tell us what chance the "average" man of sixty has to live to be sixty-one; but who is "average"?

By and large, the principles and facts of biology are comments about the way in which large homogeneous collections of individuals interact with the physical world. The variability of interaction is all attributed to the living creatures, rather than to caprice in the world of rocks and stars. And "proof" in biology is the verification that in a given percentage of instances certain physical and chemical aspects of living things will have a predicted composition, size, energy content, structure, or other objectively measurable characteristic.

There is another class of statement about the physical and biological worlds. These are definitional and they specify relationships among various properties or characteristics. An object which displays some of the characteristics will have the other associated properties as well. Thus objects which, on the basis of simple tests, are classified as "living things" can be counted on to take in materials, give out other materials, and be changed in the process. They have a course of growth, they have the property of irritability, they reproduce their kind. These statements are descriptive and they are true of objects selected to fit the description.

Classification can be based upon properties either of structure or of process. Thus plants are often characterized by physical characteristics, through the sense of sight alone. On the other hand, diseases can be classified by symptoms, which in turn are interpreted as evidence of what is going on in the body. The former is a "static," the latter a "dynamic," basis of classification. By way of illustration, the definition of an electron has both aspects: it is defined both in terms of its material structure and in terms of the possible ways it can interact with other forms of matter.

For the most part, such definitional statements are comments about functions or kinds of reactions, by which we can recognize the species or processes we wish to define. These statements are tools for thinking. They are meant to be used to solve problems; to help determine our conduct in problematic situations more wisely. If a human being inevitably performs certain functions, then it is *as if* he needs to do these things. Carrying out the functions is interpreted by us as motivated, purposive behavior. This feeling in us is reinforced by the observation that these functions can be carried out under the most adverse circumstances. If you plant seeds in a dark closet, the resulting plant is taller and more slender than one which grew in the sunlight—almost as if it were "trying" to grow out of the dark into the light, which somehow is "known" to be there.

We have, then, the notions of a physical world; of living things interacting with this world; of certain defining and characteristic kinds of interaction or functioning; of some hypothetical purpose or need to carry out these functions. We note that the "facts" are of different sorts: the physical facts give us a material frame of reference, the properties of which are stability, consistency, and generality; the biological "facts" are probable descriptions of related functions; and finally the interpretation of need gives us concepts of tendencies which "must be realized" and which have to be accepted as forces to be dealt with, whether or not we like them.

Turning to human beings, it is clear that they can help each other or hinder each other in meeting their "natural" needs. As communication and transportation developed, as exchange systems came into being, as one man became able to command more than one man's worth of energy, human organization developed. Simple biological needs originally required for their fulfilment a social organization no more complicated than the family, in which individual roles were determined by sex, strength, and age. But with newer technological developments, these simple needs began to manifest themselves through elaborate means, whose various aspects seemed increasingly unrelated to the simple drives. With them came control systems for the regulation of individual behavior and for the limitation of individual power. Maintenance of the control systems became a social end in itself.

The "facts" in the area of social reality are, first, statements about the agreements men live by—customs, laws, procedures, doctrines, status systems; and second, statements about the conditions under which these agreements obtain, who holds them, how they are to be changed. These agreements operate at all levels of explicitness, from written laws with elaborate machinery of enforcement to unwritten "rules of the game" which make possible social mobility, change of social structure, and adaptation of the group to its environment. They describe control systems of particular cultures or institutions of particular people at a particular period and place.

But such social-cultural realities are less coercive than physical and biological realities. There is more fluidity, confusion, and anxiety; less can be taken for granted. There is less universality and less consistency, as any examination by the bylaws or legal code of an old group will quickly reveal. Social reality is "legislated" by men, and there is considerable consciousness in this process. What men can arrange, men can change—provided they have the necessary agreements upon means and methods. It is our thesis that only as men learn the necessary methods can changes be brought about to enable them to find and maintain an effective adaptation to their physical, biological, and social realities.

Our technologies can and should be examined from this broad point of view. Thus the citizen participation program described in chapter 1 was created as a means to help the community face the facts about its own changing character. The notion discussed in chapter 3, that for successful in-service training the school must have direct relations with the community, can be seen as an effort to build communication in the faculty around the processes of adaptation to some reality more significant and reliable than the usual set of institutional and administrative rules. The educational importance of "learning by doing" is not so much that activity is desirable per se as that through activity one perforce comes in contact with physical, biological, and social realities about which one can then develop a stable view of the world.

It is within these realities that a face-to-face group proceeds to develop its own particular culture, its own view of reality as it is to be perceived and operated upon.

Realities within the Face-to-Face Group

In the last two chapters I have tried to indicate the genesis of the kinds of problems of individuals in groups. We begged the question of how consciously or unconsciously these problems would be worked on. Judging by the fact that so much of "human relations" training acts to make aware to the group things that are blocking it in ways only vaguely felt, there must be a considerable content and activity in the unconscious. We wish to consider this possibility further in connection with face-to-face groups, and add to our list two additional kinds of reality which are crucial to group operation and which are commonly ignored.

The first has already been given sufficient attention in the first two chapters. It is the subjective reality of the individual's world. This world is not merely of interest to the psychologist: it is actually the direct context of all acts, since there are no acts except those of individuals. We have spoken sufficiently for the time being of the individual's need to keep this private house in order; and of his need, therefore, to influence the group's definition of the membership role in such a way that his need-meeting skills also help the group.

There is a second type of subjective reality in groups, and we want to discuss it, although we feel less sure of its operation. This has been called the "group unconscious," or the "collective unconscious," or the "group mentality."

In chapter 7, we mentioned the concept of internalized groups. Although every individual is influenced by somewhat different internalized groups, it is likely that all individuals have experienced the same types of problems. Problems, particularly those invested with anxiety, are easy to communicate, to share, to know that they are shared. Assuming the universality of anxiety-problems, the fact that they can be mobilized by cues, and the possibility that such feelings are readily shared, we may be a little closer to an explanation of some difficult-to-describe periods in group life. These are periods which have the quality of sibling rivalry, of adolescent ambivalence between dependence and independence, of seemingly "self-destructive" tendencies, of sudden group "insights" which crystallize apparently within the space of a few minutes. These phenomena are difficult to explain solely in terms of strictly individual problems and needs. It is as if certain cues in the actual situation mobilized the same set of feelings in most members, as though a process of remembering were occurring, and as though the individuals were remembering the same things, the same threats, the same barriers to forward action.

As applied to groups, Bion has developed this theme in the concept of a subconscious "group mentality," which he opposes to consciously guided group achievement.[1] In the group mentality there is a shared agreement to avoid certain tasks, a resistance to allowing certain problems to become explicit. There is a conspiracy of shared emotionality which reinforces that side of all of the members' ambivalences which is resistant to "work." The resistance is easily felt, and it expresses itself in many ways. Periods during which the group mentality is in force are characterized by apathy; "running away from work" into storytelling, jok-

1. W. R. Bion, "Experiences in Groups. I" and "Experiences in Groups. II," *Human Relations*, I, No. 3, 314–20, and No. 4, 487–96.

ing, theorizing, making long lists on the blackboard, breaking up into private conversations, sudden hostility toward the leader, quarreling, and the like. Such emotional periods represent a state of affairs to which every individual, according to Bion, is a party. Applying the principle that to understand behavior is to know its purpose, it is as if the group as a whole has a "hidden agenda," a secret task into which its energy is flowing. Chapter 5 is centrally concerned with the diagnosis and development of awareness of hidden agendas in a training group.

If we judge what is real by what makes a difference, then the group mentality and the individual subjective worlds are the most real of all. For these are the spheres in which feelings, tensions, and impulses to action arise. Objective problems have a lesser reality, one derived from our need to do something to relieve tensions which arose in the other spheres during past actions. The formulation in explicit language of a problem is a process of abstraction from action to thought; and thoughts about a problem have less emotional significance than do impulses during problematic situations.

Compared to the basic emotional dynamics of the group, as represented in the feelings of individuals for or against one another, the objective problems are unreal. They provide escape from emotional travail into socially meaningful fantasy. This fantasy takes the form of a rehearsal of possible actions; and these actions, when achieved, become part of objective social reality.

The realities, which to a large extent determine what happens in a group, are at two levels of influence and are dynamically related. The reality of the objective problem is an interpretation of the relations of the group to its outside world. In this interpretation are incorporated the patterns of factors from the physical, biological, and social worlds described in the preceding section. The job of solving the problem is one of arriving at a solution which is appropriate, in terms of the sorts of facts belonging to these reality spheres. These are facts which can be obtained by measurement, polling, observation—by experimentation and statistics. They are capable of logical and rational manipulation. The problem is safe because the factors involved are part of the common community domain; they are not vested interests of individuals in the group, and objectivity is easy to achieve. Solutions to objective problems have the highest material reality. The results are incontrovertible, and the changes brought about get incorporated into the objective realities of men. These problems we shall call the "achievement problems" of the group.

But there is greater reality in the world of desire and fear of the individual and group unconscious. Problems of this sort make more difference to the group, require more energy to deal with, are more challenging to leadership, require greater self-discipline among members, and produce a greater reward for participation. Problems at this level we shall refer to as "process problems." The motivation to solve achievement problems is a reflection of the need to resolve process problems which originate in or between the actual group and other internalized groups. The obstacles to achievement problem-solving are due to one's inability to find behaviors which simultaneously satisfy both sorts of problem-solving demands. In such a case, the energy goes into the process problem because of its more compelling anxieties, and the objective problem is left untouched. We are forced to recognize that seemingly nonproductive periods of flight and emotionality exist for a reason, and that our job is to find the reason, even though it may require the help of a theory about transactions within the individual and group unconscious.

The simplest way to understand nonproductive periods is through studying the relationships between the process and achievement problems. The demands of the achievement problem come from the relatively stable and objective physical, biological, and social worlds. They provide a clear frame of reference for understanding the public meanings of behavior. We observe the group working on achievement problems. If the activity is inefficient or nonproductive, we look for process problems which would account for the trouble. Through attempts to explain these inferred process problems, we arrive at our theories about the subconscious reality worlds of the individuals and the group. If action taken on the strength of these theories rectifies the problems, then we assume that the theories were correct (pp. 51–61 discuss the method as applied to classroom teaching). Note that I am advocating here the use of the biological model set up earlier: just as we know the properties of living things by studying their interactions with the physical world, so we know the process problems of a group by studying its behaviors in working on achievement problems.

In general, then, it is the relationship between process and achievement problem-solving that we need to watch and understand. While both may be studied separately as well, the choice of the one deserving attention, the kind of attention, and analysis which is appropriate are things we learn from the relationships between the two. It is in the light of this biological model that we distrust group therapies which purport to deal only with the process problems, and planners who think planning for physical objectives is all that is required. What is needed is not a complete blueprint for the solution of one kind of problem or the other, but rather a set of policies for deciding how next to proceed under every possible type of relationship between the two.

The basic problem of the *group*, then, is to develop a rationale for dealing simultaneously with problems on both levels of reality; the basic concern of the *individual* is to deal with his own subjective world; and the basic concern of the community is to establish an environment for the various groups sufficiently stable for them to be able to formulate realistic objective problems and carry the solutions into socially significant action. But these latter concerns are by-products of the former, not separate enterprises.

The conclusion we draw from the above is that the group's major task is to steer and control its behaviors, and that it needs a methodology for doing this. The particular procedures employed in a particular case should represent applications of this methodology to the realities of the situation. This application is achieved through the process of continual decision among alternatives for dealing with the various emerging and changing relationships between process and achievement problems. We wish in the next two chapters to deal with methodology and policies for controlling group process—the function of leadership.

CHAPTER 10

As a group works, it develops its own way of life, its own culture. This culture is a set of agreements by means of which the group as a whole appears to co-ordinate the effort and contributions of individuals. When the agreements are appropriate to the task, the group is effective.

We here spell out thirteen basic principles which underlie the operation of successful groups. Then we see some of the processes by which the group disciplines itself to enforce or change its culture.

Control: Developing the Group Culture

INTRODUCTION

As can be seen from the preceding three chapters, group operation is a highly complex business. Every group, even at its first
meeting, has a long and manifold past, extending through the
history of its members. Every group is part of a larger scene, and
is continually receiving pressure from and exerting pressures on a
vast number of other groups. Every group is a microcosm of the
prevailing culture, and, at the same time, is a unique event.

The purpose of this chapter is to take a large conceptual step:
from description of what goes on in groups (chapters 7, 8, 9) to
the concept of leadership as the intelligent control of group activity. This will enable us in the next chapter to deal directly with
the problems and policies of leadership. Another way to describe
what we wish to do is to say that we shall attempt to bridge the
gap between the science of group interaction and the technology
of groups as social instruments.

Technology is the putting of science to work for conscious, human ends. It accepts scientific knowledge as the portrayal of the
processes that go on. Among these processes are some which tend
to move in the direction of the ends desired. Some of the other
processes are seen as moving toward undesired ends, or away
from the desired ends. The job of the technologist is to find the
means to increase the rate of the processes going toward desired
ends and to slow down or inhibit the processes going against
them. But he has to begin with an understanding of the processes
he has to deal with, and with some notion of their relative driving
force. Above all, he must be able to distinguish processes that
cannot happen from those that can be made to happen.

We cannot, in social science, expect for a long time to reach
anything like the precision of scientific application that the chemical engineer, for example, reaches with his science of thermo-

dynamics. There are fundamental differences, too, in approach. The chemical engineer is essentially a dominating manipulator, bending to his will a mass of chemicals. The social engineer or administrator working with people is dealing with a very different sort of entity. Manipulation, bending people to one's own will against their wishes, has been thoroughly tried at many times and places in man's history, and it does not work—at least not for long. By adding to his team the propagandist, with his arts of persuasion, the manipulator can go farther and last longer, but he can never get the kind of efficiency of which man is capable. He ultimately has to rely on force, on a terrific expenditure of energy which may well exceed what he can get from the group.

I am thoroughly convinced that the group itself has to be the engineer. It has to make its own applications of scientific knowledge to its own situation. Utilization of scientific knowledge for better group operation is not so much an engineering matter as it is a training problem. The "expert" is not the leader or manipulator of the group; he is the consultant or trainer. This is why we find over and over again, from case histories of groups that developed into effective instruments, that there was an unusual awareness of their own processes; that in these groups a significant common element was a continual effort to make explicit in the group the things the group was feeling and doing. It is only by making conscious to members the state of affairs in the group that intelligence can be effectively and systematically applied.

This chapter will describe the kinds of things of which groups need to be conscious in their own operation if they expect to learn to solve their problems more efficiently.

In meetings there are at least four distinguishable types of legitimate and inevitable problems facing groups all the time: (*a*) the publicly stated problem the group was brought together to solve; (*b*) the hidden problems of dealing with shared anxieties which usually are not explicitly formulated (problems within the "group mentality"); (*c*) individual efforts to achieve publicly stated ends (getting ideas to "take home" to another group, or learning something, or making a contribution to a worthy project); and (*d*) individuals' efforts to deal with their own hidden problems of membership anxiety and self-integration and adaptation.

The group must determine what provision, if any, needs to be made in order that each of these types of problem-solving go on. It must also control its activity in such a way that the energy going into each of the four types helps the group move toward its goals. But what are these goals?

The typical action group sees problem-solving of type *a* as its goal; some human relations trainers concentrate on type *b*; type *c* is typical of most workshops and "educational" enterprises; and group therapists are likely to strive for type *d*. There is no objection to selecting one particular type of goal to define success —unless it causes us to resist giving the necessary consideration to the other three types. Groups are well advised to acknowledge the "completeness" of people, the fact that significant achievement by human beings requires an engagement of thoughts, emotions, and actions, and that there must be sufficient scope for all these kinds of behavior in their proper and necessary integrative relationships.

Effective group operation requires conscious co-ordination and control of the four types of problem-solving; and this is not automatically achieved. The possibility of achievement is even affected by some decisions which are typically made before the meeting starts: Who will be members of the group? How shall the task be defined initially? What time limits or other pressures on our deliberations do we accept?

Control is also exerted in the opening remarks; in fact, some research workers have felt that the whole course of a meeting is determined by the events of the first few minutes. The particular reality factors to which the group's attention is directed in the opening remarks can make a vast difference in the proportions of the four types of problem-solving. Thus it may be "realistic" to want much overt participation (at least in some kinds of meetings), but calling people's attention to this at the beginning is likely to raise the amount of energy going into problem-solving of type *b*—dealing with hidden shared anxieties—at the expense of the others.

In general, we usually think of control as exerted continuously during the meeting. The conditions we are trying to safeguard through this control of process are, typically, stated in the following ways: (*a*) to keep the discussion "group-centered," so that it is of interest to all and so all can participate; (*b*) to safeguard ease of expression so members can say what they really think; (*c*) to keep the discussion at a sufficiently "practical" level that everyone can visualize what is being talked about; and (*d*) to maintain sufficient "sensitivity" to what happens that participants take account of each other's wishes and keep everyone interested and motivated.

In developing our notions about the control system and how it operates, we shall begin with the concept of "work" and its relationships to the four types of problems. Then we shall discuss productivity (actual goal achievement) as depending upon the creation of the appropriate balance between work and nonwork in all activity. Next we shall state a variety of principles of control, and this will lead into a portrayal of a number of different ways in which control is exerted.

Conditions Required for Work in the Group

Both for practical and theoretical reasons, it is useful to distinguish work from other kinds of activity. At the visceral level, we can tell immediately when a group is "working well" or "not getting anywhere." Ordinarily, work is a kind of activity in which we feel that people are "pulling together." There is a feel of co-operation about it, a voluntary, high-morale aspect.

It is evident that for this kind of work to go on, there must be publicly stated and generally shared goals. Of the four types of problem-solving listed above, types *a* and *c*, group and individual efforts to achieve publicly understood goals, are most likely to be involved when we feel that the group is "working." A characteristic of work toward stated goals is that it is easy to see what is happening. A host of decisions have to be made, but they are made openly, and people know that they are being made. They furnish precedents for future decision-situations. The decision-making processes during work contribute to the body of agreements that constitute the "culture" of the group.

The "work" involved in problem-solving activity directed to hidden problems of the individual and the group (types *b* and *d*) is mostly in the subconscious. We shall not consider such activity to be work, preferring to reserve this term for purposive goal-directed behavior in which an obstacle to the goal is overcome by conscious effort. We may, however, refer to the hidden agenda as problem-solving, because as observers we can fairly well predict behavior on the theory that the individual or group acts *as if* guided by a particular purpose—even though this purpose is subconsciously held.

For any but the most impulsive behavior in the group, there is, on the part of the individual, some conscious perception that he can and wants to contribute to problem-solving of public types a and/or c. He has motivation, and he is conscious that he has it. He is "involved" in the work of the group and wants it to "go well" so that his opportunity to participate will be protected. The publicly accepted problem gives him a basis for communication with others and for knowing how to act and choose appropriate behavior. Moreover, when his behavior contributes to the public goals, he is rewarded by the group's expressed approval or—and this is a higher compliment—by their making insightful use of the contribution.

At the same time, however, according to chapter 7, the need which has the highest priority for an individual or group is for problem-solving of the private sort to reduce anxieties to tolerable levels. The source of anxiety is in the quality of relationships with other people, even though anxiety can be mobilized by cues associated with objective problem-solving processes. Anxiety enters into objective problem-solving only to the extent that it is "contaminated" with problems of human relationship. When we say, for example, that "Mr. Smith committed suicide because he lost his money and felt himself to be a failure," we are probably only half-right. Success and failure are group determined. The unfortunate Smith's despondency was primarily, we would guess, over the feeling that people would look down on him or "sympathize" with him; that he "couldn't take it" any more. The problem-solving at which he failed was only partially of type c, his own efforts to reach a possibly stated goal. The significant difficulty was with type d, his own anxieties about himself. Had he been able to deal with the imagined problems of his relationship to other people, loss of money would be merely annoying or uncomfortable; but it would hardly produce anxiety at such a level of intensity that it had to be removed at its source.

The fact that there is most need "to do something to relieve the situation" at times when there is anxiety; and the fact that anxiety is primarily concern over relationship problems; and the fact that no two individuals have the same relationship problems —these, when added up, lead us to the conclusion that if people behave similarly in a group, they do so for different reasons. They have a common understanding that some particular behavior is possible and is relevant to public goals. In general, however, members do not behave identically. They have "readiness" for different behaviors at any given time; and there are times when some members are not really "ready" for any overt participation. And, given the same goal, they are almost certain to approach it in somewhat different ways.

Control and co-ordination of individual contributions occur through the public meanings of behavior to the group. For the individual producing the behavior, there are, in addition, meanings known only to him. Private meanings may be insights newly achieved, reassurances that an individual can meet competition, feelings that he really demolished another's silly argument, sudden realization of possibilities for friendship with another member, etc. Or, members can be gratified with the behaviors of others in the group as well as their own. They can be reassured that they are smarter or that someone really understands their point of view, or they may be glad someone finally "told off" the leader, etc.

These nonwork gratifications are characteristic of the bull-session, of private problem-solving, and of periods of emotionality. When the work-type problem focus becomes too dim, or too uninteresting, too much of a detour to more basic need-meeting, private problem-solving activity becomes greater. There is more emotionality, and the content of discussion may appear to be any set of ideas that can serve as a vehicle for communicating feeling. The group seems to be trying to maintain itself, its mutual involvement, its rate of reward, through recourse to less obvious, private problem-solving. If the group does not feel free enough to engage in such activity, or if there actually are not, for the time being, any sufficiently strong tensions, then the group may fill in the vacuum with academic argument. Sometimes it can be quite convincing, too.

In the second meeting of one training group, the leader decided to withdraw temporarily. The group members did not know why he did this, and did not feel free enough to ask. Reasonably, they started talking about the "problems of this group." But there were not enough prior agreements for the diagnosis of their group problems, and they had not yet had enough experience together to find much data for evidence.

The leader was not surprised to find them speculating about their problems with very little basis in fact. But as the conversation went on, the leader began to detect something else (later verified through interviews): the group did not feel much concerned over its own problem of withdrawal by the leader; the group did not yet mean enough to them for such details to matter. What was "really" happening was that they were simply trying to maintain their involvement in the group; they found interaction more gratifying than the embarrassment of sitting quietly. It was as if there was a particular rate of reward they were trying to establish and maintain. They did it by talking about problems, and since they had little to go on in the actual group, they drew on problems from their various internalized groups. Thus it happened that the leader listened to a learned discussion of such questions as: Are we too dependent on the leader? Does a person have to give up his independence to work in a group? Aren't we just competing with each other? The problems were those from the prevailing culture, and they were simply advanced to fill the gap.

I cite this illustration to indicate the very real drive to maintain the group through maintaining interaction; and I am also warning against the dangers of taking too seriously what people say about group problems in such nonwork situations. It is almost impossible to diagnose group problems accurately unless there is an accepted work task; only then does one have immediately useful mental images against which to contrast and interpret the behavior of the group.

To summarize: one can usually count on a group doing *some-*

thing, but co-ordination comes primarily through the work components of the group's total activity. One can also count on individuals having some readiness to participate, but the readiness is greater when there is a work job to be done because then the member role is more readily definable and individuals know how to behave. When the group is working, one finds the following by-products: first, the problem is being continuously reformulated and redefined as new meanings are consciously explored by the group; second, the culture of the group is developing, efficiency is increasing, the group is acquiring technical skills; and third, the feelings of membership in the group are increasing; the group develops more meaning for the individual, and he will work harder and take more risks to keep it going.

GROUP PRODUCTIVITY

Productivity is a concept of the amount and quality of desired change produced through group experience. The kind we refer to as "learning" means change in the way of behaving, presumably reflecting a new attitude, insight, degree of skill, etc. This sort of alteration has continuing long-range effects, and it occurs to people and groups. The productivity of classroom activity is ordinarily judged by the amount of change it produces in the pupils. But there are other types of changes that could be considered in measuring productivity: changes in the teacher, changes in the "maturity" or efficiency of operation of the class, changes in parental attitudes brought about by pupils as a result of experiences in the classroom. Let us look at three distinguishable types of stable changes which can be used to assess the productivity of group activity.

First, there is the amount of change during a period of time in the group itself. Any learned, stable change in a group would be evident as an alteration in its ability to solve problems, make decisions, meet individual needs of the members, encourage or inhibit the formation of cliques, etc. The change would be maintained as such in the "culture" of the group, the set of agreements through which the group controls its own operation. The characteristic change of the culture of a group is developmental—not from one rule to another, but from no rule to some rule. More agreements are constantly being achieved within broad policies. Thus, if a group has a "set" toward encouraging members to participate in its leadership, the cultural shift is likely to be the development of the agreements necessary to implement this policy. The agreements will be in the form of decisions about whether or not there will be a chairman, under what conditions, how selected, how recalled, how his duties are to be defined, the sort of supportive behavior expected of the others. Through experience, the group spells out in practical language the "meaning" of its beliefs about method, authority, justice, and other values. The "spelling out" is done in the development of habits and practices which are thereafter automatically used in the relevant situations.

Besides a change toward greater specificity, the culture of a group can also alter in its basic value patterns. Typically, for example, the orientation of a training group changes from dependency on the leader to dependency on itself for procedural suggestion, from reliance on the authority of the leader to reliance on the authority of its own experience.

A second way to think about productivity of group experience is in terms of the amount of change it has produced during a period of time in the behavior of other groups. This amounts to an assessment of the influence of the activities of one group on the activities of adjacent groups. For such an influence to have long-range effects, some learning, some change in the control system, must have occurred in the influenced group. Community councils, human relations commissions, and *ad hoc* citizens groups attempt to bring about changes in other groups, in their practices, attitudes, skills, officer personnel, etc. We shall present the thesis later that this kind of change can be brought about only through the agency of people who have "membership" both in the influence group and in the influenced group. We might refer to this kind of productivity as the rate of change of the community in which the group operates.

A third kind of productivity through learning can be seen in the rate of change of the subjective internalized community of the individual. Thus, as learnings occur in the actual group, one's memberships in other groups are also affected. The productivity of a therapy group's activities might be considered as the rate of rearrangement of the individual's pattern of overlapping memberships, toward a state of lessened conflict or anxiety. In so far as any group participation has therapeutic effects, one can think of its productivity partly in these terms.

In summary.—Any experience can be seen as a pattern of four types of problem-solving endeavors: of these, two types can be referred to as "work," as "achievement problem-solving," or as "culture-building." The other two types are referred to as "non-work," "process problem-solving," or as the operation of "group mentality." The productivity of group activity depends upon the manner in which these kinds of endeavors are controlled. A productive activity is one from which the group learns to control its next activity, so that it will be productive of further change in the group toward still more productive activity. Productivity is determined by the group's control system.

In Part I we have seen, either directly or by implication, a number of concepts of productivity. In the case of citizen action, productivity is primarily change of social and physical conditions in the community, and, secondarily, change within participating individuals. Productivity of in-service training presents exactly the reverse situation. Administrators are concerned with changes in working groups and in the relations among them. In the classroom, changes within students and teacher should both be appraised. Productivity in laboratory training involves changes in individuals and also in the culture of the training group.

PRINCIPLES UNDERLYING THE CONTROL OF THE GROUP

There are different assumptions about what it is that is to be controlled. A theoretician might ask: "Is a group more than the sum of its parts? Does it have properties over and above the pooled characteristics of its members?" A student of the group might ask: "Should I be looking at individuals or at the group as a whole?" A leader might ask himself: "Is my job to encourage participation of each individual, or is my job to pay attention to keeping the problem clearly defined?" The socially mobile member might ask himself: "Is it all right for me to sit next to Joe and get in a word with him now and then, or will this be resented?"

All of these questions betray the same underlying perplexity: Is the group an organic whole, made up of parts, to be sure, but basically organized as one unit; or is the group really just a lot of people reacting to each other in their own ways?

But this is not a real problem. The group is not "really" one or the other. For some purposes, such as ours when we want to talk about the "control system of the group," we find it useful to think of the group as a whole. For other purposes, such as predicting the role an individual will play in a meeting, it is more useful to think of that person as an individual and the group as his environment.

Our question then becomes: What perception of the group is most useful for a participant to have? What viewpoint, if held by the members, will result in the most productive experience for all? In the remainder of this section we wish to delineate the set of member beliefs or principles which seems to result in most effective group operation. These beliefs must rest on a basic assumption by each member that the group exists as a whole, and that every member represents that whole and partakes of it.

1. *Each individual statement, as soon as it is made, becomes the property of the group.*—"Jack's suggestion" is the "suggestion made by Jack," but Jack does not own it, and Jack does not have to defend it or prove it. It is up to the group to determine whether the suggestion is useful to itself, to test whether it is a good suggestion. On this matter, Jack himself is usually the best informant to the group; he knows most about his own suggestion and he can be used as a resource person to clarify his thought or explain its possible usefulness to the group. (For an illustration, see the case study, pp. 322–26.)

2. *Emotional expressions by individuals express the needs of the group.*—If Chris and Bud get into a scrap, everyone else appears to the others to be in it too. The chances are that the members, for one reason or another, are getting some gratification out of the fight. Therefore the fighters are expressing the need of the group at that time to fight. If a member steps in to try to stop the fight, he will

be seen as fighting, too. If a member sits by and does nothing, he will be seen as wanting the fight to occur. Emotionality is shared throughout the group, and the group responds selectively to those aspects of behavior that can be interpreted as contributing to it or being part of it. (This is the basic principle useful in steering the group. The case study in chapter 5 shows consistent use of this principle.)

3. *In all but extreme cases, problem people are to be considered group problems.*—The group does not "work on" individuals. If there is somebody in the group who disturbs everyone, and everyone knows it, the question is: "Why does this sort of behavior bother us; why can't we deal with it?" The question is not: "Why is Fred such a troublemaker?" In general, the group cannot expect to change a sick or disturbed person, but it can learn to handle the anxieties that such members mobilize in themselves. Singling out these people and giving them attention, teaches them that their disturbing behaviors will be rewarded. But if upsetting behavior is treated as a general, group problem, the "troublesome" person gets no attention at all as a person; he does get educative feedback as to the consequences of his behavior and how the group feels about it. In general, the group works only on group problems, not problems of individuals (see also "The Trainer Speaks to the Group," pp. 173–74).

4. *The question is not: "Is this behavior relevant to our problem?" but rather: "To what problem is this behavior relevant?"*—(And then: "How serious is this problem for us, and do we need to do anything about it?") All individual contributions are relevant. They arose from the situation of the group trying to do something, and they are entitled to consideration by everyone, since everyone contributed to the situation. (Meeting VIII, pp. 156–60, is a particularly clear illustration of the usefulness of this principle for diagnostic purposes.)

5. *A problem is whatever everybody feels to be a problem.*—All contributions are regarded as symptomatic of problems the group is working on or may need to work on. But no problem is accepted as one requiring action without some sort of reality test: either the group takes it up and begins working on it spontaneously, or they test to see whether it is generally felt to be a problem (see also the

discussion of "readiness," p. 61). And, of course, the group cannot and should not work on every problem; many lie outside the group's limits of operation, and many more can be endured—at least until demands of higher priority have been met.

6. *The group moves by consensus and agreement, not by taking sides in disputes.*—Minority-majority splits are generally over issues couched in global terms, rather than over concrete questions of what to do in a particular time and place. By and large, such big issues, about which no agreement is possible, are not actually used to split the group but rather to justify the fact that the group has already split. Under these conditions, the interests of the group are against finding agreement. (For a clear application, see the beginning events of the meeting described on pp. 10–12.)

7. *A decision has been reached whenever people feel sufficiently confident to act.*—The psychology of decision-making is concerned with understanding the data or concepts or preliminary experiences a group needs in order to have enough confidence or trust in itself and its suggestions to act. The most important foes of confidence are ambiguity, vagueness, and inability to assess the values and costs of alternatives. These are matters calling for more thinking, more data, more exploring of the obstacles individuals see. Steamroller tactics and persuasion are of no avail because they block the objective evaluation of consequences and the possibilities of correction if plans go awry. (General Smith showed considerable insight into this principle, see pp. 124–26.)

8. *Voting is never used to determine the right alternative, but it can be used to test confidence in a particular alternative.*—The use of voting implies a promise: we will not act unless everyone says he has confidence in the idea. In most situations, this is a more rigorous requirement than is necessary, and it is unrealistic to expect people to commit themselves in advance to something they have not yet experienced. With regard to agendas, for example, it is frequently wiser for the leader merely to ask permission from the group and then proceed if there are no objections (provided the situation is one in which it would be possible to voice an objection). This involves risk; but a group is justified in taking a risk if it has some recourse should its judgment turn out to be poor. (For amplification, see pp. 306–7.)

9. *Whenever the group does not know what it is doing, it ought to stop and find out.*—This does *not* mean that the group ought to argue over its objectives, but rather that it ought to describe to itself what it is doing. In unclear situations, there is actually discrimination against the participation of some members. When a person knows what the group is doing, then he also knows how to participate, and if he does not participate, it is reasonable to assume that he has nothing to contribute. But when a person does not know what the group is doing, he does not know how to participate, and he is blocked. Therefore, with every change in the nature of the group's activity, it is well to be sure the member roles are redefined. (Meeting IV, pages 146–48, shows an application of this principle.)

10. *All seriously intended contributions are to be responded to.*—The group understands that contributions are not only supposed to be helpful to the group, but that they also express some need of the individual to test his interpretation of the situation. Failure to respond to contributions is thus an act of discrimination against the person. If the contribution seems of no value, it is better to admit an inability to see its implications for the group than to ignore it. In general the climate of the group should be sufficiently objective and purpose-oriented that ideas out of which the group can extract no good can be rejected without rejection of the person. This is an important requirement for learning (see also the discussion of reality testing, pp. 49–50).

11. *No individual can speak for the group; the group speaks for itself.*—Each individual is a piece of the group, and he can be a spokesman for that piece. He can honestly report how he feels and what he thinks, and the group knows how to interpret such information. He can also give his impressions of the group as a whole. But no man really knows how others think and feel, and if he misrepresents them, they are entitled to defend themselves. The problem then becomes an undesirable interpersonal squabble. Members may respond to each other and the leader in various ways, but not as authoritative spokesmen for the group. (Tom's soliloquy, pp. 156–58, is an excellent illustration of what members can do.)

12. *There are individual differences, and people play different roles in*

each situation.—The way a person participates depends upon what opportunities for reward each individual perceives. Different individuals are rewarded by different kinds of participation because their needs are different and because the repertoire of roles each can fulfil is different. Those who have in their repertoire a role needed by the group are the ones who should be participants in each situation. If the group never engages in activity which needs their participation, then there is no reason for those persons being members of the group. The aim of the group should not be to get participation equally distributed among members. The aim should be to deal with its problems in a way sufficiently comprehensive that everyone can contribute if he wishes, and to see to it that there are no barriers in the group that would prevent needed contributions. (This principle is illustrated also in the discussion of resistance to change, pp. 74–76.)

13. *Every change in activity alters the prestige system and the opportunities for reward in the group.*—In general, a shift to a new activity will increase the reward possibilities for some members because they can contribute better to the new activity, and decrease them for others. Variety among activities gives more people a chance to find themselves and to achieve prestige. Although the selection of activities should be based on problem requirements, boredom and the need for change of pace should be recognized. (For further relationship with needs, see p. 253.)

The preceding statements cover a set of beliefs regarding the realities of group operation. The list can be written in other ways, and probably other lists would include more things or different things. The assumptions on which a group seems to operate reflect its control system; our list represents one such system. (It is applied to leadership problems on pp. 314–19, and to the experimental method of leadership on pp. 302–10.)

How the Control System Operates

In general, the co-ordination of human effort is obtained in one of two ways. The first is through the authority of shared ideas. The second is through the authority, backed by power, of a particular person or group. These are dealt with at length in chapter

4. The first is the ideal of democracy; the second is the ideal of autocracy.

This work is aimed at developing, in so far as possible, the democratic basis for co-ordination because it is the more effective. Beliefs such as those presented immediately above, if fully understood and acted upon by every member of a group, would provide for the greatest range of useful ideas and for their sharing throughout the group. Because each individual subscribed fully to the same minimum set of agreements, he would find his efforts joined with the efforts of others, so that his "power" would be co-extensive with the power of the entire group. He would be able to exert the most discerning initiative without having to clear his proposals with the group leadership. There would exist the maximum of freedom: the greatest scope of individual action coupled with the greatest security of group reinforcement.

I have been in groups that were reasonably close to this ideal. They were brought together for laboratory training in group operation. The individuals were highly motivated to try to reach this ideal; the twenty-four-hour-a-day culture of the environing workshop was set up to support it and to give individuals ample opportunity outside the group for reflection on what was happening in the group.

It has been interesting to discover, over the years, that this state of maturity does not mean complete "independence" in the traditional sense. A shared agreement or bargain is a social contract, a two-way street. It carries with it the implication that if in any situation I feel my action not to be in line with the policies I helped the group make, I am no longer "on my own." I must have further interaction with the group either to adjust my behavior to the spirit of the group agreements or to get an agreement within which my behavior is appropriate. Moreover, this is not strictly and exclusively an intellectual dependence; it is also an emotional one. To accept this kind of relationship to the group I also accept the idea that group policies under conditions of proper deliberation are "better" than those I would make by myself; that the experience of the group is a higher and more useful authority than the experience of any individual; that when I am in doubt as to my conduct, I can get from the group the interpretation or judgment that is in the best interests of all. The feeling that goes with the acceptance of these relationships is that of trust and of security based on trust.

Thus interdependence is always a blend of independence and dependence. The ideal is not to eliminate all dependency but to establish, protect, and maintain the quality of interdependence most appropriate for the welfare of all.

Typically, control systems in groups operate in several ways. The first is through determining the nature of responses to statements. This is the basic, continuous, pervasive operating reality of the group. *A* says something, *B* replies, *C* responds to *B*'s remark, or to a combination of *A*'s and *B*'s remarks. *A* says something more, and so on. Each response to a statement is the immediate stimulus for the next response. At the same time, every statement is a response to the general feeling of the group, to the individual's internalized anxieties, and the like.

From the group's shared agreements an individual deduces the limits within which he can choose among possible responses. The control system develops in the first place from the group's need for a stable environment—an environment in which it is possible to predict whether what one is about to do will be rewarded or punished. This possibility of predictability (and therefore of individual security) is increased as the group writes its unwritten laws of how to respond.

Suppose, for example, Al says: "Gosh, I think that decision we just made is all wrong." These replies might be made:

MARY (*with heat*): Well, this sure is a fine time to tell us that! If you didn't like what we were doing, why didn't you say something earlier?

or

MAC: I feel we won't really be sure whether its "right" or "wrong" until we have carried out the first step written there on the blackboard. In the meanwhile we all will need to be thinking about what data will be needed to assess it. Would this be a good thing to discuss now, to sort of warm up our further thinking along these lines? What do you think, Al?

or

TOM: You feel dissatisfied with the decision.

In the early meetings of a group it is to be expected that comments like Al's will evoke such different responses, and Al has no way of knowing the sort of response he will get. He does not know whether somebody will attack him, or try to use him as a responsible resource person to the group, or simply encourage him to reveal more feelings he may later regret having expressed. He also does not know how to respond further to the comments he receives, because he cannot be quite sure of the motives back of them. Mary, Mac, and Tom are operating with different and in some ways incompatible assumptions. The group will need at least to eliminate the incompatibility, if not the differences. And in doing so, a contribution will be made to the body of agreements through which the group controls itself.

The group control system is reasonably adequate when there is an understood rationale for responding to all sorts of remarks: the hypothetical suggestion, the call for action, the personal confession, the irrelevant flight, the attack, the complacent avoidance, scapegoating, diagnosing, experting, blocking, creating, etc. Of these various types of comments, the ones most requiring agreement are the emotional ones. In general, the responses should reflect the basic understanding that group deliberation is an inquiry leading to realistic decisions. The thirteen principles above specifically implement this point of view. In the case of Al's remark, the replies by Mary, Mac, and Tom might constructively follow any of the kinds of insights of the thirteen principles: (*a*) It *is* embarrassing when objection is raised immediately after a decision has been made. (*b*) It is possible that many others share Al's qualms. How about it? (*c*) Al's comment may not be a response to the decision so much as to the *way* it was made. (*d*) Al should be encouraged to state (as hypotheses to be tested by the group) his hunches as to why he thinks the decision is wrong. (*e*) It is important to weigh all valid objections carefully before taking action; but we cannot tell until we weigh them whether they are valid or not.

A second type of group control operation is in the responses not to a particular statement but to the group's general activity over a longer period of time. To some extent, of course, all responses are in part to the situation as a whole and in part to the last thing said. But there are certain kinds of statements which reveal that the member has been considering a much larger unit of group experience than merely the single statement. Thus control may be exercised through an attempt to state the "sense of the meeting." Whenever a person designated for that purpose believes that the group has reached consensus on some significant matter, he attempts to put it into words. If his statement is accepted, it becomes part of the realities with which the group consciously works.

A third control device, similarly operating in terms of larger units than the single statement, is the descriptive diagnosis. At times when the member feels that the group task or the member role is ambiguously defined, he may attempt to describe what he thinks the group is doing. Such a description attempts to relate the activity to prior planning; it raises by implication a question: Are we carrying out our plan or do we need further planning? If the plan is unclear or too general, the diagnosis may have to be based on individual rather than group data: "I am finding it hard to participate because I can't figure out the sort of contribution that would be appropriate at this time."

A fourth kind of control device is the use of a group "watchdog," possible when there has been prior identification by the group of behaviors it wishes to avoid. It can then agree that when these behaviors occur, the group's attention will be called to them, either by one person appointed for that purpose or by anyone in the group. In this case, the group is using explicit prior agreements to enforce certain restrictions on the behavior of members, in the interests of co-operation.

Another control device, the fifth, is the evaluation session in which the group simply takes time out to study how it has been operating. This provides a real opportunity to hammer out the agreements the group needs for its own operation, and it can also serve as a basis for planning next steps. But the purposes of the session must be made clear; otherwise it may become either a festival of politeness or a session wallowing in emotion.

The sixth control device operating over limited periods of time is an initial "structuring" of member roles for each activity. At the beginning of each new phase of problem-solving activity, time is spent to decide the sort of contribution which is most needed: shall it be personal experience, theories, questions, opinions? This is a useful device, because it calls for the explicit reaching of agreements, but, unlike the evaluation session, it calls for them before vested interests have become strong. The evaluation session develops agreements inductively, by reflection on immediate past experience; the prestructuring session develops agreements deductively, by applying general principles of group problem-solving to the anticipated immediate problem situation.

Finally, there can be simple advance decisions that provide the necessary control. In large public meetings, where the audience is not expected to share in determining the program, planning usually settles in advance most of the things about which agreements in a discussion group would ordinarily have to be made. The need for agreements about ways to participate is just exactly as great as the opportunity for overt participation. Suppose, for example, there is a mass meeting in which the only overt participation of the audience is in buzz groups, reporting, and filling out cards. The necessary rules for reporting and filling out cards are given by the chairman of the meeting, and his authority is acceptable in regard to those two functions. In the buzz groups, the members have to reach at least some implicit agreements, but their task is often a nonwork one, confined largely to the exchange of opinion, making no demands that people do not commonly encounter in our culture.

Some people believe that the adoption of Robert's *Rules of Order*, together with skill in using these rules, should provide adequate control. As a matter of practical fact, such adoption has advantages: first, the rules are familiar enough so that people know what to expect when they are used; second, the rules provide for a sequence of phases, so that they are at times helpful in keeping the discussion moving along toward conclusions; and third, they provide the authority for easy maintenance of order and respect for evidence. The disadvantages appear to be: first, that the rules are not of general usefulness for all tasks; their particular strength is when the task is one of legislation. They are less useful in action situations because the work is for the most part done in committees and the larger group may not become sufficiently involved in the problems of the committees to be committed emotionally to action. When the entire group is made a committee-of-the-whole, then there is a free discussion situation for which the rules give little guidance beyond the maintenance of order. A second disadvantage, at least theoretically, is the assumption that conclusions are reached through debate, with the chairman serving as referee. Energy may be diverted unnecessarily into factional quarrels, and the contributions of those people who cannot operate in a conflict situation will be lost. (This is discussed further in Case II, pp. 323–26.)

In general, however, the quality of work in groups is dependent much more on understandings and attitudes than it is on the particular set of procedures used for control. The best procedures are those that best reflect whatever understandings the group has, for under these conditions they can learn from experience how to do better. All methods of control imply the exercise of some form of authority (see chapter 4, pp. 99–101).

THE CONCEPT OF LEADERSHIP

Up to this point, I have deliberately avoided the appearance of any specific comment about leadership, but the avoidance is less real than apparent. We have been considering major aspects of group control, and leadership is the means for developing, maintaining, and modifying the group control system. It is a means, not an end; a function, not a person. But we customarily think of certain people in the group as having more responsibility than others for this function. In the next chapter we shall discuss these people, the problems they face, and the kinds of policies leaders need.

CHAPTER 11

Leadership is the set of functions through which the group co-ordinates the efforts of individuals. These efforts must result in satisfaction to the participants, as well as in help to the group in meeting its purposes. The demands on leadership are complex, and to define these demands and discover ways to meet them is essentially a job of inquiry.

The inquiry can and should be consciously guided by the experimental method. We spell out here some of the important implications of this notion, and we examine some of the common obstacles to experimental-minded leadership.

Leadership: Co-ordinating Effort toward Group Goals

INTRODUCTION

To understand group behavior, we assume that the group acts *as if* it operated within the spirit or letter of a set of agreements. At any moment in a particular group, for example, it may seem as if there are agreements that aggression must not be expressed against the leader; that the problem cannot be solved; that only people with high prestige in the group are to be listened to; that the greatest approval of the group will be given to a person who sees what action can be taken; that whenever the group gets into difficulty it wishes to break into smaller groups; that the group prefers to operate with parliamentary method; that all comments made by Jim are probably clever but erroneous; etc.

Further, it is *as if* these agreements are enforced. Violations are punished, efforts to change them are resisted; there may even be a search for ulterior motives on the part of anyone who tries to question or change the rules. These agreements may be subconscious in the sense that the group does not know it holds them, or quite explicitly debatable and reached through conscious decision-making processes. The agreements define the opportunities for participation: they set the limits to behavior by ruling out some behaviors as unacceptable, and at the same time they determine the opportunity for behaving within the limits by stipulating how the permitted behaviors are to be used (and through this, rewarded).

Group agreements have teeth in them. Their determination of what is possible, at what cost or with what reward, is the control of the group. Changing the agreements, hammering out new ones to fit the continual diagnosis of realities in the ever changing group-problem situation—this is the function of leadership. More precisely, leadership is a type of gate-keeping; it is the function of determining the susceptibility of agreements to modification, of determining the processes by which agreements can be reached or changed. The agreements most directly related to leadership are those about how the existing agreements are to be changed: under what conditions, through what kinds of representations based on what sorts of evidence, with what speed, with what degree of confidence. In other words, provision for leadership is also among the agreements of the group.

All groups have some sort of leadership, whether they know it or not. The amount of leadership is roughly proportional to the rate of change of agreements or group culture. "Good" leadership is indicated when the decisions and actions of a group become more and more in line with reality; and when there is minimum effort devoted to achieving this adaptation. We note the directional criterion: not all changes in the group control system signify good leadership; when the group operates with principles contradictory to those discussed in chapter 10, it is moving away from the realities of its situation. It is moving away from the conditions required for it to realize its purposes of obtaining maximum wisdom through maximum individual health and growth.

From the standpoint of the preceding chapters, we might think of the problems of leadership as those of taking action to resolve certain types of conflict:

First, there is the conflict between our subconscious wishes and desires and our stated purposes and conscious efforts to solve public problems. Thus the faculty group whose major wish is to avoid getting involved in additional work may, at the conscious level, be trying to set up new and demanding procedures to follow.

Second, there is the balance between acting and evaluating, as discussed in chapter 8. Our first impulse in replying to a critical statement is to regard it as an accusation: to respond to emotionalized evaluative statements with further evaluation of these statements rather than with a test of the truth of their allegations. Leadership determines the balance: whether emotional remarks are to be self-perpetuating in the group through the arousal of more emotion, or whether emotional remarks are to be taken as evidence of the need to think through a problem.

Third, there is the problem of freedom. In groups, this is the question of individual exploitation of the group versus group exploitation of the individual. The quality of leadership decides whether the group culture will be discriminatory, whether the rules will be determined by needs for limitations in the situation or by needs to suppress individuals. The most common type of discrimination in the group is against the members: it is the notion that leadership is privilege rather than hard work on behalf of the group.

A fourth type of co-ordination or resolution through leadership is the matter of finding and maintaining an appropriate but ever changing balance among the four types of problem-solving functions: process and achievement problem-solving by individuals and the group (see chapter 10).

To deal with all these problems at the same time requires a *method* of dealing with them. I shall point out that this is the experimental method. It shall be my general point of view that a group is successful to the extent that this method underlies its control system and is incorporated in the viscera and brain of the leadership, and of the members too.

The experimental method is based on two central assumptions: that useful behavior must be in line with reality; and that the way to resolve doubts is to take a first or pilot step and see what happens. Thus the "experimental" approach is to suggest a way to get the data needed to interpret reality, and it makes the collection of such data a part of action itself. There are certain deductions that follow from these ideas in the case of a group.

First, problem-solving involves continual exploration and reformulation. We cannot plan all action in advance because we cannot be certain of the factors which will be involved as we go on. Therefore we have to expect to discover some of the evidence necessary for planning action during the process of acting (and of rehearsing action in our minds). But to select from all the data of experiencing the particular facts that are relevant to the action is no easy matter. Selection criteria are needed, and these are set up through trial and error. The quest for relevance is an exploration of ideas about *if . . . then:* "If this really is an important factor, then the following things will happen. . . ." The exploration comes in studying a wide range of "this's" to find those yielding consequences which make a difference to the purposes of the group. It is because of this exploratory aspect of all action that the way we define our problems changes as we work on them; and it is for this reason that it is correct, in one sense, at least, to say that the problem never gets solved but only reformulated—even though the environment gets changed in the process.

Many of the objections to group working are due to the inability of some to tolerate the necessary uncertainty about future action. If the source of a person's confidence is that some future action is the only "right" action, then he is walking on thin ice indeed. Basically he is denying that it is possible and necessary to learn from experience; and he is further assuming that the situation is stable and unchanging between the present and some future time. The source of confidence we need is in *method;* in the faith (learned from experience) that exploration is not a sign of inefficiency or incompetence or ignorance but rather a sign of sophistication and deep understanding of the realities of human experience.

Leadership, then, guides the exploring process; it keeps its ambiguities to a minimum. It does this through proper assessment of the degree of confidence it is judicious to have with regard to all the agreements—achievement and process oriented—in the group culture.

Second, leadership guides the processes of interpreting and exploring reality, through its control of awareness of choice-points. One does not make conscious use of data except in answer to consciously formulated questions. These questions in a group can be couched in a variety of ways, but the part of a question that is useful is the part that states or implies a recognition that alternatives exist and must be formulated and weighed.

Awareness that a choice-point exists is reflected in differences of feeling about what the group is doing, that some members have severe reservations whereas others are enthusiastic. It is through the equal acceptance of the feelings of all members that the group becomes aware of the need to make a choice of action. Accepting differences in feelings is what we mean by "having respect for individuality." The group may ultimately decide that Henry's feelings are a less valid guide than Jim's, but it must take the feelings of both equally into account before arriving at this decision. This is done automatically when the group acts on the assumption that all expressions of feeling are symptomatic of group need; and when it assumes that all expressions by individuals become the property of the group.

An interpretation of equality among individuals which leads to the conclusion that everyone has equal skill, equal authority, equal wisdom, equal insight, actually shows very little respect for individuals. It results in what has come to be known as "the cesspool theory of group dynamics": that pooled ignorance is wisdom. It denies the fact that some people are brighter, work harder, have had more useful experience, etc., than others. In a group, equality exists in only one respect; the fact that all individual feelings are data which must be taken into account. But this principle is crucial.

A third deduction about leadership functioning follows from this last: that attention must be paid to finding and maintaining conditions such that each person who can make a contribution that the group needs will make it. This requires awareness of the different resources which people can bring to bear on the problems being studied by the group; and it requires defining the member role in each activity in such a way that the most useful people will feel most called upon to contribute. And the obverse also applies: individuals who are hard to understand, or who make contributions for such ulterior private purposes as punishing the group, should not be encouraged unless their contributions are obviously needed. One of the problems of leadership is to see that such people will learn that they do not have to punish the group; that they can get more reward and gratification by making helpful contributions rather than those which produce anxiety or waste time. Leadership then, is concerned with the discovery and co-ordination of member resources, on the assumption that individuals are not equal and that their differences are the group's most valuable asset.

This introductory section is, in a way, a review of some of the implications for leadership of the preceding chapters. It is also the statement of some of the key points in the reasoning behind the assumptions which are desirable for a group to act upon. The reader will see that the various items of group control presented in chapter 10, although presented simply as notions that have been found to work, can also be deduced from the concept that a group controls itself through application of the experimental method. It should also be clear that improvement of group functioning is not a matter of learning new tricks but of learning to use the experimental method consciously as the guide to behavior in the group-problem-reality situation.

In the next section, we wish to spell out in some detail how this experimental method of leadership works. Then, we will consider some common obstacles to use of the method, and try to indicate something of their nature and what to do about them. Following this, we will present a case study which illustrates many of these points, and next we will look at the question of leadership personnel. In the final section, we will comment on the relationship between the method of experimental leadership as advocated here and some other approaches which have been presented.

The Experimental Method in Operation

There are four major functions of the experimental method[1]:

SETTING CONDITIONS FOR EXPERIMENTATION BY MEMBERS

In any new group, there is initially a certain amount of jockeying for position among the members, who are trying to appraise one another. Each wants to know how he compares with the others, in respect to those qualities about which each is anxious. Each member wants to uncover the status system and, if possible, to influence it in his individual favor. Each needs to explore, to discover whether it is all right to talk freely, to express "real" feelings about the group and its tasks. Each member also forms affiliations with a few others and from this definite alignments emerge. And each needs to know what the leader is like—his strengths and his weaknesses—so that he can see how to relate to the leader. All of this is neither good nor bad; it is inevitable.

The leader knows that it is inevitable, and helps the process go on with least interference to group learning and problem-solving.

1. This material is taken in large part from Herbert A. Thelen, "The Experimental Method of Classroom Leadership," *Elementary School Journal*, October, 1952.

He can organize the work in such a way that people discuss problems with each other in small groups, so that increased participation in a wide range of roles gives them a chance to "know" each other, and the fact of a task to accomplish gives them a reason for interacting.[2] Or the members can be given the opportunity to tell of past relevant experiences. Or the leader can make listings of the problems individuals feel are important, as data to be considered.

Most usefully, the leader can make sure that every comment receives a constructive response. The easiest way to accept all comments is by seeing how they are related to the topic at hand, rather than to theories of individual personalities and background; this latter approach is difficult and in the long run, probably, inhibits free discussion. Comments from members may be seen as suggestions of facts which the group will need to consider later, guesses as to what might happen under certain conditions, diagnoses or requests for diagnoses of possible obstacles to the group, reflections of the value of a proposed course of action, and so on.

Because of his responsibility for progress, the leader cannot always merely characterize contributions in relation to the problem. He may have to protect the group from anxieties about time and energy requirements by immediate "corrective" action. Thus, if a member shows in his remark a fantastic notion of the amount of work the group can do, the leader may suggest that one thing the group will learn for itself is its own capacities. If the enthusiast suggests an outlandish project, the leader can express doubt that this particular project falls within the definition of the group's job, interesting though the proposal may seem.

Always and forever, the leader must avoid all general criticisms. His attitude is that any specific proposal may be unworkable (or impractical), but the fact that the proposal was suggested calls the group's attention to the need for better definition of the group's job. His principle always is that individuals are not to be criticized, and that seemingly useless behavior makes the group aware of some lack of clarity of its goals or ways of working.

Under these conditions, the leader maintains enough freedom

2. Thelen, "Group Dynamics in Instruction: The Principle of Least Group Size," *School Review*, March, 1949.

for experimentation so that individuals who need to experiment can do so. The experimentation referred to in this section is private, personal, and probably subconscious. It is directed to finding one's place and way of life in the group. The leader can safeguard conditions for this experimentation, but he cannot force people to experiment along some planned line. Individuals differ in their needs. Seeing to it that people can experiment if they want to, and protecting them from ridicule or loss of face or other effects that block learning from experimentation, is sufficient.

SETTING CRITERIA FOR KNOWING HOW TO PARTICIPATE

Exploration by group members helps them discover the behaviors for which they can or cannot get rewards. In the process, too, members hope to influence the group to like the things they like (and can supply) and to dislike the demands that they cannot meet. All of this can be looked upon as the development of expectations of each other, so that the group can know what to expect from each, and under what conditions.

But besides expectations based on acceptance of people as they are, there is also a need for judging the demands of the situation. Thus, during each stage of *planning* a project, any idea, however wild, should be encouraged and examined for some germinal grain of insight. Here the limits to expression of ideas and feelings are broad. But *after the group has decided* what projects to undertake, then wild ideas are merely time wasting and distracting, and probably are efforts to avoid the pain of work. At this point, the limits to expression of ideas must be narrower. One must stay on the point—or agree to change the point.

Many leaders recognize that the requirements of the situation change as the group moves forward on its task. The group knows this, too, but not so explicitly. It is very helpful to make clear these limits or demands, as the criteria that behavior must satisfy. This can be done routinely at the beginning of each new task, but additional comments will be required as needs for clarification reveal themselves. And the leader must be ready to discuss and modify, if necessary, any stated requirements over which concern is expressed either directly or indirectly.

Some examples from the classroom may make clear the nature of such statements, to help people know how to participate:

"Let's agree to devote the next 10 minutes to finding out what things in the film made the most impression on us" (Moving from a movie to the planning of subsequent work).

"This would be a good time for those who have actually taken a plane trip at night to tell us what it is like" (Trying to get better visualization of night flying as a possible plot situation for a play).

"I wonder if at this point we don't need to restrict our suggestions to the various soluble sulfates we might consider using" (Approaching the specific details of planning a chemical experiment).

"It seems to me that we have about said all that comes readily to mind about these proposed actions. Let's see if each person by now wants to go ahead on one or another of them, and, if not, what questions need to be answered before he can decide" (Testing commitment and diagnosing needed next steps).

"So far, our comments about yesterday's field trip all seem quite happy. I wonder if there aren't also some other feelings. I, for instance, felt quite uncomfortable at times, and even downright angry at some of Smith's statements" (Making it easier to say what is "really" felt so class can identify more significant problems to tackle).[3]

In communicating these requirements of the situation, a great deal depends upon how the leader talks and what attitudes he conveys. When leadership is successful, the group sees that these demands or limits come from the requirements of the situation, not from the leader as a person. The former feeling is encouraged by directness and casualness; the leader seems confident that the limits are reasonable, and that, if not, they can be reconsidered. The impression that the leader has ulterior, personal motives can be communicated by anxiety-expressing attitudes: apologies, expressions of nonspecific displeasure, tiresome explanations. These behaviors present the group with leader-anxiety as a problem to handle—an additional unnecessary and probably insuperable task.

3. For fuller exposition in a third-grade situation, see Thelen, "Social Environment and Problem-solving," *Progressive Education*, March, 1950.

GETTING GROUP AGREEMENT ON NEXT STEPS

In any group, people have an astonishing range of ideas about what makes sense in a particular situation. It is seldom that everyone really believes that any particular course of action is the best. It is unrealistic to demand commitment based on belief that any particular action is the "right" action. What agreements, then, can be made that will enable the group to act?

Assuming that people cannot fully agree on action, the group has two problems rather than one. To the problem of deciding on action there is added the problem of dealing with uncertainty and reservations about the action. Here the experimental method can break the deadlock. The group is asked, in effect, to realize that it has both problems, and then to discuss the alternative action proposals from the standpoint of the extent to which each will result in information that can clear up the confusion. Members must find that action which is informative to the group as well as useful in the situation.

In other words, when a group cannot agree confidently on particular steps, it can agree completely on its *lack* of confidence and then proceed to act to increase its confidence. The desired agreement, then, is on the method of operation, the way in which action will be taken. But it is healthy to have reservations about the action itself. No one can predict the consequences of any course with complete certainty, and it is foolish to pretend one can. Moreover, the reservations of others about the things of which one person is convinced force him to reconsider and organize his thoughts; in effect, they provide him with the need and opportunity to learn.

The leader allows himself to be put in a difficult position whenever he uses steam-roller tactics to secure a particular course of action. By doing this against the group's better judgment, he assumes full responsibility for the possible failure of action. The group members learn from this that it is all right for them not to take responsibility and that their own, often considerable, resources are not wanted. Moreover, if failure results, they learn that the leader is untrustworthy, and their motivation to participate in the next action sinks. Finally, the (often unconscious) resentment of the leader, which certainly is to be expected, is likely to sabotage the action so that it will be a failure.

On the other hand, the leader is often justified in demanding that *some* action be taken. Particularly in a training situation, the leader knows that some things cannot be learned unless one has firsthand experience with them. He also knows that if everyone experiences the same situation, the group will be able to talk together about it instead of past each other, which is usually the case when there has been no common experience from which to build.

In any case, the group can be seen as moving from decision to decision. The decisions should be about what to do and how to do it, but agreement is required only on the fact that this action will be useful to the group, not on the fact that it is the "right" action. 'Rightness" can be ascertained only through taking action and assessing the results.

The leader, then, is a methodologist, concerned with whether or not proposed action will be informative, and whether or not it can be carried out within the boundaries of the situation. His concern over its "rightness" is no greater than that of any other member of the group. To put it another way, the leader's job is to set and maintain the conditions required for the group's maximum intelligence to assert itself. If everyone leaves a meeting with the justifiable feeling that he could have reached a better decision in five minutes all by himself, then leadership has failed.

STEERING THE GROUP

By steering the group, I mean mobilizing its individual resources in such a way that it moves efficiently toward its goals. This is achieved by continual modification and redefinition of the immediate group-problem situation so that members are strongly motivated and the purposes of the group are satisfied. Steering is one of the responsibilities of leadership, whether by one man or by all the members.

We have developed a number of propositions which illuminate the nature of the problem.

First, we have seen that whatever the stated purposes, the

group is in fact working simultaneously on private and public, individual and group, problems (chapter 10).

Second, we have pointed out that the needs to deal with anxiety are compelling and will drain energy away from working toward the group's stated purposes (chapter 8).

Third, we have seen that anxiety is mobilized by ambivalence, ambiguity of and confusion over roles ("membership conflict," chapter 7), leader-member relations ("authority conflict," chapter 4), and intergroup relations ("status and value conflict," chapters 1, 7, and 12).

Fourth, we have proposed that the "reality factors" in problem-solving impose their own demands on the group (chapter 9).

Fifth, we have asserted that leadership uses concepts of the group-as-a-whole and continually attempts to diagnose behaviors of individuals as symptomatic of a state of affairs in the group-as-a-whole (chapter 10).

Sixth, we have postulated the idea that the state of affairs which leadership tries to maintain is one that will result in the creative contributions of all members (implicit throughout this book).

In practice, those concerned with steering the group continuously appraise each contribution in its context of preceding events, with the following questions in mind:

a) Does this contribution indicate anxieties which are blocking work toward the goal? If so, is this anxiety shared by many, or is it unique to the speaker? Can the anxiety be removed by clarifying our intentions, or the limits to our power, or the present state of commitment and responsibility required from us all?

b) How does this contribution relate to the steps of problem-solving? How may it be incorporated into the growing body of agreements or specifications accepted by the group as criteria or requirements of the problems to be solved?

c) What does this contribution tell us about the nature of needed activity? Should it be more problem centered, group centered, or individual centered? (More routine, reflective, emotion discovering, implication seeing.)

d) What kind of response does the contributor seek? What sort of reward does he want? Approval from the leader? Reply from certain members? Acknowledgment of his feelings? Clarification of his ideas? Invitation to explain more fully? Recognition of his status or worth?

e) What will be the effects on the group of satisfying the speaker's demands? What part of the demand, if satisfied, will reinforce or improve our ways of working? What part of the demand cannot be satisfied within the scope of our purposes and methods?

f) Would it be better strategy to try to deal with the demand immediately, to ignore it, or to incorporate it as part of the evidence for a change in direction to be proposed in the near future?

It may be helpful at this point to present a rather broad, more abstract view of the theoretical requirements of steering. We shall, in the case study later on in this chapter, illustrate its main features:

1. The group as a whole keeps, for the most part, on an "even keel." It strikes a continual balance between the expression of emotion and work. Emotional statements lead to testing with facts; factual statements call for assessment of their felt meanings. Both kinds of statements are needed, and a shift in kind occurs whenever an emotion has become recognized and shared and whenever an argument has reached tentative or speculative conclusions.

2. Each individual, however, is not on an "even keel." The fact that individuals are emotionally involved in the discussion means that they are being stimulated and challenged; personal needs arise, build up, and discharge tensions; opportunities for gratification open up. Desire and readiness to participate are a result of these processes.

3. The purpose of steering is to keep the group as a whole working on problems in a reasonably objective and rational way; and this is done through the strategic utilization of needs of individuals to participate in specific ways that will reduce their individual tensions. Steering seeks always for ways of channeling tensions into group work, not for ways of suppressing or denying tensions of individuals.

4. When the tensions of most members become very high or

very low, the group loses its focus on group purposes and shifts to individual private purposes. Under these conditions, the "climate" needs to shift toward greater informality, and this is brought about by reorganizing the group through the use of buzz sessions, role-playing, leader withdrawal, coffee breaks, etc. Under conditions of most efficient working, there is a wide range in the amount of tension felt by the various individuals at any one time.

In this theoretical view, then, steering deals fundamentally with work, emotionality, organization, and individual and group needs. It tries to relate these to continually clarified demands the group must meet to achieve its purposes.

The production of steering behaviors appropriate at all times to the state of affairs in the group is an artistic job. Leaders internalize the guiding principles and understandings so thoroughly that their leadership roles appear to be a spontaneous implementation of attitudes rather than the end product of a set of calculations. This sort of artistry is learned through reflection upon one's own experience. Chapter 3 makes explicit the institutional conditions required for self-training a faculty in a school; the underlying assumptions of the plan are appropriate to any self-training situation. (Striking similarities between the roles of leader and trainer can be seen by comparing the present discussion with that of the trainer's role, pp. 169–77.)

Symptoms of Breakdown in the Use of Experimental Method

Since effective problem-solving is an application of the experimental method, we should expect to find groups learning to use the method simply as a result of trying to work better. There are, however, a great many culturally sanctioned ways to avoid the method, a great many problems of individuals and groups that indicate the operation of negative forces. Let us examine some of the common devices which are violations of the experimental method, and then turn to some of the reasons why they are used.

We are grateful to Paul Diedrich for his delightful research into the matter, and we should like to present it in his own words:

Most educational discussions become, sooner or later, a desperate attempt to escape from the problem. This is often done clumsily, causing unnecessary embarrassment and leaving the group without the comfortable feeling of having disposed of the problem. A "cultural lag" is evident in this situation. Educational leaders have long since worked out an adequate battery of techniques for dodging the issue.

In the course of a misspent youth, the writer and his friends have sat at the feet of many eminent practitioners of this art and have compiled a list of their devices. The list, of course, is only tentative, partial, incomplete, a mere beginning, etc., but it should at least give group leaders a command of alternative modes of retreat, enabling them to withdraw their forces gracefully and to leave the problem baffled and helpless. In the interest of promoting the Christian spirit, we must dispense with acknowledging the sources of the following items. Additions to the list will be gratefully received.

1. Find a scape-goat and ride him. Teachers can always blame administrators, administrators can blame teachers, both can blame parents, and everyone can blame the social order.
2. Profess not to have *the* answer. This lets you out of having *any* answer.
3. Say that we must not move too rapidly. This avoids the necessity of getting started.
4. For every proposal set up an opposite and conclude that the "middle ground" (no motion whatever) represents the wisest course of action.
5. Point out that an attempt to reach a conclusion is only a futile "quest for certainty." Doubt and indecision "promote growth."
6. When in a tight place, say something which the group cannot understand.
7. Look slightly embarrassed when the problem is brought up. Hint that it is in bad taste or too elementary for mature consideration or that any discussion of it is likely to be misinterpreted by outsiders.
8. Say that the problem "cannot be separated" from other problems; therefore, no problem can be solved until all other problems have been solved.
9. Carry the problem into other fields; show that it exists everywhere, hence is of no concern.
10. Point out that those who see the problem do so by virtue of personality traits: e.g., they are unhappy and transfer their dissatisfaction to the area under discussion.

11. Ask what is meant by the question. When it is clarified, there will be no time left for the answer.

12. Discover that there are all sorts of "dangers" in any specific formulation of conclusions: dangers of exceeding authority or seeming to, of asserting more than is definitely known, of misinterpretation, misuse by uninformed teachers, criticism (and of course the danger of revealing that no one has a sound conclusion to offer).

13. Look for some remote philosophical basis for settling the problem, then a basis for that, then a basis for that, and so on back into Noah's Ark.

14. Retreat from the problem into endless discussion of various techniques for approaching it.

15. Put off recommendations until every related problem has been definitely settled by scientific research.

16. Retreat into general objectives on which everyone can agree but which suggest no content and no changes in the present program.

17. Find a face-saving verbal formula (like "in a Pickwickian sense") which means nothing but which everyone will accept because he can read into it his own interpretation. This is the highest art of the good administrator.

18. Rationalize the status quo with minor improvements.

19. Retreat into analogies and discuss them until everyone has forgotten the original problem.

20. The reverse of "begging the question." Begin with a problem like "What should be the content of our core course?" End with the conclusion that maybe we ought to have a core course.

21. Explain and clarify over and over again what you have already said.

22. As soon as any proposal is made, say that you have been doing it in your school for ten years, even though what you have been doing bears only the faintest resemblance to the proposal.

23. Appoint a committee.

24. Wait until some expert can be consulted.

25. Say, "That is not on the agenda; we'll take it up later." This may be extended *ad infinitum*.

26. Notice that the time is up. If other members of the group look surprised, list your engagements for the next two days.

27. Conclude that you have all clarified your thinking on the problem, even though no definite conclusions have been reached.

28. Point out that some of the greatest minds have struggled with this problem, implying that it does us credit to have even thought of it.

29. Say forcefully, "Do we really want this laid out cold for us?" Obviously we don't. Therefore, wet-nurse the problem.
30. Be thankful for the problem. It has stimulated our best thinking and has therefore contributed to our growth. It should get a medal.

Certainly with all these techniques, there is no excuse for awkwardness in problem-evasion.[4]

THE PROBLEM OF LEADER ANXIETY

Back of these devices there is anxiety—anxiety over the possibility of failure, over the maintenance of prestige by the leader, over the feeling that the group is incapable, over the ambiguities and lack of certainty that are so inevitably a part of discussions prior to decision. In many cases these anxieties are needless, and they can be dispelled by placing one's faith in tested methods, and in the ability of people to learn these methods. Lack of such faith creates an impossible position, in which one must either be an "autocrat" or a "manipulator."

We are convinced, as a result of much research as well as from generally agreed-upon observations that the behavior of the leader is of vast importance. It is of so great significance that part of the method of leadership we want is one that can reduce this influence, that can distribute the chores of leadership more broadly within the group. The leader who sees his role as a lonely one, who feels that the whole weight of the enterprise is on him, cannot afford to fail, even in situations that are "impossible." He sees the success of the group not really as the success of the group but as a tribute to himself; and the group never fails—it is he who fails, even though he may feel that it is the fault of the group that he failed.

Just as we see decision-making as the process of developing enough confidence to take action, so we see leadership as a set of behaviors guided by confidence in one's understanding of adequate methods, and by confidence in the skills of implementing these methods. There are many "personal problems" with which leaders must come to terms in one way or another. Knowing this, and having some notions of their solution, is helpful in dealing with them. If a leader burns up all his energy worrying about

4. Paul Diedrich, "How To Run Away from an Educational Problem," *Progressive Education*, Vol. XIX, No. 8 (March, 1942).

them, he not only will have little energy left to apply to the job of leadership, but he may also have distorted perceptions of what is going on, and of the group "realities."

I wish to mention here some problems of leadership and to suggest some helpful insights into the ways they can be dealt with. I shall not attempt a deep interpretation of the leader's feelings, but will try to show what guidance can be obtained from understanding the experimental method of leadership.

Case 1: "We are going to have democracy around here or I'll know the reason why." In these words we can sum up the attitude of thinly veiled directiveness used by teachers who want to force the students into agreement on plans.

Comment: There is great concern over "being democratic." It has become an emotional word used to connote approval rather than a defined criterion for appraising reality. Most of what people seem to mean by being "democratic" is already safeguarded in the formulation of the experimental method given above. Therefore the leader may safely spend his energy in leading rather than in worrying about whether he is meeting such additional and inadequately defined criteria.

There are certain stereotypes about "democracy" that can stand in the way, not only of experimental leadership, but also of democracy itself. One of these is the unrealistic view that participation should be evenly distributed all the time. Another is that there is only one "democratic style" of leadership, as, for example, that shown by the benevolent autocrat. It is useful to reject this view; leadership should be appropriate to the situation, and the experimental method is the only known means for securing appropriateness in any conscious and systematic fashion. There are times when it is appropriate to hold the group to its task. There are other times when the group can be encouraged to explore widely in an effort to help define its task. The help we need comes from understanding principles, such as those on pages 62–67. It only adds a needless anxiety burden when the former is called "autocratic" and the latter "democratic."

Case 2: "I wish I could say what I really feel." This is a common plaint of leaders after meetings.

Comment: It is true that a leader accepts a higher degree of responsibility and self-discipline than is required from the others in
the group. He is in a position of greater influence, and his abuses
of that position have graver consequences. On the other hand, it
seems unreasonable to make the leader a second-class citizen, deprived of his rights, and depriving the group of the kinds of contributions expected of others. Under parliamentary procedure,
when the chairman wants to enter into controversy, he hands the
gavel temporarily to someone else. This is the key for solving the
problem.

If the image of group problem-solving is one of a battle between
opposing camps, then the chairman is required to be "neutral."
But if the image is one of the collection of data which are accepted
and judged as the property of the group, then the chairman can
present his data, too. If the required data are opinions, then the
leader may state his opinion. Any contribution which the group
needs at a given point should be given by anyone with the ability
to do so. The leader can usually present his opinions safely if a
few others have been stated first, so that the group does not feel
that the leader is trying to shift the activity into new directions
simply out of self-interest. If he feels a need to alter the course of
action, then he should make his wishes explicit and give the group
a chance then or later to react to them. But the leader, like the
administrator, needs to understand possible long-range consequences of his behavior (see p. 113).

Case 3: "Aren't there some other factors you should take into
account?" This is a common device used by leaders to bring the
group to a particular desired decision.

Comment: Inviting the group to guess what the leader has in mind
is possibly a useful teaching device in situations in which the
members acknowledge their job to be one of learning to think
"like teacher." It turns the discussion into a game, and sometimes it is flattering to a class to feel that the teacher thinks it
capable of thinking the problem through in the same way he
does.

In adult groups, however, it seems a wiser policy for the leader
to say what he has in mind, rather than to obtrude his own self

into the discussion in this way. If the leader is afraid to make explicit suggestions because he feels the group may simply accept them without thought, then the problem might better be tackled as one of setting up conditions for thoughtfulness. A similar attitude is shown in a leader's tendency to respond only to suggestions he likes, or in his unwillingness to make clear the fact that plans have already been laid, or in his keeping silent at times when the group turns to him for advice. He will do better to explain why he does not want to participate rather than simply to ignore requests. Withholding relevant data from the group, or acting capriciously both tend to make the group dependent on the leader's criteria of judgment as the ones to be used. They remain in his mind rather than out in the open where everyone can help to apply or develop them. Members, too, can be less than candid—particularly around the boss (see pp. 110–11).

Case 4: "Are you with me?" This phrase recurred over and over again in a long rambling report delivered by an air force officer to a group of his fellows.

Comment: In this particular case, the other members of the group said they were following him, and he need not have worried. But in general, a leader should indeed worry about whether the group is "with" him if he goes too long without testing his performance against reality. A few good questions, or any kind of requirement for action, may be the means for testing, since, if the group is not following, they will not be able to answer the questions, and they will not know what action to take. The leader role, as distinguished from the resource-person role, can best be implemented by short, concise interventions, rather than by a rambling monologue with punctuations by the group. In a reporting situation the simplest principle seems to be to go ahead and give the report (being sure one knows what it is to be about) and then deal with questions or misunderstandings later. (The air force officer should study principles 1, 3, and 4, pp. 181–91.)

Case 5: "I have the feeling that Joe's unfavorable feelings are due to the fact that he is a newcomer to the neighborhood and hasn't had time yet to see what it is really like." Thus spoke the leader in one citizen block group during a meeting in his house.

Comment: This is, of course, a very mild interpretation compared to such remarks as "I think Joe is having trouble because he is all tied up in guilt feelings." We have already proposed that statements need testing rather than "psychologicizing." The leader should accept the fact that he is not a therapist and that, in any case, his comments are no way to give therapy. In a group, such interpretations are likely to be antitherapeutic, because they may arouse anxiety in others who fear they will be picked on next, or who feel sympathy for Joe which they cannot easily communicate in the face of the leader's example. It is not the group's concern to diagnose why individuals feel the way they do. It is its concern to know what feelings people have and use the fact that such feelings exist as symptomatic of conditions in the group that need to be made more explicit and studied. (Besides violating principles 2, 3, and 10, chapter 10, this leader has forgotten principle No. 6, p. 16.)

Case 6: "Boy, did I get a surprise! I thought I had Tom all set to raise the question about the Groober case, but he just sat tight." This is a comment from a leader to a friend after the meeting.

Comment: That's the trouble with "planted" questions; the leader cannot really count on their popping up "spontaneously" when they are wanted. It is better for the leader simply to tell the group that a rump session, over beer in the back yard, produced a few questions the group might need to consider. Then the leader is free to call on Tom directly for his question.

Many things which affect group meetings go on outside the meetings themselves. For every "official" planning session there may be several "unofficial" sessions. The leader should help the group adopt the attitude that such sessions may well uncover ideas the group needs, or make diagnoses of difficulties about which something can be done. A plan is not necessarily a better plan because it developed during the meeting, and people should feel free to meet outside and then should be invited to contribute their findings to the group. (Tom was caught in a divided loyalty situation; see pp. 235–37.)

Case 7: "Aren't we wasting a lot of time?" One leader injected this comment several times into a long, wandering discussion.

Comment: Passing over the rather tactless implication that the group is engaging in irresponsible discussion (that the leader himself is supposed to help to avoid), it is clear that this leader felt the pressure of time. Indeed, there are often situations in which time is inadequate to cover the agenda; but if the leadership is effective, then this shows only that the agenda is too long. When many decisions have to be made too rapidly, nobody has any confidence in the results, and such decisions often do not result in action.

Worry about "wasting time" almost always is a worry about something else, that could be approached in its own right. Impatience can be dealt with either by accepting what the group is doing as necessary, or by redefining the activity so that it will be more productive. Time pressure as such can be handled by whittling down the agenda, delegating some of it to a subcommittee— if a subcommittee can handle it—or agreeing to meet again to finish the work. Since it is not easy to know how far a group can get within a specified period of time, it should be understood that it will get as far as it can and report whatever accomplishment it has made. This is also a common problem for school principals (see pp. 81–83).

Case 8: "Now children, I hope you will love me." This was the opening statement of a student teacher who had finally, after observing the class for several weeks, gotten up the courage to begin trying to teach it.

Comment: There is nothing in the experimental method that tells whether the leader should be loved or not. Under conditions of sound leadership, the group experience is rewarding, and most individuals know whom to thank. If a group has a significant job to do over a long period of time, members begin to have more and more personal meaning for each other. They can share more of their own ideas and inner thoughts within the context of problem-solving; they can learn to use their own resources more effectively. The problem for the leader is that sometimes he feels that he must choose between helping the group solve problems, on the one hand, and being "loved," on the other. Uncertainty about the group's affection may reflect the leader's own reservations about his planned course of action. If so, the group should be given an opportunity to accept or reject the plan, or at least to choose among the possible courses. In any case, the only anxieties a leader should share with the group are those concerned with problem-solving, not those concerned with his wish for affection or with other matters the group can do nothing about. (The administrator, p. 109, and the leader in Case I, p. 322, also had difficulties of this sort.)

By all odds, the most common source of anxiety for a leader is the expression of hostility toward him. It may therefore be worth while to investigate this phenomenon in some detail.

The leader is a visible person who is always seen as representing the demands of the institution. Whenever the group members become frustrated, regardless of the reason, they are likely to believe that it is the leader's fault. In many ways they will express hostility to him; and he has to be wise enough to realize that hostility is being directed at him as the target simply because they are unable to discover and define what they are *really* upset about. When group members need to express hostility and cannot focus the problem that gave rise to the hostility, they will find somebody to use as a scapegoat. Sometimes, of course, they scapegoat another group—Jews, Negroes, Catholics, etc.—this is most often the case when they fear the leader too much to express feeling against him. Scapegoating outsiders is an attempt to evade responsibility for one's own behavior by blaming others who are not involved. Scapegoating of a clique within the group is not uncommon; some leaders tacitly give approval to this.

The tendencies of a group to blame the leader and to be unable to tolerate frustration through development of a "wait and see" attitude can be upsetting to a leader. It arouses his anxieties and makes him doubt himself, and, when a person is insecure and unconfident, he tends to do stupid things. In general, there are two opposite sorts of traps into which anxious leaders fall: seduction and dictation. Thus, when a leader cannot see the group's hostility toward him objectively, he is likely to punish himself or to punish them. In the former case, he does so by accepting the notion that trouble *really* is his own fault, and he may begin to try to win the group over with blandishments, gold stars, outside conversation with group members, etc. He spends all his energy trying to be seen as a "nice guy"; in effect, he attempts to seduce the group. The trouble is, of course, first, that he is likely to be unsuccessful because he is overanxious, and this overanxiety is what he will communicate. Second, he has no energy left to lead the group toward the solution of its problem. Third, he makes it hard for the group to express its hostility toward him because it will feel guilty at kicking a man when he is down; the group members either have to suppress their hostility or direct it at some even sillier target.

The other trap, dictation, is even more familiar; particularly in situations where status hierarchies are well defined. As soon as the leader feels the group members are hostile, he begins to blame them and, in effect, treat them like wayward children. This does not work, because the group now has to spend its energy in an undercover effort to placate or sabotage the leader. It has nothing left with which to do its work.

But seduction and dictation are at least positive (even if misguided) efforts to do something about the situation. Another possible behavior is withdrawal. This is essentially running away from the situation because the leader cannot handle himself in it. In many areas of life this is not only permissible but intelligent, particularly if one knows he is running away and trains himself to meet the situation next time it occurs. But in a group leader, running away is not permissible, because it is his job to lead. The withdrawn leader is seen as sulking or anarchistic. Some leaders build up elaborate rationalizations for their withdrawal: it makes the group "freer," "gives the members a chance." Actually it does not do either; it only aggravates the group frustration and makes a bigger problem out of what may be only a little one.

In general, when a leader gets anxious about himself, he loses his objectivity, his ability to diagnose accurately in terms of the realities of the situation. He may have fantasies that the group has somehow "found out" something about him of which he is ashamed, or that it is punishing him for being a minority group member, or for being a teacher rather than a father, dentist, housewife, or whatever he would rather be.

These observations may serve to illustrate some useful principles:

First, the leader does not have to take responsibility for everything that happens. When all is said and done, responsibility belongs to the group, and the leader is merely its instrument. His job is to get responsibility shared, and he does this by helping the group learn and work with its own methodology of control. If the job is too big for the leader, he needs help and should get it; there should be a leadership team. (We shall discuss this later in this chapter.)

Second, the leader has only one purpose—to help the group. As long as this is clear (as shown by the fact that the group feels free to give him advice and criticism), then he can also meet some of his own needs without jeopardizing his usefulness as leader. Under conditions of mutual trust, leaders can express indignation, anger, enthusiasm, and the like. The group chimes in or simply waits for the interruption to finish. It is not the feeling expressed by the leader that adds to the group's burden: it is the anxieties about his feelings that become additional demands which the group usually cannot meet. Leader anxieties are harder to deal with than are member anxieties because the leader also controls the means the group can use. In the areas where the leader is anxious, he will not be able to help the group find these means.

Third, the leader has to accept his own skills and limitations as realities in the situation. More than others, he has to know the sorts of situations which cause him to become angry, for example, so that when he becomes angry he can tell what part of that feeling should be attributed to the situation, and what part to his own personality make-up. Only the former is of concern to the group. It is not always easy to accept one's own limitations, particularly when the group is dependent, because at these times the members try to get the leader to run the show; they may use flattery and other seductions and blandishments to do so. But if the leader does not know and accept his own limitations, he has plenty of opportunity to discover them. As a matter of fact, the most effective and rapid way to learn about group leadership is to try to act like a leader and then study what happens.

The Dynamics of Leadership—a Case in Point

After so much discussion of the experimental method and of the kinds of problems leaders face in using this method, it may be helpful to illustrate some of these notions in their practical setting, namely, the meeting of a group of people. The following case study takes a group up to a rather embarrassing position and then shows how two different leaders might deal with the situation, and what might happen as a result. Following the case study, we shall call attention to some of the points which, from the preceding discussion, appear to us to have considerable significance.[5]

Let us imagine a group of twelve people in its second meeting. We find the group trying to define its "goals." There has been a rapid interchange of opinion, and everyone who wanted to has spoken. No agreements have emerged, the group has already expressed all its ideas about goals, and people are perplexed and rapidly becoming frustrated about next steps. Not knowing what else to do, four individuals repeat their original suggestions. The repetition is more expanded, and the effort to persuade is increasingly evident. The individuals seem less tentative, and the proposals are offered with overtones of exasperation. They seem to be saying: "Look! We want to move on. We can move on if we can all agree on a statement. Here is a statement. It's a good statement. Let's not be stubborn."

Each of the four presentations is followed by uneasy silence, except that one person tries to make a joke after the second.

Let us now describe two different ways in which the situation drawn from a leadership training group could develop from this point:

Case I: An argument develops among the four proposers. The others look uncomfortable. Two members attempt to make peace by pointing to elements common to the proposals. They are rudely interrupted. There is an increasing number of glances at the leader. The leader finally, after clearing his throat several times, suggests tentatively that "it might be a good idea to see what is involved in these proposals." The argument takes a fresh turn. Someone asks the leader point-blank which he prefers, and

5. This case is taken from Thelen, "Basic Concepts in Human Dynamics," *Journal of the National Association of Deans of Women*, Vol. XV, No. 3 (March, 1952).

someone else answers that this is of no importance—the group must make its own decision. A member who has been quiet so far, but was chairman last meeting, takes the floor and tells a long personally oriented anecdote; this falls of its own weight and trails off into silence.

Somebody suggests (as someone inevitably does in such a situation), "Let's vote," and asks how many favor proposal one. He is shouted down but someone else takes it up and tries to get a vote on proposal two. A few people listen. Another member says with considerable force, "Let's start over."

One of the proposers, with a great deal of controlled heat, says that the group is behaving childishly, that the leader should have settled the debate, that since the leader didn't, he, the proposer, insists that the group consider his proposal. He urges that if anyone can give a valid objection to it, he should do so now, and that otherwise the proposal should be taken as accepted by the group.

There is excited muttering, out of which a few phrases can be heard. The group is demurring, but nobody comes forward. The proposer says his suggestion is the group's wish. "Next question is the way to implement it," he says. "Any ideas?" (He looks belligerently at each member of the group.) One member, faced with the real threat of action, says: "This is outrageous!" Another says: "Why don't you go home and sleep it off?" A third says: "Whatever happens suits me. I came here to observe group process, and I'm certainly seeing plenty."

The leader suggests appointing a committee composed of the four proposers and the two noisiest objectors to bring in a consolidated statement of goals for the next meeting. Nobody says anything, and the session is adjourned.

Case II: The leader steps in, after the four proposals, by pointing out that they do not seem to be something the group is able to deal with at this time; he feels this may indicate that the task is premature. He then asks why it is hard to deal with the proposals, and what might be done to make it easier. A couple of people try to state reasons, but have difficulty with introspection along these lines. One states that it is hard to find the words in so large a group.

The leader suggests breaking into groups of three to find the difficulty, with all the reasons given then to be listed on the board as a basis for possible decision. There is some hesitation, and someone says he doesn't like to break up the group. This is discussed for five minutes until a member says: "Look, I don't like to see us break up, but I don't think we will get anywhere this way, and I would be willing to try it as an experiment. If it doesn't work, we'll know better next time." Several people say: "Fair enough."

The threesomes form. They are slow to get started. They seem unsure of what they are supposed to do. Contributions tend to be autobiographic, and ease of discussion increases as they take cues from one another. After about ten minutes, someone in each threesome suggests that they ought to list the difficulties they see. A recorder is selected and, in effect, becomes chairman for the purpose of organizing a list.

When the total group reconvenes, it listens to the lists. Many specific suggestions are made, and each is accepted, rejected, or tabled until a later time. The group members finally conclude that what they really want is not a set of statements about goals, but rather some activity whose focus is *not* their own group. They suggest making observation forms for studying some other groups. This is not accepted, but it leads to the formulation of the criteria the desired activity should meet: that it be a shared experience, that it involve study of phenomena outside the group, and that it be directed to the question of what is the role of the member in some types of situations to be decided on the basis of interest.

The first ending portrays increasing frustration, loss of objectivity, undirected and uncontrolled emotional expression. It is as if the group were in the grip of powerful forces which drove it inexorably further into conditions nobody wanted. A host of new anxiety problems arose: the "weakness" of the leader, open competitiveness, feeling that voting for a proposal is really voting for a person, lack of clarity as to what a decision is, weakening of group self-confidence, member feelings that participation is inhibited, participant feelings that they are not doing justice to their own ideas, etc.

Yet something was going on. Much energy was being spent, but it dissipated itself within the system in the development of cliques and of hostility among them, in individual escape into destructive fantasies, in aggression ineffectually directed at the group. Bion would say that the "group mentality" was in control: the group acted as if its major purpose was to keep any decision from being made (see pp. 269–70).

The second ending portrays a group in control of itself, with willingness to act in spite of some reservations, and with an organization for work appropriate to the task. And no new anxiety problems were created. At all times during Case II, behavior was in response to stated problems rather than to hidden ones. Each person was responded to. The original problem was reformulated as a problem on which action could be taken. Moreover, the group "culture" was developing—i.e., the group was learning procedures which it could use from its own experience. The gratifications of success are reinforcing to such learnings.

In Case II, we see certain major principles in operation:

1. Correspondence is preserved between feeling and action through making explicit the facts about the state of affairs in the group; steering of the group proceeds from interpretation of these facts. There is continuous feedback.

2. An unanxious climate is maintained in the group so that individuals can think objectively. The leader is leader of the group and controller of group process in the name of the group; he is not leader or controller of the behavior of the individual members. This means that individuals are "free" to experiment; that whatever they do is taken as an expression of *group* need and therefore as something to be responded to in terms of an evaluation of the requirements of the group situation rather than in terms of evaluation of individual worth. More particularly, the individual contributions are examined at one level for suggestions about the group enterprise, and at another level for their reflection of the emotional state of affairs of the group.

3. The method of control is not through the opposition of individual wills or of the group's will against the individual, but rather through the opposition of emotion by thought. An emotional expression is accepted as a tentative diagnosis that calls for confirmation; this is secured from inferences about how effectively the group is working. And a proposal for action is seen as a

tentative emotional commitment which calls forth processes for ascertaining the degree to which feeling is shared. Leadership determines the magnitude of the excursions into these two phases. Poor leadership and irreversibility is characterized by one emotion calling forth another; by one action proposal unleashing a host of competing proposals. In short, emotionality in Case II is assimilated in thought and action; and action is built into the permanent dynamics of the group through its consequent emotional reorientation. Each is resisted by the other, and, through this, a delicate balance is maintained—a balance sensitive to all individual influences.

The Personnel of Leadership—the Leadership Team

On the whole, in the thinking of students of leadership the ideal of the one-man leader, the paterfamilias, is on the way out. There is some doubt that the monolithic leader, working out his lonely destiny entirely by himself, ever actually existed—or at least that he existed in the numbers claimed by some of our contemporary "rugged individualists." Generals had their confidants, politicians their wives, presidents their "kitchen cabinets."

At any rate, the present tendency is to think of leadership as a team operation; and to think that the various functions of leadership are distributed among selected individuals within the total group. There have been efforts to formulate the various roles that belong in a leadership team. The most widely tried team is the leader-observer-recorder combination, as used in subgroup meetings in large conferences. We do not feel that any final conclusions can yet be safely accepted about the composition of the team. We are more inclined to look for the criteria to be used in forming such teams in each different situation than we are to try to write the role specifications for all of them.

In this section, we wish to discuss a number of "team" relationships, and examine them in the light of what has been said above about the experimental method in leadership.

TEAM RELATIONSHIPS

1. *The confidant.*—The more complex, subtle, and demanding the leadership job, the more difficult it is for the leader, and the

more likely he is to suffer from anxiety and loss of objectivity. In general, the novice leader is also conscious of his difficulty in meeting a bewilderingly large set of criteria. These people need someone with whom they can communicate readily; someone who was at the meeting; someone who is not himself hurt by possible mistakes; someone who has a secure relationship to the leader and a desire to help.

This is the role of the confidant. He is there to be used, and his skills are the skills of listening, and of taking his cues from the anxiety problems of the leader. The confidant works with the leader outside of meetings, and helps him diagnose what was going on and what sorts of difficulties may be anticipated next time. He is a person on whom the leader can try out his "bright ideas" without committing himself fully to them. Basically, the confidant helps the leader deal with his confusions and thus frees the leader's intelligence to help the group. The confidant may have little to say during the meeting, and when he speaks it is likely to be simply as a member.

2. *The co-leader.*—This functionary operates during the meeting. His role appears mostly in groups whose objective is intellectual activity, unrelated to emotional reorientation or action. He may operate to "spell" the leader, to allow the leader to withdraw temporarily so that he can develop new arguments or prepare himself for the next major issue. He may operate as a sort of supermember, presumably identifying himself with the group and formulating some of the questions other members hesitate to ask. He could also have a group protective function, in that he would feel freer to demand more adequate explanations by the leader. And he could serve as a sparring partner, engaging in argument with the leader as a way of developing emotional involvement in the other members of the group.

The co-leadership situation is probably seldom one of equality of leadership. One of the two is bound to dominate, and this is workable provided the fact is accepted. There have been instances in which the group tended to see one leader as the acme of all virtues, and the other as a gruesome epitome of evil. Co-leaders can attempt to avoid either too unequal roles or a fight for leadership, by planning in advance what each will do. This works if the meeting goes as planned, but if it does not, both leaders are likely to run into the embarrassment of stepping into each other's preserves or otherwise violating their agreements.

The fact is that unless the hierarchy of designated authority is unambiguous, the group suffers. In cases of confused authority, no decisions can be reached because no one can be sure whose word, in case of doubt, is to be considered final. It is our impression that the concept of equal leadership as a goal is unrealistic and stultifying. The second person should be an assistant, or handyman, or apprentice, or anything else that accurately assists the role relationship.

3. The planning committee.—There are clear advantages to the leader in being able to discuss the last meeting with a small group and get their assistance in thinking about the next meeting. During the meeting, too, members of the planning committee can help in clarifying plans, explaining assumptions, keeping the group on the topic. Such a committee is most useful in situations where the leader can lay his cards on the table, and when full consideration of problems is desired.

The selection of the planning committee is of some importance. If the personnel rotates, there is less likelihood that it will be seen by the group as a bunch of leader-dominated henchmen; but there is then also the problem of working with an occasional hostile or uninvolved planner. The rotating committee is a good training device, particularly when the leader serves as a resource person to the committee and then does not have to feel wholly bound by their planning. In the training situation, the committee's functions are mostly diagnostic and advisory. The practice of composing the committee from all those with complaints works well if the group accepts its planning responsibility seriously and if the complaints are responses to the situation rather than projections onto the situation. It is not unusual to try to get all "the various points of view" represented on the committee.

Probably the best method of selection of members depends upon the specific functions of the planning committee. If it is required to work out proposals for the group, those who know and care most about the proposals may be most useful. It is thrown together simply as a way of getting the group out of frustration—

if the problems are dumped on the committee—then the most useful people are likely to be those who can tolerate frustration and who have some sense of humor. If it is to organize topics for discussion, then it should include people who know how to organize subject matter. And so on.

4. *The natural leaders.*—When a person from the "outside" is designated to serve as the leader of a group, he may need more support than can be secured without special provision. This is especially true, for example, in the case of a university consultant stepping into a group of foremen for the purpose of helping them see their need for training. Here the leader has everything against him—class, salary, education, inability to communicate, lack of membership or acceptance in the group.

The greater the gap between the leader or consultant and the others in the group, the more useful are the "natural leaders." These are people with influence; they are watched by the others to see what reactions they have. The group takes its cues from them. The leader is well advised to talk with them in advance, not as the basis for "manipulation" but as reality-testers of his plans and approach. In a word, they know the situation and he does not. The fact that their opinions are respected by the rest of the group is the evidence that they are actually in touch with group realities. If they support the outsider in the meeting it is because they think the group ought to do so, not because they "sold out" to the consultant (who usually has nothing to buy them with anyway).

The other advantage of working with the natural leaders is that they have contact with the group members outside of the meetings, and can continue to further the objectives in the absence of the leader or consultant. When one works outside the group with the natural leaders, one has the opportunity to keep the leadership where it belongs—in the group—and to define his role as adviser realistically. It is strange that teachers make so little use of the natural leadership within their classes.

5. *The functional team.*—There are two bases for a team of persons whose special skills are complementary. One basis is to help the leader, by dividing some functions of leadership among themselves. The other basis is to provide special "services" to the

group. The leader-observer-recorder team is more often not a team so much as a trio of service functionaries, acting independently of each other, but each giving assistance to the group. The leader is chairman, methodologist, and, frequently, resource person. The observer may be anything from a "depth analyst" to a watchdog on participation, interruption, or audibility. The recorder is the "group memory."

There are times when such a division of service roles is helpful and, in that event, the group should give thought to defining the roles and getting the most competent people into them. This is especially true of the observer, whose task is usually so poorly defined that his observations are of no help, and he has to fight to get a chance to give them. He should be selected only after the group has decided that a watchdog will be needed during some particular activity, to keep a check on simple overt behaviors such as interrupting, passing from one issue to another without decision, and the like.

A planning committee might feel that meetings would be more productive if there were more effort to formulate agreements as soon as they seemed imminent; if someone would summarize progress so that the group could maintain its perspective with regard to the business agenda; if someone more sensitive than the leader would make an effort to clarify emotionally tinged contributions which the leader seems unable to "understand." If such roles seem useful, the committee might then divide them up among themselves and try to perform them. No special co-ordination of these roles would be necessary. Each would be active when the occasion and need for it arose naturally during the meeting. In a training group, the committee might decide to discuss these roles with the group, let members know who is trying to deal with each function, and encourage others to practice the roles too.

The ideal team for leadership is the total group. Either each person can produce all the needed behaviors or else each knows the roles he can play, and among the group all needed roles are provided for. The more nearly this ideal is reached, the more efficient the operation. As a group goes on meeting, it normally tends toward this ideal, although few groups ever reach it.

One last important concept about designated leaders is the principle of noninterference. In a word, the *designated* leader operates only when needed. In a training group, which accepts its own development as a major objective, the trainer may stay out of the discussion completely for a period of time in order that the group can find out what its missing roles and needs are. In the case of a group that meets only once to consider a proposal, the leader is not so much concerned with helping the group understand its process problems—but quite the opposite; his job is to get the group over the agenda as smoothly as possible.

Thus the definition of the leadership role at any time has to be given in terms of the long- and short-range goals of the group, the realities of leader and member skills, and the requirements of the problem.

SUMMARY

There are several approaches to leadership. Some writers, like Cantor,[6] emphasize the threat-defense principle: good leadership provides a "climate" in which members of the group do not have to be continually on the defensive. Lee[7] emphasizes the approach of general semantics: good leadership clarifies relationships between words and the objects they represent, and distinguishes between people and the ideas they express. Bion[8] puts stress on leadership as the facilitation of group skill in diagnosing its own state of emotion. The usual military concept appears to be that logical analysis of the problem is the fundamental act of leadership. Leadership in the Quaker business meeting is concerned with the continuous effort to locate and test the "sense of the meeting."[9] Thelen and Tyler[10] see leadership as the business of maintaining harmony between the "process" and "achievement" problems of the class.

6. N. Cantor, *Learning through Discussion* (Buffalo 2: Human Relations for Industry, 1951).

7. Irving Lee, *How To Talk with People* (New York: Harper & Bros., 1952).

8. W. R. Bion, "Experiences in Groups. I–VI," *Human Relations*, Vol. I, No. 3, *et seq.*

9. Stuart Chase, *Roads to Agreement* (New York: Harper & Bros., 1951).

10. Herbert A. Thelen and Ralph W. Tyler, "Implications for Improving Instruction in the High School," chap. xii in *Learning and Instruction*, Part I of the 49th Yearbook of the National Society for the Study of Education.

These various approaches are not mutually exclusive. They merely represent somewhat different starting points in thinking about an obviously complex phenomenon. Basic to all of them, and to the procedures spelled out by the various authors, is some concept of the experimental method. We have, therefore, attempted to "get behind" these procedures to state directly at least a few ideas as to what this experimental method is.

Any change from one style or method of leadership to another requires, as Kurt Lewin pointed out, the "unfreezing" of old habits and the formation of new ones. It is a process of breaking loose from the traditions, stereotypes, role expectancies, and group sanctions which maintain the older habits, plus the development of new supportive mechanisms to reinforce redirected efforts.[11] Even when an individual teacher works by himself, his effort is essentially a social one.[12] This leads us back to the recognition that groups do not operate alone. They exist in a community, and the next chapter, which is also the last, will take us back to the community—not as a set of forces operating on individuals, but as the interactive environment of all groups.

11. Kurt Lewin and Paul Grabbe, "Conduct, Knowledge, and Acceptance of New Values," *Journal of Social Issues*, December, 1945.

12. Roger G. Barker, "Difficulties of Communication between Educators and Psychologists: Some Speculations," *Journal of Educational Psychology*, September, 1942.

CHAPTER 12

For a group-as-a-whole to exist, it must be interdependent with other groups in a larger community. Only thus can it have purposes of "acting on" a situation to change the situation. Groups arise through the coming together of "like-minded" individuals within the community, and their methods of operation are seriously affected by the over-all culture of the community. Conversely, whatever changes occur within the community come about through the changes within and between groups.

The fact that people belong to different groups for different purposes produces the situation of "overlapping group membership" within each individual; and this concept closes our circle of concepts and takes us back to chapter 7.

Community: The Context of Group Operation

To develop a framework of ideas, one has to choose a starting point and then build the argument according to some more or less logical scheme. We chose as a starting point for Part II the existence of membership conflicts within individuals, for we saw such conflicts as the stuff from which most if not all social needs elaborate. We then inquired as to the ways in which individuals deal with such internal problems, and we suggested that behaviors of evaluating and acting (including thinking) serve as the means. We next recognized that not all behaviors are helpful; that there are realities in each situation that must be taken into account. Since knowledge of reality factors is obtained and tested through interaction with other people, we were led to the question of how individuals participate in groups and to the idea that groups provide for and control participation by means of shared ideas and attitudes. At this point, we presented a set of principles on which we believe successful groups base their behavior; in effect we spelled out a moral code for groups, even though we maintained that it was developed through study of group operation rather than by deduction solely from "larger" ethical principles. The fact of group self-control or discipline then led us to inquire how the group provides for these functions, and this resulted in our last chapter on use of the experimental method in leadership.

This development of ideas is required from certain hard facts about language; that only one idea can be presented at a time, and that ideas therefore have to be arranged in sequence. In experience, however, ideas do not come one at a time, but come imbedded in impressions. Thus, in a given group a person is almost simultaneously aware of, for example, one member's discomfort, the group's lack of clear goals, the fact that "we are behaving like children," and the pressure of time. Moreover, as a person reacts in a group, he behaves as if he were influenced by many more factors than he is aware of: his rejection of the leader's authority, his own wish for status, his need to impress some other member, and, possibly, the fact that he is talking angrily.

These additional factors, not comprehended by any one person, may be in the awareness of others. After the meeting, for example, there is usually a wide range of perceptions and feelings about it (unless the group has been working productively on clear problems); different people see and respond to different things—cues and gestures and ideas which did not seem to exist for others.

All of these considerations can be boiled down to the primary fact that we are constantly dealing with part-whole relationships, rather than with simply interrelated units. Whatever "figure" we give attention to is created out of the larger pattern of "ground" conditions by our own processes of giving attention. Many people "see" only the leader, or the "problem," or themselves. All our approaches to thinking about human behavior are learned, selective, and limited, and this is why they aid thinking. No one can think about everything at once, even though his feelings may be widely reponsive. Thinking about groups is a procedure of extracting from felt impressions useful ideas of directions, causality, or progress.

The chief difficulty of an approach necessarily limited to what we are aware of is not that the "wrong" parts will be looked at so much as that they will not be related to an adequate "whole." It is all too usual to regard groups as autonomous. This is a real dclusion, much like trying to think of individuals apart from their relations to others. *In a word, to understand and improve group operation you have to see the group as part of a larger community.*

The fifth-grade English class, the Rotary Club, the Nathaniel Hawthorne garden section of the Coriolanus Club, the board of directors meeting—all these have their social meaning through their impact on the social and physical environment, even though the means of impact is through the group members. All are affected by a larger community and have much greater effectiveness when they can call these "outside" factors into account. Not only from a long-range social standpoint, but also from the standpoint of better day-by-day operations, many characteristics of the larger community make a real difference to what a group can do and the means by which it can do it.

The purpose of this chapter is to relate individuals and groups to the community, to fill in the larger "whole" against which the parts of the discussion so far presented are to be understood. In Part II, our first two chapters saw the individual as the whole within which various psychological behaviors could be examined; our next three chapters saw the group as a whole within which individual acts could be examined and determined. This chapter sees the community as the whole within which the groups are to be understood as parts.

We shall begin with a description of the community as an interwoven network of processes of communication and communion; next we shall look at groups as subcultures within the community, and then we shall examine the nature of intergroup conflict and the dynamics of resolving it through the operation of the "bridging group." We shall then study more explicitly the part played by the community in intergroup conflict. Against this background we shall develop a model of group-community development. Such a model is useful because the state of affairs in the community determines how far and in what ways groups can grow; and the means groups employ in their operation determine the state of affairs in the community. Finally, we shall develop a series of basic principles useful for realizing this model.

BASIC PROCESSES IN THE COMMUNITY

A community may be thought of as having two simultaneous sorts of processes constantly going on. One kind of process, communication, is the influencing of one part by another. Some identified person says some describable thing to some other identifiable person. The network of communication channels, whether via engraved stationery or over the back fence, keeps the parts of the community in relationship to each other. The content may be knowledge others ought to have so as to plan their actions wisely; it may be attitudes expressed to others and tested against their reactions; it may be orders or instructions handed down within organized institutions.

A second kind of process, communion, is the sharing of feeling about commonly experienced problems, ideas, physical features, and incidents. The processes of communion relate each part of the community to the community as a whole, rather than to particular other parts. The kinds of experiences that are available to all include past historic events (battles, disasters, revelations to local prophets), shared aesthetic experiences (scenic views, pioneer or prestige houses, monuments), common social experience (the first families, the colorful characters, the tragic ones, and the strange ones), "literary" experience (legend, folklore, and local customs), and so on. The important thing to note about communion is that something *outside* the individual or group, and available to all individuals or groups, seems to focus reaction. It may be a view, a story, a stereotype of other communities, a civic problem, an anticipated hardship. It may exist "on the ground," like Seattle's view of Mt. Rainier, or the garden courts and ironwork balconies in New Orleans. On the other hand, it may be merely an idea, like the notion that "our troubles are caused by in-migration of foreigners," or the notion that our town is the "best little city north of the Smokies."

A stranger moving into the community is first admitted to communion with respect to the existing and obvious landmarks; he can guess with some accuracy which are objects of pride or melancholy and the communal meanings of these objects are easily shared. After he gets settled in his own house and job, the stranger next becomes aware, let us say, of the problems of bad streets, sordid taverns, individuals and groups which are discriminated against. He is advised to "take it easy" at this point of problem recognition, until he finds out what these conditions mean to the community—what the common interpretations are. He may discover that bad streets are maintained as a smug gesture of defiance against the "world outside"; that the rowdy life of the tavern is required as a horrible example to keep moral teaching alive; that discriminating against a particular group is the accepted channel for expression of hostilities arising from many sources that "cannot" be examined objectively. The stranger may find that these interpretations are carefully guarded, or he may find they are easy to discover; but he does not fully belong to the community until he knows these meanings, indentifies with or against the values involved in them, and accepts their existence as part of the realities within which he must operate.

It is noteworthy that these processes of communion are most facilitated in a small town and, possibly, one with an open interest in its present state of affairs. When the town gets too big, there are too many local events for any of them to become a symbol incorporated into communal experience in any significant fashion. The communality in a big city tends to revolve around big physical objects such as a waterfront, or colorful or influential buccaneers of industry, graft, government, or society, or complex abstractions like rent control or "the crime syndicate." Things happen because "they" managed it so; but nobody knows who "they" are. And there is little you can do with a waterfront parkway except admire it and curse Sunday traffic; a big industrialist or labor leader is known only through the newspaper, and you either wish you were like him or are thankful that you are not; the "crime syndicate" is reacted to as a sinister force but it is not something I even imagine I can do anything about.

Under these metropolitan conditions, the formation of groups may serve a number of purposes. Thus we can see the informal tavern group as arising out of bewilderment and a need to escape a feeling of nonparticipation and lack of place in the functioning of the community. The ethnic group may maintain its customs and language, not so much because it feels that these are "better" but because they are shared and known to be shared, and provide the basis for a higher degree of communality than is possible in the sprawling city as a whole. The minority group may be created by stereotypes whose operation represents a sort of perverse effort on the part of the majority to find belongingness; majority people may not have very much sense of groupness with each other, but they can try to reassure themselves by pointing to minority groups that assuredly do not.

The citizen group is likely to have limited civic objectives like beautification or delinquency, because the whole is too staggering and unavailable for comprehension by the average member. Because of weak communion with comprehended civic realities, such groups may pick other groups rather than objective problems as their "enemies." The amount of hostility and anxiety between "do-good" organizations, the jealous protection of their jurisdictional rights, their feelings of guilt and sudden stirrings of activity when a more powerful group is rumored to be in formation—these are signs of the lack of common bases for communion. People in the same and in different groups cannot share feeling about problems because any identified problem is too insignificant and any significant problem is too complex.

Probably of all the groups in the city, communion is greatest in the neighborhood group, existing partly for individual welfare, partly for maintenance of property, partly to put pressure on city officials, and partly to educate and induct newcomers into the neighborhood. A badly run rooming house is not insignificant to the neighborhood, even though it is only a drop in the city-wide bucket. The moving-in of a new family can be noticed and discussed formally. People are known as people, and the consequences of what they do get back to them. In effect, there is neighborhood provided and maintained interaction among individuals; there is expectancy and opportunity to talk together which is not all a matter of initiative by individuals who are seen as deviates. "Belongingness" is automatic at the point of communion, of shared meanings of salient aspects of neighborhood life. There is no need to bother with membership rituals, initiation ceremonies, or common alliance against "others."

What I have called the "neighborhood group" is, in effect, what exists in the village. The major difference is that such groups in the large city do not have the freedom for decision and the autonomy of the village group. They work within a set of prescriptions resulting from city-wide systems of politics, education, sanitation, etc., and they have comparatively little freedom to change these things. The neighborhood group must perforce put more emphasis on amelioration and adjustment and less on the creation of new political or organizational forms.

Our picture of the community may be summed up as follows: First, each individual experiences more or less of the same events or problems and knows that he shares the meanings of these events with others. Second, individuals and groups form a network of communication and mutual influence, and every person has some place in this network. Third, the nature of the spontaneous informal groupings depends upon the amount and quality of communion possible and needed. Fourth, there is discernible in all organizational life the acting out by citizens of needs for relating themselves through the group to the larger community. The technology of chapter 1 exemplifies these propositions.

GROUPS AS SUBCULTURES

We see that in any community there are more or less commonly experienced and felt objects, customs, stories, personalities, and institutions. These remind people of physical, aesthetic, moral, administrative, and educational facts about what people believe, how they shall behave, what they shall call good, etc. In short, every community has its culture.

Each individual reacts to the various facets of this culture: its authority, its complexity, its confusion, its form, its ethical assumptions, its images of individual and collective goals. The reactions of individuals differ. Some—the "100 per centers"—believe that they accept the culture; and others see them as trying to maintain their notions of the culture against all doubters. The people we call "antisocial" appear to be in revolt against the parts which are perceived as exerting "authority" or curbs to individual impulses. These people may form gangs to continually test the ways in which the boundaries can be breached. Those who react to confusion may, in their quest for authoritative interpretations, attend Great Books classes or a church. Or they can join the National Guard, the "Y," or any other movement which provides for them the discipline and clarity of goals they cannot find in everyday living.

Thus, in a general way, we can say that individuals are concerned about different aspects of the culture; and that individuals with similar concerns tend to affiliate with each other and become a "group." As a group, they state their purposes by differentiating out of the community culture as a whole certain particular objects which best represent their concerns.

The school, for example, formulates its goals by identifying those individual behaviors through which the culture is maintained and improved, i.e., through whose learning individuals will develop their greatest potentialities. As more and more individual behaviors are found to influence the community, these become additional objectives of the school. Thus, to the school curriculum have been successively added natural science, commercial subjects, health, social science, and human relations. As complexity of living develops, more and more "private" behavior is examined for its consequences for the welfare of others. Those behaviors whose consequences are appraised as significant must then be made consonant with the community control system (culture), and the school, as the primary instrument provided for bringing about the socialization of youth, has another objective to add to its list.

In the same way, but more informally and voluntarily, the fraternal organization, club, action group, and others, pick out certain objectives which imply communion within the group, and imply the objects to be investigated, the means to be employed (study, action, entertainment), and the bases for belonging. In effect each group develops its own subculture. It may be an "improvement" on the prevailing culture, thus giving the members protection and peace—and substituting the group for the larger community. In this case, withdrawal from the community plus effort to maintain the organization at all costs may result. On the other hand, the group subculture may merely be a reinforcement and refinement of *avant guarde* or regressive tendencies within the larger culture. These may be illustrated respectively by a modern art society in which the members actually paint and experiment avocationally with new ideas, as compared to a juvenile "gang" or a modern art society in which members listen to lectures on "art" criticism. Or, as some psychiatrists suggest, the subcultures may simply protect and cultivate in pure forms certain basic emotional drives. Thus Bion proposes the army as the maintainer of "fight," the aristocracy as the maintainer of "pairing" (sexuality), and the church as the maintainer of "dependency," in their most direct expressions.

Because a group has to be able to define its purposes explicitly or implicitly, and in a way acceptable to its members, it follows that the purposes of a group are always limited to those things which are common or acceptable to many people rather than being extended across the whole gamut of needs of any individual. Thus it is that from the personal standpoint, groups become limited instruments, and one may need to belong to several groups to satisfy all of the needs active within him. This, then, sets the stage for chapter 7, and the problems of overlapping group membership.

We see that the function of a group in the community can be defined in terms of the needs, arising from individual-community interaction, that it is concerned with, and that the flavor of its subculture depends upon these concerns.

In fact, however, it is only "as if" a group has a concern over such facets of culture as authority, poverty, and so on. A "cultural facet" is nothing that can be seen, touched, tasted, or felt, as such. What is experienced are the daily contacts, conversations, and feelings we have in the situations of living. We do not usually think of ourselves as reacting to the "culture," because that is statistical abstraction. A more accurate statement about what is going on is to say that all individuals do form some "world-view," some picture of the general conditions under which they live, and they also learn and use certain interprctations as to why conditions are what they are, and whether this is pleasing, discouraging, challenging to action, and so on. This "world-view" is tested through daily experience. One acts as if his view were correct (since he has no other view to operate with), and then sees what happens as a result of his action. If the results are as anticipated, or are merely comfortable, no problem is raised, and the part of the world-view concerned in the action is strengthened. If the results are uncomfortable, a problem may arise; that of bringing one's private world-picture into enough relationship to "the way things are" that one can operate more directly and with greater reward.

The notion that groups or individuals have a concern over some facet of the culture is only a way of saying that there are certain problem themes that run through enough of their experiences that they need to do something about them. A problem is what somebody sees to be a problem, and in that sense, it is always a projection from within one's self to targets outside one's self. Thus, it is by no means unusual for "liberal" groups to see and attack as a problem the fact that many individuals are subjected to discrimination. But the means they use often curtail the rights of others, and one is justified, perhaps, in feeling that the reason discrimination was selected as the problem was concern over the hostilities of the group members themselves, coupled with a need for reassurance that they really are not hostile to others. "Discrimination" is a socially approved target which makes possible the identification of people against whom hostility can be safely directed.

I hasten to add that this is not "bad"—it just is. And I should point out that there are many other motivations for working against discrimination. The point is, first, that there are reasons why the particular people working on any problem are the ones to be working on it; and second, that the subculture of a group is the set of operating agreements erected to make possible the attack on problems which are personally important to the group members. In the example given, the experience of "working on" discrimination is motivated by the uneasiness one has that his "world-view" is inadequate in some areas that have to do with the experience and expression of hostility.

There are some classifications possible of group subcultures in terms of the "kinds of people" who belong and, by implication, the "kinds of needs" characteristic of each category of person. I refer to the concept of social class. For our purposes we may note that people have different living standards, opportunities, incomes, occupations, etc. We note further that some characteristics tend to be found together. Thus we associate in our minds such things as professional occupation, relatively high income, a home in a "nice" part of town, many years of education, expensive clothes, membership in exclusive clubs, support of charitable and artistic ventures, and so on. We note, too, that people tend to find their friends among others similarly "placed" and that clubs tend to draw more or less the same "kind" of people into membership. Associated with these patterns of living are also, in general, certain more fundamental characteristics: the way in which people control their aggressive and sex impulses, the amount of inner freedom and of guilt in individuals with respect to different things, the tendency to plan in long-range or in short-range terms, and the ability to tolerate frustration versus the need for immediate gratification.

When these patterns of behavior, attitudes, motives, and manners are arranged along a scale, there are usually found to be clusters with breaks between them. Each cluster along the scale is termed a distinguishable "class," and as many as nine "classes" have been discerned in one city.

Practically all societies have this kind of class stratification. They differ in the rights and privileges given to each class as compared to the others. They differ also in the ease of moving "up" or "down" from one class to another. We in America probably have the fewest legally and socially recognized differences in privilege among classes, and we certainly have the greatest amount of moving upward. Class characteristics are not inherent in people—they are learned in and out of school, and they are practiced in social experience. To move upward requires that one learn to behave like members of the next higher class.

The categorization by "class" is one of prestige, power, opportunity, and contribution. Classification is also possible using criteria of skin color, religious preference, occupational status, ancestry, taste in literature, hobbies, etc.

For our purposes, there are two major consequences of the fact that communities are stratified, or, to put it more dynamically, the fact that people's voluntary associations tend to be with others "like" themselves. The first consequence is that communication is relatively easy within a class, and relatively difficult between classes. Thus many a "community organization" ends up only with people from the same class level, talking to each other rather than to others whose co-operation is necessary to solve the problem. The second consequence is that under these typical conditions, the organization is likely to have only its own class view of community problems and to arrive at poor, or at least partial, solutions, because the problem was never really seen realistically as a whole.

INTERGROUP CONFLICT

Our image of the voluntary groupings in the community is as follows: First, that we should expect each group initially to be formed from people who can communicate readily together; and we suspect that, generally speaking, such people will have similar "cultural backgrounds" or ways of life. Second, we should expect each group to attract to it people who have similar fundamental concerns or targets of communion; these people acknowledge the same goals and ways of working. Third, as each group works, it develops its own picture of the community, defines civic problems from its own point of view, conducts its own investigations, biases its members in favor of its own viewpoints, identifies its "enemies," and demands loyalty from its members.

If the groups are all just "talk" groups, the only problems produced are within individuals who happen to belong to two groups with different viewpoints, as portrayed in chapter 7. But, if the groups are action groups, trying to change and improve the community, and if there is inadequate direct experience shared among the groups, then there is likely to be considerable conflict between them. Each group has planned its own strategy independently of the others, and it comes as a rude shock to discover a competitor operating on different or opposite assumptions. They cannot both be right. So it becomes necessary for each group to do one of several things: (*a*) discredit the other group as a way of "disposing" of its solutions; (*b*) pretend in public that the more different solutions the better, but in private go around with a worried frown; (*c*) reconsider its own ideas, probably tapping new resources that should have been used earlier; (*d*) merge with the other group; (*e*) put on a big campaign to establish its rights to the problem and thus squeeze out the other group.

An illustration may bring this down to earth a bit: Two groups were formed independently in different parts of the community, and both decided to take action in cases of illegal conversion of houses into smaller dwelling units.

The strategy of organization *A*, in part, included calling on the city building inspector's office, telling him of their concern, and asking him to send out inspectors to check on suspected construction. After several proddings, the inspectors would go out, and, in a fairly high percentage of cases, would report that the construction was legal. The secretary of group *A* would accept this verdict

—for a day—and then call back and suggest that another inspector go out because the neighbors just reported (let us say) that thirty-six telephones were being installed in the six-flat building. The secretary would further respectfully suggest that the inspector sent out this time should not be the one sent out the day before yesterday (so that the owner would at least have to pay graft all over again to the new inspector). This time the report would be honest. Any publicity from the group would give the inspector's office thanks for its splendid co-operation. After several months of this treatment, the reports were prompt and honest the first time, and the inspector's office acted promptly enough to curtail attempted violations before the construction had gone very far.

Group *B* followed a somewhat different strategy. The inspector would be called up and told point-blank to send a man out to inspect the property. After several days, during which nothing happened, the inspector would receive a bawling out for being so slow. After that, he would be "out" when group *B* was on the phone. Group *B*, then, through its president (a reasonably wealthy lawyer) took the city attorney out to lunch and complained about the inspector's office. The president also committed his organization to foot the bills necessary to prosecute the owner in court. The city attorney put pressure on the inspector's office, the construction was found to be illegal, and the group had to raise the money to prosecute the owner.

The same differences in tactics characterized the approaches of the two groups to the police captain, the alderman, and others. Three years later, we find group *A* still trying to co-operate with people, and group *B*, as the result of a "deal," merged with another organization which has relieved it of all responsibilities and functions. During the entire period, there was much rumor-mongering and bad feeling between the two organizations, and a great deal of time and energy wasted by both in verbal forays against the "enemy" group. And many citizens, living in the area served by both organizations, became disgusted with the whole thing, sat on their purses, and were "too busy" to participate in community improvement programs. I leave to the reader's imagination the plight of two men who were on the board of directors of both organizations. (The heads of groups *B* and *A* were probably similar to the two executives, pp. 103–8.)

In general, conflict between two organizations will probably be greatest under one or more of the following conditions:

a) The two groups have approximately equal power in the community.

b) The two groups have a small core of common values within their subcultures; that is, their psychological motivations are different.

c) Very few members of one group belong to the other.

d) Both groups are nonexperimental in their methods of operation, so that there is no means for reality-testing solutions.

e) Both groups fail to be aware of their own internal process problems; this implies that members have little security and the groups therefore tend readily to become touchy and defensive.

f) Both groups have inflated and unrealistic notions of their own power and prestige.

g) Both groups are competing for the same members and the same rewards.

h) The *raison d'être* in both groups is a need for protection against real or fancied aggression by others.

i) Neither group has defined its objective problems comprehensively; and, in particular, little attempt is made to relate long- and short-range goals.[1]

Intergroup conflict should not arise when both groups operate along the lines discussed in the preceding chapters, because—

a) each group would feel "secure" enough that it could communicate with the other;

b) both groups would be in communion with the same problem, which they could talk about together as a problem in its own right;

c) both groups would develop their strategies a step at a time on the basis of evaluation of each step and would use substantially similar realistic methods;

d) each group, through overlapping memberships, would

1. Adapted from Herbert A. Thelen, "Educational Dynamics: Theory and Research," *Journal of Social Issues*, VI, No. 2 (1950), 24.

know about the other's existence, and it would develop a working relationship to complement the other's resources; and

e) the groups would clarify their separate and joint spheres of action, and refer inquiries to whichever was appropriate.

It is only in a riot situation that intergroup conflict is actually an overt war between two groups. Intergroup conflict is the aggregate of behaviors of individuals who behave emotionally or unrealistically as a result of feeling trapped in the struggle. The struggle is, as a matter of fact, within themselves. (Compare with principle 6, p. 287, and also the discussion of vested interests, p. 232.)

We turn now to the dynamics of resolving intergroup conflict. We shall present the thesis that all successful methods boil down, fundamentally, to the operation of a "bridging" group.

RESOLVING INTERGROUP CONFLICT: A MODEL

The most commonly accepted examples of intergroup conflict represent one special case: when group *A* and group *B* are both easily identified and both maintain hostility toward each other. There is often a rationalization in the surrounding community that these two groups are "natural enemies." This amounts to saying that the state of conflict is either approved of or is deemed inevitable and "naturally" right even if morally awkward. Examples of accepted "natural" enemies are labor and management, whites and Negroes, haves and have-nots, young and old, fundamentalists and liberals. Needless to say, a climate of expectation of conflict not only tends to maintain conflict but also makes its reduction difficult, because the parties involved would have to re-establish their place in the community if the conflict were to disappear. Moreover, the community would be deprived of one of its emotionally involving "interests"; those people not in group *A* or *B*, who work on their own needs vicariously through unacknowledged identification with the conflict situation, would have to find some other situations on which to focus their fantasies. Almost everyone in the community shares the conflict between groups and contributes to the conflict climate, even though he maintains that he is not "personally" involved.

Experience has shown that in this special "natural enemy"

situation, there is a perfectly simple solution. All that is required is that members of groups *A* and *B* work together on some project in which *A*-ness and *B*-ness are irrelevant, but in which the efforts of members of both groups are required for success. Labor-management luncheon projects, Friends Service Committee week-end camps, Negro-and-white army and shop groups, parent-teacher workshops (not the usual PTA meetings)—these are types of "working together" in which the participants can and do, over a period of time, learn for themselves that in the situations in which they normally have contact, the "differences" between their groups do not have to matter. And, of course, it helps if there is community agreement "against" rather than "for" conflict. This may be one reason why there are so many reported instances of reduction of conflict among "natural enemy" groups of young people; none of the older people likes gang wars, even though they are probably carrying on precisely the same thing emotionally at the adult level.

Let us examine in detail what must happen for conflict to be reduced between groups *A* and *B:*

First, we must define the problem by locating the conflict. Groups *A* and *B* do not actually interact with each other as groups except in the situation of battle. The conflict is demonstrated by members of *A* and *B* in their behaviors toward each other and toward bystanders, under a variety of circumstances. The reduction of intergroup conflict, then, is something that has to happen to members of the two groups, and it will be easier or harder to achieve depending on the community's interest in having the conflict maintained or eradicated.

In the "work together" situation, members of *A* and *B* are brought together to work on some problem or toward some goal which is important to them. They thus form group *C*. While they are working on this problem, group *C* is the directly experienced group, the one in which the members get immediate, actual responses to whatever they say or do. Group *C* develops its own culture, its own agreements, leadership, and expectations of its members; it also develops its channels of reward and of gratification for individuals. It must, however, keep its activity separate from the activities of group *A* or *B*. That is, its goals must be defined in such a way that there is no jurisdictional overlap with *A* and *B*.

Jurisdictional overlap occurs in many groups, such as community councils, and this explains why community councils (made up of representatives of other groups) so frequently are both ineffectual themselves in problem-solving and unable to help the cause of interorganizational peace. Suppose, for example, that groups *A* and *B* are trying to get a new school building, and that *A* wants to run a survey to establish the population trends among school-agers, whereas *B* wants to make immediate demands on the school board. If representatives of *A* and *B* are called together in group *C* to consider what to do about overcrowding in schools, Member *A* will suggest and defend a survey as the first step, and Member *B* will call for action. They cannot do otherwise without being disloyal to their groups. Both representatives, along with the chairman in group *C*, will quickly see that there is need for the survey, and then for taking whatever action the survey shows is required. But the representatives will find it hard to admit this because they are expected to report back to their own groups, and neither is prepared willingly to explain that his plan, presented by the representative, was rejected. If there is already hard feeling between members of *A* and *B*, then it is impossible to vote for a plan offered by either group: the vote would be for the group and not for the realistic solution of the problem. Community councils are therefore well advised to define the member role as "consultant from" rather than "representative of" the group.

An example of the significant *C*-type group in which there is no jurisdictional overlap is the meeting of whites and Negroes on a city block to work for better lighting. Here the fact that one is white or Negro, or has strong feelings about the other race, is irrelevant, because there is no "white" or "Negro" solution to the problem. It may be difficult to listen to each other at first because of the intrusion of fears, but if lighting is important, under good leadership the people will soon get absorbed in the problem. Here nobody is "representing" his race, and there is no need to attack the other or defend his own; such activity is out of bounds and, as such, is either ruled out of order by the chairman, or simply ignored by all.

Assuming that members of *A* and *B* dislike each other simply because they are known to hold these memberships (that is, they are strongly prejudiced against each other), then the first discovery that must be made is that you can work with people you do not like, in a particular group *C* situation. It is trust, not liking, which is essential for co-operation. The feeling of trust does not necessarily have to include admiration for other's ideas, or feelings of "equality"; its positive component is communion with respect to the same goal, and its negative expression is lack of suspicion that the other fellow says what he does as a means of supporting his own group.

The second discovery is that members of the other group can be pried loose from their group. To put it in more prosaic language, members of the "other group," present in group *C*, do not fit their image or stereotype. The conclusion must be either that the stereotype is wrong or at least of only limited applicability, or that these particular people are not typical of their group. This discovery frees individuals to act in accordance with the feeling of trust. Active co-operation is not with the enemy, because the other fellow is not really the enemy. Therefore there is no disloyalty to the groups, and there is freedom to try for the rewards of spontaneous participation in group *C*.

As participation becomes more spontaneous, member behavior in group *C* gets freer and more revealing of self. Members of group *A* may casually refer to or quote other members of group *A* who may have useful ideas for the discussion. Members of group *B* may talk about their place (and, by extension, group *B*'s place) in the community. In the discussion of lighting, for example, this might come out in considering a plan for voluntary installation of lights by owners: A Negro might contrast the position of the Negro home owner with that of the white owner.

This is a significant landmark in the progress of the group. The members feel free to acknowledge their "outside" affiliations, and to feel this freedom means that they perceive that the others will accept these associations. In effect, there is suggested a broadened identification: the group *A* person who could identify with and interact with a member from group *B*—under the special circumstances of group *C*—can now identify with group *B* as a whole. This amounts to an acceptance of group *B* and this in turn means potential membership in group *B*, at least with respect to problem-solving of the type going on in group *C*. When people accept each other they accept each other's affiliations—which is why the engaged girl wants the prospective groom to visit her family. The feeling of potential membership in the "enemy" group is evidence that the enemy no longer exists. There is a feeling of escape from conflict, and, instead of feeling immobilized and blocked emotionally, one is now "free" to bring conscious and objective thinking to the task of understanding the conflict, appraising its causes, inevitability, and relevance. Presumably this phase should mean the end of emotionally contaminated panic behavior toward members of the other group.

During the meeting of group *C*, the members from *A* and *B* maintain some sort of psychological relationship with their own groups. Since the problem of group *C* is not directly the concern of group *A* and group *B*, the relationship is not through the feeling of need to defend solutions from one's own group. The major "cue" for activation of person *A*'s feelings about group *A* is the presence of people from group *B*. These people initially are symbols around which are mobilized within person *A* attitudes learned in group *A* toward group *B*. And these attitudes are found to be irrelevant in the group *C* situation.

As the meeting goes on, assuming that the problem-solving is successful, the member learns to *accept* the fact that these attitudes are irrelevant, and he can now participate more spontaneously because he does not have to use a lot of energy in keeping himself from making a blunder. It should be noted, however, that this learning may be temporary; it is maintained by the climate of group *C*. When person *A* goes back to group *A*, he may at first reinstate his earlier stereotyped attitudes toward group *B* because having such attitudes is part of what it means to be a member of group *A*. It is likely that people pass through a period of flip-flops: of feeling one way while in group *A* and another way while in group *C*.

This is the point of "acting out" ambivalence in feeling toward the other group. The violence that goes with prejudice is the effort to maintain and justify prejudice when one also feels that prejudice is unsound or bad. Most hostile behavior would not be necessary if one could be completely *sure* that the other group was worthless. So that we are brought to an important recognition: bad feeling between groups *A* and *B*, expressed through stereotypic reactions, is a means to an end, rather than the inevitable behavior of "natural enemies."

The next phase of reduction of intergroup conflict is brought about by the need for integration within the members of group *C*. They cannot indefinitely go on having opposite feelings in meetings of group *A* and of group *C*. Will they succumb to the prevailing hostile attitudes assumed toward group *B* in the culture of group *A*? Or will they simply leave group *A*?

The probability is that the member from group *A* will now begin in group *A* to try to change its feeling toward group *B*. This prediction is based on an important learning from group *C*: that members of group *B* are *not* necessarily all the bad things group *A* "says" that they are; and that one can work with them. In other words, experience in group *C* has enabled the group *A* person to reality-test the attitudes of his group which have been maintaining the conflict. And he has discovered that these attitudes make no sense as long as one puts the problem first, and all have a defined part in the problem-solving.

The likelihood that one person *can* change the culture of his group depends on a number of factors. If he is an influential person in the group, his arguments are more likely to get a serious hearing. If he attacks group *A*'s attitudes directly, with all the zeal of a new convert, he will, in effect, be invited to join group *B*, where he belongs. If he acts consistently to insist that the planning of group *A* stick to the problem to be solved, and that decisions be made realistically in terms of who is needed to help, rather than in terms of whom do we like, then he may have some effect. If several influential people from group *A* were also participants in group *C*, the chances for success are much greater. And finally, if group *C* is run with skilful leadership which gives the members a chance really to understand the assumptions on which they are operating—then success is even more likely.

Group *C* was set up as a "bridging" group between *A* and *B*.

It built a communication bridge and provided for communion over a problem lying "outside" the groups in conflict. For group *C* to be successful, it had to retrain members of *A* and *B:* first with respect to their attitudes toward each other, and second, and much more fundamentally, with respect to *methods of group operation.* In short, for group *C* to be successful, it must, through members from *A* and *B*, bring about changes in the ways those groups work. The change is away from concern over the group's "position" in the community toward concern over solving community problems; this is a change from the effort to legislate reality to the effort to operate realistically. And this means a change away from pressure tactics and demagoguery toward objective analysis, recognition and development of individual potential, and adoption of the experimental method as the means for keeping contact with community realities. And finally, under these conditions the individual achieves integration because he can live simultaneously in all the groups of which he is a member; he can move without member conflict from one group to another within his subjective world.

The salient features of the operation of the bridging group re:

1. Bringing about communication between members of the opposing groups under conditions such that neither has to "defend" his group.

2. Developing the bridging group itself into a strong one with its own culture and appeal to members.

3. Operating the bridging group as a training situation in which the members can learn the experimental method of group problem-solving.

4. Facilitating acceptance by members of each other and of the groups they represent.

5. Influencing the members of the home groups toward gradual change of their ways of operating, toward a more problem-reality oriented approach.

It is our belief that in every successful effort (such as that reported in chapter 1) at reducing intergroup conflict these steps can be discerned.

The Community's Part in Intergroup Conflict

The average community contains many groups, and to some extent they act as bridging groups for each other. If I am in group *A* and you in group *B*, but both of us are in the Men's Chowder-Tasters Society, the chances are that we will use this common group partially as a bridging group. Or we may have a close friend in common, and, through him, test our attitudes toward each other's group. Possibly the local newspaper, through editorials and news coverage, makes it easier for us to accept each other's groups.

It is through common approaches to groups and problems that the culture of the community develops. And it is at points of choice or conflict that the prevailing culture tips the scales one way or the other. I have indicated that community expectancy can be "for" or "against" conflict; it can be "for" or "against" experimentalism; "for" or "against" problem-solving rather than empire-building. These matters are determined by hundreds of seemingly unrelated acts performed, wittingly or not, by many people. Let us pick out a few of the acts that probably tip the scales against co-operative group action—the acts that show the existence of forces against the kind of group operation we advocate.

ACTS AGAINST CO-OPERATIVE GROUP ACTION

1. *The reporting of news.*—Newsworthy events are ordinarily either sensational or significant or both. The tendencies to report incidents between individuals as if they were intergroup phenomena and to report group decisions and actions as if they were individual phenomena tip the scales negatively. The first tendency (e.g., to identify sex criminals as Negroes) is disappearing, but the latter tendency remains. Group meetings are reported primarily as the sounding board for comments by individuals with high prestige. "Names make news" but they may not have much relationship to what is actually going on. Back of every annual banquet with a name speaker there may be a far more important tale of average people banded together in common cause. Editors should recognize the significance of grass-roots

movements, of hard, unspectacular, volunteer citizen activity. Mass media can do a great deal to keep up morale, and to give organizations a sense of common cause; perhaps even to assist the co-ordination of efforts of various groups through well-placed editorials, and through serving a clearing-house function. Editorial policy, including news coverage policy, may reflect too much the particular class and other group affiliations of the editor. Like any teacher, the editor needs to know how well the attitudes of his group represent the community as a whole.

2. *The preaching of ideological exclusiveness.*—The most pervasive and widespread model for intergroup competitiveness is the system of churches, each supporting, sometimes defensively, its own brand of religion, including nonsectarianism. The notion that people should be segregated on the basis of belief has been the undoing of many citizen groups. It automatically excludes nonbelievers, who are just the ones who ought to be reached, and it invites status competition over whose interpretation of belief is to be considered authoritative. Too much energy is spent in arguing beliefs and prejudices. The more churches work together for civic betterment, not as individual churches but as a part of a city-wide movement, the more likely they will be to involve new members and alleviate civic apathy by means of operating faith. When religious work is used to tear people apart, it tips the scales one way; were it used to pull the community together, it could be a powerful force for promoting a healthy community climate.

3. *The relations between citizens and officials.*—Policemen, firemen, health officials—all the official denizens of city hall and precinct —represent civic authority to the citizen. The kind of reception and follow-up of complaints and suggestions made by citizens may well have more to do with the state of citizen apathy than any other single factor. It is astonishing that so much of what is good and hopeful in the life of the community bypasses the whole political structure, even though civil servants are hired by the people for the express purpose of maintaining their welfare. There is hardly a major job in city hall that would not profit from the help of an advisory board of citizens, and it is all too rare that school improvement begins within the school. Very few citizens

feel close to the processes of civic decision-making, and therefore very few citizens discharge their civic duties with any other feeling than one of being imposed upon.

4. *The self-discipline of special interest groups.*—Taverns, stores, architects, landlords, transportation arrangements—all these and many more give the community its flavor. The institutions with which citizens have their daily contacts, and which rely for their support on community patronage and good will, could profit by taking the larger view, by thinking in terms of long-range consequences of promotion, merchandising, pricing, and favored-customer policies—not to mention such things as an ideal of service, promptness, and accommodation to unusual individual circumstance. Such proprietor groups might well get together, formulate joint problems, and work with citizens in thinking them through. Anything that improves one part of the community rapidly affects the community as a whole.

This listing is of course very incomplete. The operation of courts, industries, real estate and property management, mortgage policies, medical care, and so on, through all the complex facets of living—all these services communicate attitudes of respect for people or of denial of worth; of open-minded optimism or of closed-minded defeatism; of concern for all or of flinty self-interest; of entrenchment of power groups or of co-operation in common cause. And thus the community climate and culture is built; and it determines what is possible, what activities will be rewarded, what aspirations the community can have; whether people will live in serenity and at peace with themselves and each other. These things people learn.

The operation of the community culture is through the consistencies of biases and attitudes expressed by the many acts of everyday living. The acts of the "influence people" contribute most because they are visible and make a difference to the welfare of a large audience, and because they "set the standard" for others who aspire to influence.

I have chosen to deal at length with the community because it is the underlying substratum of learned reactions, which, in ways hidden from the group members, for the most part, enter into all phases of group operation. But the relationships are mutual: change of community attitude is also the result of learning, primarily through interaction between people in formal and informal meetings.

There is a type of subcommunity in which all the same dynamics are at work, but in a more readily controllable and ascertainable way. This is the institution: college, factory, large store, art center, hospital. The institution mediates between most formal groups and the larger community. Studies of institutions lead to one highly significant generalization: the attitudes and biases which pervade an institution—its culture—filter down from the top. These are transmitted either as learned reactions taken over by lower echelons, or as problem areas fraught with anxiety which give the institution its continuing self-obsessions and concerns. It is because of this fact that leaders need to assume considerable responsibility for attitude-communicating behavior. At the present time, for example, there is beginning to be interest in the problem of feedback: how to get evidence for decisions about internal policy, from reactions to previous behaviors up and down the hierarchy.

The operations of large institutions penetrate many more dimensions of community life, and do so more directly, than do groups. We have, on the one hand, the company town, like the army town; it is an extension of the company which gives the town culture its basic framework and direction. On the other hand, the company may be one of many industries which ignore the community and are largely unaware of the mutual interactions which so vitally affect costs, labor policy, training designs, and, probably, creativity in research and production methods. In either case the troubles within the large institution tend to be elaborated more generally in conflict with the surrounding community; and the methods used for dealing with intra-institutional conflict provide a model throughout the community for dealing with many other conflicts arising in a host of other enterprises. (Adoption by industries of proposition I, pp. 114–17, would set a desirable model for the community.)

GROUP GROWTH AND COMMUNITY DEVELOPMENT: A MODEL

The development and growth of a voluntary citizen organization demonstrates most clearly the mutual relationships between groups and community. We shall trace such an organization from its inception through the various stages of growth, and attempt, in the process, to point out some of the ways in which the group and community interact.

First, a movement or organization starts in the mind of some one person, more sensitive or socially conscious than others. He is aroused about some felt problems, such as delinquency, defeatism, or the schools; and he talks about this to the people with whom he can communicate best, his friends. If the issue is anxiety-producing he may talk about it under cover of some safe activity like a bridge game, to which he can escape if necessary. Finally, he finds one or more friends who respond by sharing similar feelings about the problem; he gains a cohort, and both are now reinforced in their feelings and begin to work rather vaguely toward the goal of taking action. The ease with which he finds cohorts, as well as the way he presents the problem to them, will be much affected by the amount of freedom of expression in the community, and particularly the quality of tolerance for the disgruntled and sensitive individual.

Second, the leadership clique develops from the first conversations, primarily through the induction of close friends. This group shares many social activities, and has considerable internal freedom for expression of their power fantasies, identifying target groups and "enemies," and talking over people who for one reason or another it will be "strategic" to involve next. The amount and quality of organization of the community helps the clique decide who is strategic, as it helps it decide how big the problem is. The more organized the community, the greater the ease of communication and involvement of others.

Third, as a result of their own conversations, backed up by discreet inquiries directed to "outsiders," a few strategic people are located and added to the group, probably under the guise of a quasi-social meeting. These new people are likely to belong to the same social class, and they are strategic because they have needed

technical knowledge about the problem, are in a position to influence large numbers of other people through their own organizations, or are officials who will have to take action later in connection with the problem. These "strategic" people are explored
warily, and are flattered by being put in the role of consultants.
The clique attempts to reality-test ideas, and to get half-promises
of co-operation; but at the same time it retains power by offering
to do all the work. Of course, some of the strategic people may at
this point be admitted to the clique—after considerable testing of
their amenability and value. Once more, the community culture
enters. These strategic people are likely to be leaders; their reactions show how large a "bite" on the problem can be taken in
the first action step, and their attitudes, the realism of which is
assured by their record of successful operation, point to the probable forces of resistance and facilitation that must be taken into
account.

Fourth, two things happen simultaneously: the over-all plan
begins to take shape, and, in the process, the functional roles of the
clique and the strategy people begin to get defined. Through discussion of objectives the individuals assess how meaningful the
movement will be to them; through discussion of leadership roles,
the people find out what sorts of gratifications they can get and
what price in assumption of responsibility they will have to pay;
through discussion of the groups to try to involve next, the new
group develops its own self-image, as powerful or dependent, as
active or as promoting the activity of others, and so forth. The
group is likely to consider whether its proposed activities will
raise or lower its position in public opinion.

All these decisions are conditioned by estimates about the ease
of communication of objectives, the potentials for action believed
to reside in other groups, the previous examples of success or failure along similar lines. In addition, the grand plan itself, particularly with respect to its boldness and creativity, suggests quite
clearly the freedom for daring or the habits of dependence which
characterize groups in the community.

Fifth, the first action step is taken. Assuming that the group has
decided to play a central action role, rather than merely to study
the problem by inviting in prestige speakers or to turn it over to

some existing agency, this step involves bringing in other people. Several important things happen at this point. For one thing, a set of bylaws is worked out to protect the clique leadership and to define the steps in the prestige hierarchy of the organization. This enables members to estimate the effort required for the rewards of "moving up." Second, the informal group of strategy people is formalized in the board of directors, made up of a mixture of experts (who become heads of working committees) and prestige people (who help with membership, fund raising, and public relations). Third, the leadership group hammers out its basic methodology of either co-operation or pressure.

If the group feels sufficient internal security, the policy is likely to be co-operation. There is likely to be a strong effort to find a place for everyone who wants to help, through description of a wide variety of adequately supervised and rewarded jobs. There will probably also be an effort to maintain continuous involvement in the membership, through the feedback of policy decisions and reporting of progress.

If the group does not feel secure, and is basically more concerned with the protection of its power strivings, the policy will be very different. The first action may be to hire an executive secretary responsible to what now becomes an inactive board of directors; this really means that the group remains dominated by the officers of the original clique, and the secretary is given all the routine work. The group tries to get members not so much to work as to swell the number of people the officers can say they represent when they make demands on officials and other groups. The test of membership is therefore not willingness to work but rather similarity of belief, of readiness to "go along" with actions taken by officers who can give the beliefs expression.

Here, as always, the decisions are made in terms of existing models in the community. If there are no generally accepted patterns of co-operation, there will be no co-operative models to consider or emulate.

Sixth, along with the first action step, "public opinion" begins to enter the picture concretely. The right of a group to talk within itself is accepted as part of the right of freedom of assembly. But when the group goes outside itself to influence others, then a host of perceptions arises. The nature of these perceptions again depends upon the stereotypes already existing in the community, and the interpretations made of the first action steps accurately reflect the state of intergroup communication. If the problem is one which lies within the jurisdiction of other groups, these may get defensive and hostile; they may get very active to allay their guilt feelings at having done little themselves. There may be whispering campaigns and smearing of the officers. There may be tentative proposals made from other groups, ranging from threats to offers of merger.

Seventh, as action goes forward, working alliances with other groups have to be developed. This is likely to involve a redefinition of the problem and of the jurisdictions of the interested parties. If the group tries to ignore other groups it will gradually find there are limits to its action and growth. It will not be able to reach new types of people, it will stop developing new techniques, it will become more conservative and tend to rest on its past accomplishments. The excitement goes and self-training stops. The group gets ready to attack any new group that tries to start work in the same problem area.

If, however, the group has developed enough security so that it now exists as an institution apart from the original officers, it can form relationships with other groups. This is a crucial point, involving acceptance by the community and by the group of the worth of its functions. There develops the expectation that people will join, work hard for a few years, and then go on, without prejudice, to other experiences. A sufficient body of tradition and stabilized policy grows so that the group is no longer vulnerable to threats. It can contemplate with equanimity considerable change in the means it uses to achieve its goals: and these have been whittled down and redefined as realistic aspirations.[2]

Eighth, the group takes its place in the network of community organizations. It may engage in joint fund-raising activity. There is referral of potential members from one group to another, depending on the kind of participation the prospective member wants. Mass meetings tend to be sponsored by at least two or-

2. Much of this section is built on presentations of Professor Martin Loeb to the Chicago Workshop in Community Human Relations, 1952.

ganizations, and interpretation of the work of the group puts it in the context of action by other groups as well.

I have to confess that I have yet to see this last step developed very far. But that does not deter me from going on to suggest a further logical development that would ideally follow, assuming that the group and the community were growing. This step would be a joint membership campaign, supervised by an interorganizational group. Through mass meetings and other publicity, people would be acquainted, first, with the needs of the community, second, with the kinds of actions required to meet these needs, and third, with the various organizations trying to take these actions. The aim would be to help each person in the community find his niche, through the kind of participation he most needed and could be rewarded for. This is clearly a goal for the community as a whole, not for any one organization. Other possible developments, such as community centers operated interorganizationally, and total campaigns for limited objectives, are consonant with this stage of development. The interorganizational group referred to here would be the community council, new style.

Ninth, as time goes on, the objectives and methods of the coordinated network of groups would become elaborated and assimilated into the culture of the community. Individual behaviors and decisions would tend to be in line with the program. What had been the action program of one group would become a community movement in which most of the relevant forces were aligned. The movement would, in effect, define a generally sanctioned way of life with respect to its broad objectives. City officials would gradually become the functionnaires for its implementation, and necessary guiding roles would be provided within the planned official structure of community maintenance.

The original groups continuously redefining specific goals, would have—and will always have—a place. It is that of the active social conscience, the prophet of change, the formulator of new values. And it is only through such groups that individual insight, sensitivity, and creativity can be utilized for the development of the "humane community" toward which man's nature (including the processes described so far) is driving him.

It seems reasonable to suppose that this image of group growth is also an image of how the community can be built: with adequate communication and communion, maintaining realistic organizational structure and opening up the widest opportunities for individual growth and development.

BASIC PRINCIPLES FOR GROUPS IN RELATION TO THE LARGER COMMUNITY

The development of groups is accompanied by the taking of action. The taking of action changes the community. All the groups affected by this action react to it. Under favorable conditions within the climate of the community, they then begin planning action together, and eventually co-operate in realistic community-wide programs. So goes our model. Our argument has been that the growth of any group, and, with it, the possibilities of community development, can be truncated at any point in this progress.

In this section we wish to single out in brief recapitulation the assumptions basic to group operation which we believe will enable this social process to reach completion:

First: Community problem-solving is put ahead of organizational power as the objective.

Second: Anyone who can help with the problem-solving is welcome, regardless of professed belief or our theories about his personality.

Third: Efforts are made to seek out and reach working agreements with other groups working for the same objectives.

Fourth: The group serves as a bridging group to reduce conflict among the other groups to which the members are loyal.

Fifth: The group adopts an experimental methodology, determining action at each step on the basis of evaluation of results of preceding steps.

Sixth: The group pays attention to self-training and to its own development so that leadership is strengthened, goals are kept realistic, individuals make satisfying contributions, and workable solutions to problems can be formulated explicitly and passed on to other groups and communities.

Seventh: The group collects adequate data about the problem: the attitudes of all those involved, the "real" reasons why its actions have the effects they do, the objective picture of progress made so far, the phase of the problem the community is most ready to tackle next.

Eighth: The group realistically appraises its own resources and skills, and gets professional help when needed.

Ninth: Throughout all action, the group defines its "enemy" as objectively defined conditions in need of change rather than in terms of individuals or other groups to be demolished.

This is the last list. As I bring this book to a close I turn back to its other lists:

8 principles for neighborhood leadership (pp. 14–18)
3 basic aspects of experience (pp. 46–50)
34 generalizations about organizing activities for specific purposes (pp. 62–67)
9 specifications for in-service training (pp. 91–92)
7 problems of administrators (pp. 108–13)
6 summarized principles for organizations (pp. 126–27)
7 principles for trainers in human relations (pp. 171–77)
4 basic principles for all technologies (pp. 181–90)
13 principles for control of the group (pp. 285–89)
4 major functions of leadership (pp. 302–10)
8 problems of leaders (pp. 314–19)

and now:

9 principles of relationship between groups and their communities.

Twelve lists!

In the Preface, we said of the six technologies: "Behind these differences, however, are fundamental similarities." We now say: "Behind these twelve lists is one fundamental set of principles— the principles of human interaction." These are the principles we live by, and each of us must formulate them for himself in response to his own needs and in terms of his own experience. And we shall communicate them to each other through our actions, as we try, through understanding, to build our better worlds.

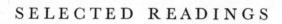

SELECTED READINGS

Selected Readings

On January 1, 1954, Hare and Strodtbeck released an authoritative listing of books and articles which describe or explain matters in face-to-face small groups.* They found 1382 of them, covering the period 1900–1954. There are many from which to choose!

Of the publications which have contributed most to the thinking in this book and which seem memorable to me, I suggest for additional reading, the following:

1. BETTELHEIM, BRUNO, and SYLVESTER, M. E. "Therapeutic Influence of the Group on the Individual," *American Journal of Orthopsychiatry*, XVII (October, 1947), 684–92.

Explains how emotional conflict, expressed openly between two members of a group, may assist another member to deal with similar conflict within himself. Suggests use of this principle to compose groups for maximum need-meeting and growth of the members.

2. BION, W. R. "Experiences in Groups. I" and "Experiences in Groups. II," *Human Relations*, I, No. 3 (1948), 314–20; and No. 4, 487–96.

In these articles, the first two of a series of seven, Bion presents assumptions central to our discussion: that the state of the group-as-a-whole depends upon the relationships between emotionality and work; and that individual behaviors are interpreted as expressing needs of the group-as-a-whole.

3. CHASE, STUART, in collaboration with MARIAN CHASE. *Roads to Agreement*. New York: Harper & Bros., 1951. Pp. 240.

Presents stimulating descriptions of different ways of working of successful groups. Excellent material on which to try out your generalizations.

4. DAVIS, ALLISON. *Social Class Influences on Learning*. Cambridge: Harvard University Press, 1948. Pp. 100.

The first forty-six pages present a concise summary of the concepts of social class and how class differences operate to produce differences in children.

* Fred L. Strodtbeck and A. Paul Hare, "Bibliography of Small Group Research," to appear during spring, 1954, in *Sociometry*.

5. DE HUSZAR, GEORGE. *Practical Applications of Democracy.* New York: Harper & Bros., 1945. Pp. 120.

On the assumption that the meaning of democracy is expressed in the ways people work together, the author has sought out and here presents democratically promising (and psychologically sound) innovations in ways of working in a variety of situations.

6. DEWEY, JOHN. *Experience and Education.* New York: Macmillan Co., 1939. Pp. 116.

The concept of interaction and the significance for education of individual-group relations are here presented by this psychologist's philosopher. Presents a lucid and concise discussion of authority, freedom, control, and other concepts central to our book.

7. FRENKEL-BRUNSWIK, ELSE. "A Study of Prejudice in Children," *Human Relations*, I, No. 3 (1948), 295–306.

Prejudice is here seen as one part of a patterning of needs, approaches to problems, and personality. Makes clear the central importance of the way people accommodate to authority.

8. HILLIARD, A. L. *The Forms of Value.* New York: Columbia University Press, 1950. Pp. 330.

Adds considerably to our understanding of the nature of goals through scholarly and systematic analysis of values and their influence on behavior.

9. JENNINGS, HELEN HALL. *Sociometry of Leadership.* (Sociometry Monograph No. 14.) New York: Beacon House, 1947. Pp. 28.

Explains the psychology of socio-groups and of psyche-groups and the different needs they serve. A classic study which supports the notion that task-oriented groups must, at times, recognize emotional phenomena.

10. LEWIN, KURT, and GRABBE, PAUL. "Conduct, Knowledge, and Acceptance of New Values," *Journal of Social Issues*, V (December, 1945), 53–64.

A penetrating analysis of the way change is produced, particularly in organizations.

11. REDL, FRITZ. "Resistance in Therapy Groups," *Human Relations*, I, No. 3 (1948), 307–13.

An illuminating diagnostic picture of the psychology of individual change at various stages of relationship between individual member and group leader.

INDEX

Index